100 Countries

by

Colin E. Rice

100 COUNTRIES

Copyright © Colin Edward Rice
2016-2019.

Colin Edward Rice has asserted
his right to be identified as the author
of this Work in accordance with the
Copyright, Design and Patents Act 1988.

All Rights Reserved.

No part of this book shall be re-printed or circulated
without the written consent of the author.

First Published 3 November 2019 (Printed Edition)

Outside cover: Temple of Bacchus, Baalbek, Lebanon.

DISCLAIMER

This book is a work of fiction.
The names, characters, events and
incidents in this book are completely fictional –
they really, really are.
If you think you recognise anyone,
or anything, then you are sadly mistaken.

Anything I claim to have done in this book
is my own feather-brained decision.
You should not emulate my choice of lifestyle.

DEDICATION

*Dedicated to Andy
for his gallant effort to beat me to
100 countries.*

CHAPTERS

PROLOGUE
Getting Ahead

THE BULK OF THE BALKANS
1. Bombs and Bullets of Bosnia
2. The Good, the Bad and the Ugly

OVERTAKING ANDY
3. Back-Busting Bangladesh
4. Glowing Report from Chernobyl

ODDS AND SODS OF EUROPE
5. Tobacco Mountain
6. Monty's Malta
7. Ribbentrop Runts

STALIN STATES
8. UFO-Spotting in Slovakia
9. Commonwealth of Commies
10. Baltic Balls-Up

INTERLUDE
Warning Bells

THE BATTY BALKANS
11. Bonky Bunkers of Albania
12. Routemaster Rip-offs

VIKING CLEAN UP
13. It Ain't The Arctic Circle
14. A Stone's Throw to North Pole
15. Final Dose of Vikings

GRAND FINALE
16. Howdy There, Hezbollah

EPILOGUE
The Journey Continues

LIST OF COUNTRIES

PROLOGUE

Prologue: Getting Ahead

If you have read my first book, *7 Continents*, then you will sympathise with my serious ailment – a deep and prolonged case of the travel bug. It consumes all my spare time: reading travel guides, watching travelogues to gain ideas for exciting destinations, researching overland routes on Rome2Rio and monitoring flight prices on Skyscanner. I am well and truly hooked.

One matter gnawed away at me, though. An old friend of mine, Andy, who I had travelled overland from Europe to Asia with, had visited more countries and territories than me. His tally had expanded to 77 by August 2015, and I was trailing at 65 following a trip to Cambodia. I desperately needed to add another dozen or so countries. Or maybe I should round my tally up to 80? Or 85? Where should I stop?

That made me consider what would be a fall-off-your-barstool number of countries. Or perhaps another way, was there an impressive, world-renowned traveller I could beat? If I could beat him, or her – now that would be a mightily impressive pub tale.

My starting point would be a list of the world's greatest travellers. According to Paul Simpson of the British Independent newspaper, aside from historical figures such as James Cook and Charles Darwin, the most traveled was Michael Palin.

As a younger fool, I was envious of Michael Palin.

An incredibly funny man, the ex-Monty Python star had taken to making travel programs after a stint as a train-spotter. He starred in series such as *Around the World in 80 Days* and *Pole to Pole* and was a confessed travel nut. The BBC had paid handsomely for his travels around the globe; surely, he was esteemed as an impressive traveller.

After further research, I found that Palin had been to 96 countries by 2012 – according to an internet article that had painstakingly catalogued all the countries he had visited on his various travel shows. Palin was also working on a new travel show based on a tour through Brazil. So, let's assume I needed to visit 100 countries to beat him. If I could achieve that, then I could win a pub argument with Michael Palin. And resoundly beat Andy.

The next question on my mind was which countries and regions to visit. Certain countries such as India, Brazil and South Africa are vast with dozens of UNESCO World Heritage Sights, cities and once-in-a-lifetime things to do. I needed to savour these trips – to rush them would be sacrilege.

No, I concluded that I should concentrate on countries that were travellable in a short period; preferably those with neighbouring countries I could rapidly visit in clusters. As Andy and I called them, *tickfests*.

Besides camels and rug salesmen, the Middle East was stuffed full of small states I could readily tick off. And I could conveniently stopover at these places on long-haul flights between the UK and the Far East. Some Scandinavian territories stubbornly remained on my tick-list, and the Baltic States and Balkans were one giant tickfest connected by Soviet-era railways. Other routes came to mind, but those above would be my initial target along with Western European holiday destinations served readily by stuff-them-in airlines like Ryanair and Easyjet.

I was determined to reach my goal – but would I have enough time and money? And would my wife agree? Let's go for it, I thought.

This is my tale of trying to reach 100 countries and territories.

Andy – time to eat my dust.

Michael Palin – you had better watch your crown.

THE BULK OF THE BALKANS

Between 1991 and 2003, the Socialist Federal Republic of Yugoslavia had fragmented into six independent states. Despite the notoriety of the brutal civil wars, and Serbia's propensity to snuff out ethnic groups who didn't want to be under the yoke of Belgrade, how could I resist an opportunity to add six countries to my tally?

I managed to find a dirt cheap passage from Manchester down to the Northern Balkan region on a £50 JetStar flight to Venice. From there, I took a train and bus-ride to the capital of Slovenia, Ljubljana. That was country number 72 – and I was advancing on Andy's tally of 77. Next, I took the *SAVA* Express to Zagreb, Croatia – that was country number 73. *Tickety tick.*

I had visited Eastern Europe in 1990, around the time of the fall of Communism, and had had amazing fun riding in Trabant and Lada cars, travelling on USSR-made trains, eating stodgy food and drinking beer all night for one pound. Call me nostalgic, or call me daft, but I had futile hopes of rediscovering some of that Communist charm.

However, Slovenia and Croatia were largely tarted up, and the great interfering hand of the European Union and hordes of package tourists had done wonders to cover up the decades of command-economy degradation under communism. Leonid Brezhnev would be choking on his chicken Kiev.

I was gasping for something more hard core: for off-the-beaten-track places where the package tourists still feared to tread. I had had enough of neat eurocities – get me outta here.

So, I decided to press ahead to the allure of postwar Bosnia-Herzegovina and bought a train ticket to Banja Luka. Bosnia ought to be satisfyingly dilapidated I thought to myself. The Intercity B397 was scheduled to depart at 9:18 a.m. and arrive at Banja Luka at 1:34 pm. before continuing onwards to Sarajevo.

Shortly before 9 a.m., several blue passenger carriages with red-white-and-blue go-faster stripes were shunted along the platform by a yellow shunting locomotive. At the rear, a brakeman was hanging off a grab-rail furiously waving a red flag to make himself look essential to the operation. The carriages screeched to a deafening halt, and the brakeman leapt off like a spider monkey, unhooked the tiny locomotive then it rumbled away in a choking cloud of diesel smoke. A few moments later, a red diesel-electric locomotive reversed up to the carriages and coupled up. A conductor magically appeared several metres in front of me.

'Banja Luka?' I enquired.

'Banja Luka,' affirmed the smartly dressed conductor.

The steel steps of the second-class carriage were as steep as the Inca Trail and at least four-feet high. I struggled up with my two bags and squeezed into the train corridor, which was built for anorexic fashion models. I was quite wedged in and had to lean forward like a rugby player in a scrum to pass the toilet and reach the passenger cabins on my left. Experience told me that the compartment next to the toilet would smell like a Glastonbury Festival field toilet, so I hurriedly took the second compartment since a crowd of excitable passengers had appeared at the other end of the corridor.

I opened the compartment door and was greeted with six ancient and mouldy-looking sky-blue velour seats. They had giant boxy armrests and U-shaped headrests generous enough to accommodate the head of a hippopotamus. Perhaps this was a delightful carriage 40 years ago, I thought. This was exactly what I was looking for.

The seats to my left were less grotty, whereas the ones to my right had headrests encrusted with black hair grease and looked most disgusting. But then I realised that the cleaner seats would be facing backwards, so I grimaced and took a hair-grease seat to get a decent view facing towards the approaching scenery.

Shortly, a middle-aged lady dressed smartly in a beige raincoat mumbled to me in a Slavic language and took a seat next to the compartment door. The conductor shrilled his whistle at 9:18 a.m., and the locomotive loudly tooted its horn. Just then, the compartment door opened again, and a fit-looking young man with a US Marines Corps haircut entered. He wore a grey hoodie and blue trousers and took the middle seat opposite me; poised on the edge as if he had decided to chat to me as a matter of grave urgency. I gave him a warm hello, and we almost immediately began to chat.

Zlatan was a businessman running a small software development company and was on his way home to Sarajevo. We chatted enthusiastically, and he was an eager and intelligent man who had travelled quite extensively around the Balkans and Europe. Deep in conversation, the journey passed quickly, and by about 11 a.m., we had reached the Croatian border and the train screeched to a halt.

We were in the hills, and the neat beige-painted border post was flanked by a pair of ten-metre flag poles: one with the blue-and-red-striped Croatian flag, and to its right, the European Union flag flying proudly with its yellow stars representing the wildly differing opinions of the member states.

Soon enough, the train pulled away – and hurrah – I was in country number 74. Zlatan and I continued our enthusiastic conversation.

1: Bombs and Bullets of Bosnia

Bosnia-Herzegovina (No. 74)

My plan of attack was to take the train from Zagreb to Banja Luka in Northern Bosnia – a tolerable five-hour train ride. Then from Banja Luka, I would hop from city to city taking three to four-hour journeys; I didn't have the stomach to spend all day on a bus or train.

'Why don't you visit Sarajevo?' Zlatan suggested.

'I will. But I want to visit Banja Luka first,' I replied.

'There's nothing much there. Why don't you come with me to Sarajevo,' Zlatan persisted.

I thought about his invitation at length, but the journey from Zagreb to Sarajevo would be over ten hours long – and I would have to suffer the whole day in this greasy hippo seat.

'Maybe,' I replied.

The train snaked through valleys between green hills and alongside rivers where crystal-clear water gushed over gravel beds and rocks. Rustic cottages were dotted about the hillsides.

I couldn't reconcile that this beautiful country had been the scene of unimaginable horrors and myriad casualties in the Yugoslavian wars. Slovenia had suffered dozens of deaths. Croatia had suffered tens of thousands. But Bosnia had lost hundreds of thousands of soldiers and civilians. The exact losses were not known, exacerbated by the mass genocides committed by the Serbians and their efforts to cover up, but it was somewhere in the region of 100,000 to 250,000.

Bosnia was an ethnic and religious cocktail. The Bosniaks were practising Muslims who represented two-fifths of the population at the outbreak of hostilities. The Serbs, who were Orthodox Christians, constituted a third of the population; and the Roman Catholic Croats represented the remainder. The Croats and Bosniaks bravely declared independence for Bosnia and Herzegovina in March 1992. This act predictably enraged the Serbian government in Belgrade, which was planning a Greater Serbian state.

By May, the Bosnian Serb general, Ratko Mladić, had control of the Yugoslav army, the Bosnian Serb military and various paramilitary groups. They took control of the majority of Bosnia, and the Muslims were rounded up or encircled – and the genocides and sieges began.

The entire tragedy had unfolded on international television, and footage of civilians in Sarajevo being picked off by snipers and artillery fire was a daily occurrence. Now here I was, over two decades later, entering the interior of this ex-war zone on a communist-era train.

I realised that I needed to respond to Zlatan.

'I can't ride to Sarajevo because my ticket is only valid to Banja Luka,' I finally decided after much thought.

'No problem,' replied Zlatan, 'I can talk with the ticket guy.'

Later on, the conductor entered our compartment to check tickets. After a rambling discussion in Serbo-Croatian, Zlatan advised me that I could pay an extra

32.90 Bosnia-Herzegovina convertible marks (£12.30), or *ka marks* as they called it, to extend my ticket. I paid the elderly conductor and thanked Zlatan.

We arrived at Banja Luka station at 1:30 pm, and the lion's share of the passengers disembarked. I watched them waddle along the gloomy platform into the utilitarian station building wearily dragging their refugee-looking baggage. I sighed to myself that I was not going to be dragging along behind them.

On our way again, an hour later the scenery started to turn an ominous brown, and Zlatan tugged my shirt and pointed out of the grimy, stained window.

'Look. That is Zenica. It looks like Russia, huh?'

'Oh yes. It does. How awful,' I replied in admiring disgust.

Rusting, angular factories surrounded the railway line and were topped by towering red-and-white-striped chimney stacks billowing filthy-black smoke into the air. Industrial plants bristled with lights in the grey dusk, and steam and smoke spurted from them in random directions. Hundreds of rusted train carriages and cargo wagons lay abandoned on the railway sidings like dead cattle, service roads were unkempt and street lights leaned at alarming angles. The whole scenery was reminiscent of my trip to Russia in 1990 with a miserable air of industrial decay and pollution on an alarming scale.

The scenery improved remarkably after we left behind the region around Zenica, and my mind wandered to more pleasurable thoughts. The conversation with Zlatan waned, and we took to reading novels. By 6:30 p.m., our grotty train slowly rolled into Sarajevo Central Station like a weary beast crawling the final metres of its migration. I grabbed my bags and followed Zlatan off the train – taking extreme care on the steep stairs.

'Colin, I have a friend who has a hostel in the city. Well, I stayed there many times when I was looking to start my business in Sarajevo, and I became good friends with them. It is a safe place. Would you like me to show you?'

Normally I would avoid any offers like this, but Zlatan seemed a genuine character and I trusted him.

'Sure, how do we get there?' I asked.

'We will take the tram, but we need to walk to the main road first.'

'Can I buy my onward ticket to Mostar first?' I asked.

'Yes, I will help you.'

The station was a typical communist-era concrete dump with dull, disinterested workers hiding behind the glass-screened ticket booths. The concourse reeked of cigarette smoke from the passengers lounging about the station cafés who nursed espressos and encrusted ashtrays. I located the train timetable, which looked like it had not been changed since the days of Marshal Tito. The Mostar train departed daily at 7:13 a.m., so I bought a ticket for two days later from the zombie-worker under the watchful eye of Zlatan for 10.90 ka marks (£4.00).

Outside the station, it was eerily deserted, and we crossed the deformed tram tracks and walked past the United States Consulate. It was an enormous compound; quite why they needed a Pentagon-sized complex in such a small state such as Bosnia was extraordinary. Were the Americans using it as a forward listening base against Russia? Was it a military storage facility? For sure, it would be incredible that such an impressive facility was necessary just for processing visa applications of the donkey-cart load of

Bosnians with the available funds to visit America.

We crossed the main road, which was a wide boulevard of unweeded paths and concrete car lanes patched with abandon, and reached the tram stop on the opposite side. The cars were predominantly old bangers, which rattled past at reckless speed belching blue smoke – it reminded me of the acrid air in Canton and Budapest in the 1990s.

'This is Sniper Alley where the Serbians shot Bosnian Muslims during the war,' Zlatan informed me shaking his head in disbelief, 'the Serbians were hiding in the hills in front of us and picking-off the civilians. Terrible. Terrible.'

There were ample trams on Ulica Zmaja od Bosne and within a couple of minutes, one rotten red-over-white specimen rumbled up to the platform, and we clambered on. A young man felt pity for me and offered me his seat. Either that, or he was worried that me and my weighty luggage would tumble on to him at the first corner.

The interior of the tram was utterly decrepit: lined with white glossy panels smeared with graffiti and meagrely lit by rusted fluorescent light fittings. The narrow aisle was crowded with standing passengers, and the seated ones were squeezed into bottom-shaped, yellow plastic seats attached to enamelled tube frames worn down to the bare metal. The residents of Zenica would feel right at home in this depressing carriage, I thought to myself.

A shoebox-sized ticket machine was attached to the handrail pole, and I rummaged in my wallet for change.

'No need to pay,' Zlatan advised, '*nobody* pays. The conductors stop work at 5 p.m. – nobody will check for tickets. I guarantee you.'

The train rumbled off clumsily and waggled along the deformed rails at a cautious pace. I carefully surveyed the buildings along Sniper Alley looking for evidence of artillery damage. They were a mixture of grim communist-era office blocks, shrapnel-damaged Bosnian war relics and gleaming post-war skyscrapers. After ten minutes of a bone-shaking ride, the line split at the edge of the old city, and the right track snaked to the riverbank of the Miljacka River. I was admiring the view when Zlatan hailed me across the heads of the expressionless passengers.

'Here. Let's get off – the hostel,' he hastened.

After some initial disorientation, Zlatan led me across Obala Kulina Street and down a narrow street lined with low-rise buildings to the Traveller's Hostel where he pressed a door intercom. A joyous voice crackled from the intercom, and after some Slavic banter, the gate lock clicked open with an electrical buzz, and we climbed the worn alabaster steps to the first floor.

A bearded man greeted Zlatan warmly and gave him a Middle Eastern-style embrace, and they joked and laughed at each other. He looked like a gaunt bricklayer not a hostel receptionist. They paused their excitable banter momentarily while I was checked-in, then they continued their hearty chatter in reception while I transferred my bags to a lower bunk in dormitory number one. A few minutes later, I returned to the reception where Zlatan was standing.

'Okay, I must go home now. I hope you like your stay in the hostel,' he told me.

'How about something to eat?' I invited.

Zlatan hesitated then humbly declined.

'Oh, come on. You've been a great help,' I pleaded.

Zlatan agreed and hugged goodbye in a Middle-

Eastern sort of way again with Beardy-Bricklayer, then we headed to a nearby pizzeria. After a Neapolitan pizza and a few local Sarajevska Premium beers, Zlatan bade goodbye and I crashed for the night.

After a decent nights sleep and a quick shower, I took a city map from reception and walked to the Sacred Heart Cathedral on Strossmayerova Street. Outside was a statue of Pope John Paul II who had held a service at this Catholic cathedral. The Sacred Heart had been seriously damaged in the fighting and rebuilt post-war; it looking like it was brand spanking new. I peeked inside, but my stomach was complaining that it was empty. Where could I eat breakfast? I walked around the market square and found plenty of café-bars about, but oddly, they were only selling beer or coffee – nothing to eat. How ridiculous.

Despite my hunger pangs, I visited the boutique museum of the Massacre of Srebrenica. During the conflict, United Nations troops were supposed to protect the Bosnian Muslims in the refugee camp in Srebrenica but had withdrawn under Serbian attack. The Bosnian Muslim civilians were despicably left to perish at the hands of the Serbians and brutally murdered in one of modern history's worst genocides. The men were loaded on to buses and transported to the woods where virtually all the men between 15 and 60 years of age were exterminated by Ratko Mladić and his henchmen. A total of 8,000 were slaughtered.

Saddened by the story of the brutality, it was truly time for breakfast. I continued to Mula Mustafe Baseskije, where a three-storey hotel had its walls blown away during the siege. I crossed the street and saw, to the left of a narrow cobbled road, a building had its gable wall heavily scarred by artillery fire and bullets. You didn't need to look very hard to find evidence of the siege. Yet, investment had been streaming in, and much of the city had been renovated and tourists were returning to rejuvenate the economy.

At the next block, I spied a bakery. So I hastened along and found the traditional store was spartan, yet clean, with glass and stainless-steel cabinets displaying local breads.

'*Kava*?' I asked for a coffee.

The young lady in a white apron and headscarf shook her head then pointed to the glass-fronted chiller cabinet full of Western-branded tins of soda. It didn't make any sense: I could find cafés with coffee but no bread and a bakery with bread but no coffee. Was I asking for too much? I reluctantly took a can of Pepsi and surveyed the *sirnica* bread displayed in the cabinet.

They were giant spirals of flaky pastry the size of a dinner plate and introduced by the Ottomans. They had plain *sirnica* or ones stuffed with meat or sheep's cheese. I ordered two slices of the cheese variety and wolfed them down – most delicious. After my unconventional breakfast, I continued down Ulica Mula Mustafe Bašeskije in search of Zlatan's home turf, the Turkish old town.

Bosnia was under control of the Ottoman Empire for four centuries and ruled by the Muslim caliphate. Yet, the Ottomans were a moderate bunch and tolerated Christianity and other religions. Consequently, churches and synagogues were allowed to continue with their services, which would embarrass our modern intolerance.

I zigzagged to the Turkish bazaar, where I located the Gazi-Husrevbey Mosque named after an Ottoman governor. Old Gazzer founded several mosques and developed the city in the sixteenth century. Inside the courtyard of the walled mosque, worshippers washed their feet at the fountain in the shade of the stone arches and trees before straggling-in for the midday prayers.

I retreated to the east entrance of the courtyard where Gazzer's mausoleum stood to observe the scene. It was a well-maintained mosque with stone walls and green Islamic flags hanging from wall-mounted flagpoles. The mausoleum had the lowest front doors imaginable for a homo sapien- they only reached my stomach. Facing the mausoleum stood the lemonade-pink Islamic literacy centre with an equally diminutive door, and I watched a moustached man stoop like a hyperkyphosis-ridden chimpanzee to enter.

I wandered the narrow lanes of the Turkish bazaar where charming outdoor cafés were patronised by locals puffing away on hookah pipes and sipping Turkish coffee from espresso-sized brass cups. After a lunch of Bosnian steak – whatever that was – I walked to the banks of the Miljacka River, which ran alongside Obala Kulina through a rock-lined causeway.

The clear, shallow river tumbled over rocky beds two storeys below, and a javelin-throw away, the river was spanned by the quadruple-arched Latin Bridge. It was near this Ottoman bridge that Archduke Franz Ferdinand was assassinated in 1914 triggering the tragic chain of events leading to the First World War.

Sarajevo was bequeathed a stunning backdrop of low hills cloaked in rust-red roofed houses set among coniferous trees dotted along the steep streets. The sun fought with the fluffy clouds in the pale blue sky pierced by white rocket-like minarets. I couldn't believe that this beautiful riverside view was both the scene of the start of the First World War and the horrific Bosnian genocide.

My main objective of the day, which appealed to

my love of dark tourism, was to visit the Tunnel of Hope which was dug under the airport runway during the conflict. I hailed a taxi which headed west along Sniper Alley, past the monolithic USA consulate and after several kilometres reached the tram terminal at Illidza. Down some narrow rural roads and through open farmland, Sarajevo airport came into view.

The driver dropped me outside a heavily war-damaged house with its back to the airport runway. I thanked him and reluctantly paid the rather steep 34 ka mark (£12.70) meter charge. He probably retired after that windfall.

The sand-coloured detached residence was built from square cement blocks, and the front wall was peppered with holes from artillery fire, which were large enough to place my fist inside. This house was the start point of the tunnel that the Bosnian resistance had dug – and now housed the Tunnel Museum.

Behind the museum lay the runway of Sarajevo Airport, and I watched a turboprop plane glide in and land in the early afternoon sun. Behind the airport lay the hills which had been controlled by Serbian forces and overlooked the encircled Bosnians in the city centre.

The scenery was all too familiar to me. The Siege of Sarajevo began in April 1992 – just two months after I had returned to England from my third cavale – and I remember watching the events unfolding on the nightly news. Unbelievably, the siege was still running – almost four years later – when I emigrated to Hong Kong. It became the longest-running siege in modern history; even longer than the German siege of Stalingrad in the Second World War. During the Siege of Sarajevo, the mounting death toll and fleeing civilians had reduced the population by a tenth.

Monitors from the United Nations had recorded an average of 330 shells a day pummelling Sarajevo; at its peak, 3,700 in a single day. An estimated 600 snipers, 250 cannons, 650 mortars, 26 multiple rocket launchers, 3,700 rocket launchers and 120 tanks were aimed at the unfortunate Sarajevans.

United Nations peacekeepers had taken control of the airport during the siege but wouldn't allow the Bosnians to cross from Bosnian-controlled Illidza, where I now stood, to the besieged city centre. The Serbs believed they could lay siege to Sarajevo – and starve out the 70,000-strong Bosnian defence force and its citizens – but they didn't bank on the Bosnian's resourcefulness. The crafty Bosnians dug a supply tunnel from the house right in front of me, almost half a kilometre under the airport runway and the noses of the United Nations peacekeepers, to the city of Sarajevo. The Bosnian moles had dug right under the waiting hound dogs.

I paid the 10 ka marks (£3.70) museum entrance fee then ventured inside. I began my visit by watching a video of the role of the tunnel in the Siege of Sarajevo. The Bosnians had laid steel rails in the narrow tunnel to transport people, supplies and even livestock through to the city. After watching a video of the siege and wandering the small museum, I ventured down into the preserved remains of the tunnel.

The section under the runway had unsurprisingly been filled-in after the cessation of hostilities, but this section had been preserved and allowed me to see how cramped the conditions were. The hand-dug tunnel was propped-up by shaved logs and lined with wooden planks. It was barely wide enough to accommodate my ample body, and I had to stoop low in the tunnel to avoid banging my head on the roof-beams. Perhaps the tunnel was constructed by the same builders who built the diminutive doorways of the Gazi-Husrevbey's mausoleum, I thought.

Fascinated by the ingenuity and resilience of the Bosnians, I thanked the curator and left the museum. My mind must have been so cluttered with thoughts of the epic siege that I hadn't even a whiff of thought about how I was going to return to the city. There seemed to be no transport: just a couple of tourist coaches and a private car. So I decided to walk back along the route that the taxi had brought me – hopeful I could perhaps catch a bus back to the tram terminal.

The late autumn sun was radiant and the air was crisp as I ambled along the narrow road flanked by sunflower fields and vegetable plots. I passed an allotment of cabbages and watched a couple of farmers with white headscarves and lilac shirts tending the furrows with their hoes. They noticed me after a moment, leaned on their hoes and watched me back – probably with equal fascination. 'That idiot tourist looks lost?' they must have been thinking.

Past the cabbage farmers, a destroyed farmhouse had a collapsed roof and its front wall was blown away. Football-sized holes were punched through the outer wall, and the interior walls were peppered with unmistakable small-bore artillery holes – I safely assumed that it had been destroyed in the war.

I continued down the streets retracing the taxi route. I surveyed the houses dotted along the road and estimated that around one in ten were still war-damaged. Yet, aside from the houses being sprayed with artillery, this seemed a typical rural scene reminiscent of perhaps Holland with steep-roofed houses and white picket fences. I picked up the main road to Illidza and walked for about an hour, passing rustic houses which were preparing for the winter months ahead with piles of chopped logs stacked neatly along the wooden patios.

At the tram terminal, the rickety line formed a turnaround loop and the shoddy trams were lined up at the low concrete platform to take passengers back to the city. The lead tram was full, so I boarded the red-and-white one behind and sat at the rear. This putrescent and vandalised tram specimen looked in far worse condition than the one I had rode the previous night. I imagined the decrepit yellow seats collapsing through the floor at any moment. Shawled women, grey-faced old men and giggling teenagers in love boarded one-by-one, then after a short wait, we trundled-off down Sniper Alley.

The tram was so slow we were being overtaken by shawled grandmothers with walking sticks. On the positive side, I had a better opportunity to inspect the buildings along Sniper Alley as we trundled along at a snail's pace. One building, six storeys high and about a football field long, had all its outer walls blown away and sported large artillery fire holes.

Back in the city, I took a table in the market square fronting the Sacred Heart Cathedral and enjoyed several *kava* and a few Café Crème cigarillos in the chilly evening air. By now, the bars were cranking-up. On the way back to my hostel, the music blared out, and the young men and girls laughed, drank and flirted on the street. I calculated they were probably born during or shortly after the siege – and possibly owed their existence to the Tunnel of Hope.

I set my smartphone alarm for 6 a.m., as usual, anxious not to miss my morning train. I probably took a couple of hours to sleep planning how I would get from country 74 – which was now a respectable number – to

Andy's tally of 77. Or better still, reach 78. Andy had emailed me earlier in the day and nervously teased that I would be grinning when I reached 78 countries. 'No,' I replied, 'I will be grinning when I reached 77 and cheering when I reach 78.'

Somehow, I slept through the ruffles and scuffles of my seven fellow bunkmates. A New Yorker and a couple from Ontario had just arrived and were excitedly sharing travellers tales with an Asian guy lying on the threadbare rug. I would have concerns at just walking on it barefoot, never mind lying down on it. I somehow fell into a slumber then later awoke to the sound of the muezzin calling the morning prayers
'Allahhhhhh, Akbar.'
The Sarajevo night was still upon us, and the putrid trams had started noisily and were trundling heavily along Obala Kulina Street. They must have weighed 100 tons because their sound was like a house-sized boulder being rolled along a granite floor. I reached for my smartphone; it was only 5:16 a.m., and I needed to pee. And I knew for sure I couldn't sleep when I needed a pee.

I tip-toed to the toilet then lay down again. It was useless: I began thinking of how to reach Albania, and my mind was running away on overdrive. After a while, I looked at my smartphone again – it was 5:41 a.m. Sod it. I decided I would get up now and be early for the Mostar train.

Slowly and quietly, I packed my backpack and crept out of the dormitory, where I found Beardy-Bricklayer snoozing on the reception sofa with his blanket pulled up to his chin. He was as alert as a junkyard guard dog and jumped off the sofa in a flash. I apologised and asked him to call me a taxi. I handed in my room key and padlock, thanked him with a *hvale* and clumped slowly down the worn stairs to the dim street.

A taxi was lurking in a small alley to my left with his amber taxi light on. Was he the one I had ordered? Not sure. Ah well, I needed to get a move on. The taxi driver dropped me at Sarajevo main station. A café-bar was open at the station concourse, and I woke-up the middle-aged owner and ordered two slices of *sirnica* bread and *kava*. At 7 a.m., I paid my bill and walked to the platform, where I was as surprised as Archduke Franz Ferdinand's bodyguard that the train rumbled-up on time.

The carriages were pulled by a red-and-white JŽ class 441 electric locomotive originally built in Romania for Yugoslav Railways. It was damned ugly, like a Sarajevo tram on steroids, but I immediately loved the brute. I boarded and took a mouldy window-table seat on the right, and a giggling couple sat opposite me. The seat covers were faded red and new velour headrest covers had been stapled over them – presumably to cover the original head-grease stains. Soon I was on the way at the scheduled departure time of 7:18 a.m.

My adrenalin was buzzing at the thought of being on the road again. And what's more, to see Mostar bridge – the site of another notorious event in the Yugoslavian conflict – with my own eyes. Yet, I was exhausted due to lack of sleep and soon dozed off. I awoke with a startle just ten minutes later; the old brute of a locomotive slammed to a halt at a station, and the carriages noisily smacked their buffers against each other.

I was at Hadžići Station, which was a dirty-cream station house in Nowheresville – it didn't even have a platform. A wiry old man in a cheap black suit and a frumpy *babushka* in a lilac head-shawl, black traditional dress and green cardigan scuffled across the gravel and rails to the awaiting train. Why do they not have a platform, I wondered? Why bother stopping an Intercity train for just two pensioners? Is it safe to let old folk wander across the tracks? Who knows.

Brute honked indignantly and smoothly pulled away. Soon enough, it entered a steep green valley shrouded in the morning mist. Simple white detached farmhouses with blush pink roofs were dotted here and there in inconsequential corners of nowhere. It looked vaguely like a scene from Sichuan province in China except that the vegetation was different: bamboo was replaced with pale-green ferns and bushes tinted with yellow hues of the oncoming autumn season.

After ten minutes or so, we stopped at an infinitesimal station in the mountains, and a lady clambered off the train and crunched across the gravel and tracks. Off again we went. The couple opposite me looked like castaways of 1970's Albania going on holiday. The gaunt and lanky man sported a childish basin haircut, had a giant hooked nose and wore a brown jacket. He stared excitedly into the eyes of his Gallic-looking lady, who had wavy, mousey hair and wore a neat beige raincoat and blue neck-scarf. He took a photo with his point-and-shoot camera and wound the thumbwheel. Had I entered a Bosnian time warp?

After the red-capped station guard had disappeared from view, we were into green-bushed mountains: the Dinaric Alps. The peaks were shrouded in mist at this elevation, and it was so nowhere that even the nowhere-houses were – well, nowhere to be seen. Then we passed through tunnel after tunnel until the clouds and mist were far below us – suspended in the valleys in feint wisps and great clumps.

The train continuously climbed, the mountains became even steeper, the mist ever further below us and the dark noisy tunnels became lengthier. The trees became more sparse, with spruces and evergreens dotted among the sheer rock sides of the railway cuttings. The tunnels became more frequent: every minute the train would pop out into a cutting to spectacular views of mountain peaks, then a minute later, dart into another tunnel. Each time, Basin-Head made a cooing sound like a deranged pigeon at his woman and shrugged his shoulders.

By 9:16 a.m., the train rumbled into Jablanica Station, which was surrounded by jagged, wild mountains rising a thousand feet above me. The white minaret of a mosque reached high into the sky with a slender, round tower and pointed black spire – it appeared like an Iraqi scud missile. Another 15 minutes journey later, the September mountain sun had burnt-off the morning mist. The Brute snaked slowly past emerald-green dam lakes surrounded by craggy, steep treeless mountains. Sparse bushes with light-green and pale-red leaves cloaked the mountainsides.

At 10 a.m. all the passengers, including Basin-Head and his woman, scrambled for the carriage exit. This was it – Mostar. I hurriedly packed my things and followed them out, delicately treading down the treacherously narrow and steep steps.

Fortunately, the bus station was adjoined to the train station, and I hurried along the smooth concrete terrace into the bus ticket office. I was greeted with an empty floor the size of a tennis court lined with empty window kiosks. At the far end, I noticed one occupied by a woman who was tending to a couple. At my turn, I asked for a bus to Dubrovnik. The stern lady, who looked like a portly librarian, peered over her glasses at me then wrote assertively on a scrap of paper and pushed it to me.

'8. 12:30?' she demanded.

'12:30 p.m. today, please,' I cordially replied.

'35 ka mark,' she replied without a drop of empathy.

'Pay euro?' I asked. Stern-lady rolled her eyes and tutted.

'Okay.' Then, after tapping on an oversized Casio calculator, she showed me 17.89 on the LED display.

'18 Euro,' she grizzled.

Fine. I gave her a 20-euro note, collected my change in *Republika Kyska* money and deposited my backpack in the luggage storage. I then scurried off to find the world-famous bridge, Stari Most. Walking briskly down the narrow road, I eagerly looked for ordnance holes in the brickwork of the buildings crowding the path. I was mildly disappointed, but a third of the way down Maršala Tita, I passed an abandoned hotel built of pre-fabricated concrete panels.

The two upper storeys were clad with sand-coloured vertical panels decorated with *bas-relief* images of Bosnian stick figures in various poses of farming and fighting each other. The building was punctured by shell holes and the roof panels were caved in – a stark reminder of the fierce fighting that took place in the civil war.

Past two blocks of bakeries and bars, I took a right-left into the cobbled tourist alley of Kujundžiluk Bazar. It had probably barely changed in over four centuries with trinket shops and Turkish *kava* bars lining the street. Brass Ottoman-style coffee pots and jewellery appeared to be the hot sellers for caliphate-loving tourists.

Many of the souvenir shops sported a mini-workshop where a chap leisurely hammered on brass plates. I wondered whether this was a charade: carefully choreographed to mislead the tourists into thinking that they were buying locally made souvenirs. I hazarded a guess that all the stuff was probably imported from Turkey. Or China. But there was no time to investigate the authenticity.

I strode along the cobbled path for another ten minutes dodging puddles and middle-aged Western-European tourists who were admiring the displays of hammering skills. Further down the path, I reached the River Neretva flowing in the valley to my right. Straight ahead was the great arched bridge of Stari Most.

It was a postcard-perfect scene with peanut-brown craggy bluffs towering over the valley leading to steep banks of scrub and boulders plunging to the river. Rough-stone houses with the ubiquitous blush-red roofs loomed precipitously over the steep riverbanks in higgledy-piggledy lines punctuated by the missile-like white minarets of the mosques.

Mostar developed in the fifteenth to sixteenth century as a frontier post of the Ottoman empire. It all looked rather harmonious and idyllic in the brilliant autumn sun under a powder-blue sky: Bosnian Muslims, Christian Orthodox Serbians and Catholic Croats had lived peacefully side-by-side for centuries.

But of course, the peaceful existence came to an explosive conflict in the early 1990s. Following Bosnia and Herzegovina's declaration of independence from Yugoslavia, the Croats and Bosnians fought the Serbian-dominated Yugoslav army in the first siege of Mostar in spring 1992. The iconic bridge was destroyed in November 1993 – a haunting moment for those who watched it on television. By the time the hostilities had ceased, 90,000 residents had fled Mostar and countless buildings were badly damaged.

Following the end of the war, the town was rebuilt with assistance from UNESCO to much of its former glory. Stari Most was reconstructed between 2001 and 2004 with the original stone fished out of the river. They had done a magnificent job, and the stone town looked picturesque nestled among the crocodile-green bushes and trees.

The bridge itself was a high arch with straight approaches making it look thin and fragile close to the apex – much like the Rialto Bridge in Venice. It hung between the hillsides with low-rise stone buildings on its shoulders. Yet, it was a little plain in real-life and looked far more exquisite on the night-shot cover of my Lonely Planet guidebook with all the town lights illuminated it.

I continued towards the bridge, where I realised the approach was a marbled pathway only two metres wide. I had thought it was a road bridge. It had raised step ridges every two feet to avoid slipping and the sides were black wrought iron and stone. At its apex, a bronzed man in his late twenties stood in his red budgie-smugglers on the bridge wall – a member of the Mostar Diving Club. He swivelled his head side-to-side looking for tourists he could scrounge some euros off before making one of his daring leaps.

I kept my eyes staring down at the marble walkway to avoid him cadging me for money – or avoid accidentally looking as his budgie – or maybe both. At the other side, a group of elderly Italian ladies were in a huddle watching Mr-Budgie-Smuggler posing on the apex. They waved their arms about like Italians always do shouting *'Si. Si'*.

I stood near the blushing Italian ladies and took some shots of the river far below. Within moments, another diver in budgie-smugglers badgered me with an open hanky of euro coins.

'You want photo [of a] diver? Pay money or no photo,' he grumpily informed me.

'I'm taking a photo of the bridge, thank you,' I retorted then took an indignant last shot before venturing back across the bridge.

Time was scarce before my 12:30 p.m. Bus journey, so I headed back down the cobbled alley to search for lunch. I passed all the expensive tourist restaurants and found a cheap eatery. I took a wobbly table outside and ordered a Turkish coffee and some sort of meaty dish called *mitick*. I whiled away 45 minutes watching the Italian tourists hobble past, a shadowy figure still merrily hammering away on bits of brass in his trinket store and some Slavic schoolchildren laughing and joking on their way to the bridge.

It was time to head back to the bus station, so I paid the waitress and re-traced my steps back to Maršala Tita and the bus station. I retrieved my backpack then sat at an outdoor café near bus bay number three. I ordered and drank two espressos then began to get nervous, so I walked back and forth along the departure bays and checked every bus that arrived in case they were in the "wrong" bay.

At 12:25 p.m. a coach arrived in the correct bay. I stowed my bag in the luggage hold and paid a euro to the driver for a sticky label to attach to it – for some reason only known to him – then took a seat on the offside before the bus pulled away.

The road to Dubrovnik snaked through light-coloured foliage with patches of dirt and rocks protruding. It reminded me of the Greek countryside.

After I dozed off for a while, we ground to a halt at what looked like a road toll-gate. I then realised this was the Bosnian immigration post. The relief driver in a faded yellow shirt with dark-yellow armpit and neck sweat patches made his way down the coach aisle. He collected passports and identity cards as he went, but those with European passports were not collected. Engine turned off, he left for ten minutes and then returned with the passports and handed them out as the bus roared away.

We were now in no man's land, and my adventure in Bosnia Herzegovina had concluded. This was a stunningly picturesque and fascinating country, that is, except for the grotty factory city of Zenica. Mountains, Russian Orthodox churches with onion domes, slender minarets of mosques, clear mountain rivers, bazaars and cobbled streets.

Following the ravages of the war in the 1990s, Bosnia had come a long way. Intrepid tourists were trickling in to see its world-famous heritage, and I could feel the pulse of the potential of this fascinating country.

Bosnia definitely deserved a spot on my favourites list – and I was now just three ticks behind Andy.

2: The Good, the Bad and the Ugly

Montenegro (No. 75)

After exiting Bosnia via Mostar, I travelled through Croatia to the ancient, marbled city of Dubrovnik. I planned to head down the Dalmatian Coast to Montenegro and try to continue onwards to Albania. After I visited the astonishing marble-clad Venetian city, I walked to Dubrovnik Bus Terminal on Obala Pape Ivana Pavla II and bought a ticket on the bus departing at 8:30 p.m.

The bus arrived horribly late. By the time everyone had boarded and the driver had unnecessarily scrutinised the tickets, it departed at 9:22 p.m. It was going to be well after midnight when the bus arrived in the seaside town of Budva, Montenegro. Still, I was not uncontented, for I was about to enter country number 75.

Onboard the bus, I got chatting to a young Australian lad who was also on his way to Montenegro with a pal he had met along the way. The bus stopped at the Croatian border and the driver turned off the engine and did the passport-collection routine. Presently, he returned with a neat pile of freshly stamped passports, handed them to a lady passenger in the front row and we set off. No sooner had she passed them out to everyone, then we were at the Montenegro border and had to collect them all back again.

Montenegro was the smallest of the ex-Yugoslavian states – a third less land mass than Wales and a population smaller than the population of Leeds. It emerged from the break up unscathed in human loss – since they were buddies of the Serbians – and they created the Union of Serbia and Montenegro in 1992.

I had scarcely heard of Montenegro until I took a cursory read of my Lonely Planet guidebook in preparation for my visit. I had heard of Montenegro in the James Bond movie *Casino Royale* – Bond played poker with the baddie Chiffre in the Hotel Splendide – but I had thought it was a fake country. I decided I would have to find the Hotel Splendide in Podgorica.

Back on the road again, we soon hit Herceg Novi where some passengers disembarked. Then we hit the stunning Bay of Kotor and snaked around the bay with the lights of the towns and villages dotted around the shore and up the hillsides.

The coast road hugged the hills, and we wound around and around the bay – often in sight of the town we had left a long way ago – yet close enough it seemed like I could throw a stone across the bay at it. By 11:30 p.m. we were at Kotor, and a loudly snoring European lad was slapped by his partner and they alighted. The Australian lad began to assemble his stuff to alight, but I told him we were a long way from Budva and showed him my map.

The bus trundled into Budva after midnight, an hour late, thanks to getting stuck behind a car transporter for much of the way. We said our goodbyes, and I followed my hand-drawn map to the Apartment Butua. After 20 mins walk – and asking a staggering drunk for directions – I located the hotel. I needed to make a lot of ground the next day, so I slept without washing to save precious sleeping time and woke early at 7 a.m. to clean and get checked out.

The wheelchair-bound receptionist was very polite, and he offered me breakfast at the all-in rate of 3 euros (£2.20). I sat down for breakfast and was highly excited when the waitress offered freshly cooked sausage and eggs. I was stunned when my plate arrived – in the centre stood a pink boiled sausage. It looked like a severed digit and was not fried in any manner.

After my house-of-horror breakfast, I approached the receptionist who assisted me to call the bus station. It seemed there was an 8:55 a.m. bus to Albania, but it might not run today. I hastily checked out and fast-walked the route back to the bus station.

Sadly, the Albanian bus had been cancelled. The only option to get to Albanian was to take a series of short-haul buses, known as *furgons*. With little sleep, and a hard day travelling from Dubrovnik, I didn't want to abuse my back.

'Any buses to Podgorica?' I enquired.

'Yes, at 9 a.m. The cost is 6 euros,' he replied. That was only £4.40.

'Fine. One ticket please,' I decided.

So, it was time to pull the toilet chain on my dreams of visiting Albania - at least for now; I didn't have enough buffer time in case something went wrong and I missed my flight to Manila. I took my ticket and Lonely Planet guidebook and sat down for an espresso in the café to study my options.

Transport links to Belgrade were still there despite the breakup of the Yugoslavian state; maybe I could try running-up to Belgrade on the overnight train from Podgorica? From there I could take the train back down to Sofia. That would leave me with one country less than planned, but it would be a safer bet as far as timing and the risk of missed connections. However, it meant that I couldn't overtake Andy on this cavale.

The 90-minute bus ride up to Podgorica was pleasant enough, with the famous black mountains spanning the horizon and the Adriatic sea below as the road coiled upwards to the mountains. This was a highly mountainous state – 60 per cent of the land was over a kilometre in height.

The midi-sized bus swayed heavily side-to-side as it negotiated the steep sharp bends leading up the hills from sea level. A while later, when the views of the sea were no more, we wound our way through the hills until we reached a low-rise city. Which looked rather like a small town. Podgorica.

After dropping a few passengers along the way, the bus stopped abruptly at the bus station. I had to get my ticket out of here – maybe the train to Belgrade didn't run daily? Or they might sell out of tickets? So, I grabbed my backpack and scurried off the bus to find the train station. I yomped past taxi drivers, who all looked mind-numbingly bored and under-utilised, and they hollered after me for business.

I located the jaded train station and approached the ticket counters. A grim-faced, middle-aged ticket lady with a long thin nose and outlandish jewellery like Dame Edna confirmed that the Belgrade train was running at 20:05 that evening. I paid 34 euros (£25) for a couchette in a three-berth cabin, then she drew a little diagram on a post-it note.

'See. Loco. See. Train 463. You train 463,' she stabbed at the post-it note with her pen.

Ah. My carriage was the second one behind the locomotive. Oddly, there was no luggage storage at the train station nor any decent cafés. Everything was in the busier bus station next door, so I trailed back past the same touting taxi-drivers, paid 2 euros (£1.50) to deposit my backpack then headed off up Octobarske Revolucije Road.

The streets were quiet, except for a little car traffic, and mostly lined with poorly maintained, Soviet-style pre-fabricated apartments. Rivers of rust ran down from the balcony railings, ground-floor walls were spray-painted with graffiti and the walls and windows were generally grotty. Unkempt potted plants and washing lines of T-shirts adorned the balconies.

The apartment blocks were painted awful dull colours as well: two-tone with either scrapyard-Robin-Reliant blue, out-of-date-pork-chop brown or baby-poo yellow contrasted with dirty-concrete white. It was a worthy adversary to the most deprived inner-city council estates in the UK and was thoroughly grubby and depressing.

I passed a few men of fighting age, and they stared menacingly into my eyes. Not just a glance – a real hard look. Their eyes were sunken and red around the outside as if drunk or taking some drugs. Or maybe they were Balkan zombies? It became disconcerting. What were they staring at, I wondered a bit nervously? Are they looking for a fight? Or planning to pickpocket me? Or just damned rude? On the contrary, the polite ladies ambled by, mostly talking to themselves.

Another odd thing I noticed in Zombieville was that nobody was smiling. Or laughing. Or giggling. They all looked so serious and miserable. Well, I suppose I would be pretty miserable if I had to live in one of those Soviet-era council flats, I thought to myself.

I reached the end of the road and encountered my first landmark, the Prirodnjacki Clock Tower. It was a simple grey stone tower about six storeys high with a few cut-out windows and an arched belfry of sorts.

However, there was no clock. There was no building attached. You couldn't go inside it. Or up it. It looked like a tower hacked off a pre-Norman church. A couple of young men sat nearby and hollered to me with what I presumed was a Slavic version of an angry 'Hey you!'

I stared intently at my city map for the Hotel Splendide. I couldn't find it. Would anyone be insane enough to build a casino among this socialist council estate? Did it actually exist? I swore under my breath and resolved to investigate this further when I found some WiFi signal and internet.

I turned right and headed down Petra Prlje straight past the Osmanagica Mosque. It was a major tourist sight but looked just like a Welsh stone cottage with a tall white chimney stuck on the top. Not much to see here, I thought. I then turned right over the Union Bridge over the Morača River. According to my guidebook, there was a palace located behind the US Consulate. I said to myself I would eat my backpack if there was a palace in this dump.

The consulate was sitting in a spectacular compound of low walls topped by a steel-spiked fence. As I turned the bend just past the entrance, I suddenly realised that it was a deathly quiet road. A pack of stray dogs had taken-up position in the centre of the road, and any passing car or motorbike was game for being chased. I wasn't frightened of the dogs *per se*, but I was afraid of getting rabies if they bit me. As I passed them, I gave them my best angry stare and was ready to scream and scare them off, but thankfully, they just stared at me like the men of the town.

Past the consulate, I turned right into Petrovića Park and located a light-pink building set among the evergreen and deciduous park trees. Was this the House of Petrović Summer House? There was no-one around to ask, and the building was closed-up anyway. Returning to the main path, a Yorkshire terrier spotted me from 200 metres away and began growling and charging towards me. I stood my ground, and surprisingly, a couple became the first Montenegro folk to smile at me – or indeed for that matter – at anything. A foreigner getting bit by a dog? That's funny, huh?

I decided that my last hope for any kind of interesting tourist spot was to see the Saborni Hram Hristovog Vaskrsenja – a modern Serbian Irthiday cathedral which had been under construction since 1993. I walked back up Bulevar Revolucije then turned right down Moscow Road, where I passed the most atrocious apartment blocks that I had ever clapped eyes on. Even a cockroach evicted from a heap of dung would refuse to live there. After two blocks, I found a gravelled car park the size of a football field, and in the centre stood the ivory-white basilica.

It was a typical Orthodox Christian central plan design with a grey dome set above a squat cross, pitched-roof transepts and apses bolted all around the perimeter. The two lower storeys were shoddily clad in huge ill-shaped slabs of stone, but above this, the church was ornately decorated concrete. I shielded my eyes with my hand to imagine what it would look like if the caveman-style bottom was chopped off.

Deliveries of bricks, piles of builders sand and a CAT backhoe loader occupied the car park – it was more like a builder's yard than a place of worship. I circled the building looking for an entrance and came across a middle-aged couple on the east side. They looked typically British, so I approached them and asked if they knew the way into the cathedral.

Sure enough, they had Birmingham accents. For inexplicable reasons, the unfortunate couple had chosen to stay in Podgorica for three days. I was bored after 30 minutes – what on earth had they been doing with their time, I asked?

'Well, we spent a day at a monastery out of town. And it was...' then the husband paused – as if to say it was interesting – then changed his mind, 'it was OK. We just walked around it and wanted to go after an hour.'

They then proceeded to tell me about all the other interesting adventures they had on their adventure – none of which involved Montenegro.

'Do you know where Hotel Splendide from Casino Royale is?' I asked them.

The husband chuckled, 'That's not a real hotel. I think they filmed the scenes in Czechoslovakia.'

'Ah well,' I lamented, 'that's hardly surprising – there's nothing of interest in Podgorica. Why would you visit a casino in this place?'

After goodbyes to the unfortunate Brummies, I followed their directions to the entrance. Once inside, I was surprised to find a polished granite floor and gold-leaf walls adorned with Orthodox frescos. The images of saints were massively overdone: some walls were like football crowds of saints watching a cup-final match. The centrepiece of the cathedral was a huge two-tier brass chandelierf which hung ominously low over a priest in the crossing. He was talking to a young lady who seemed to be in the process of being Christened. The interior was probably the most beautiful thing in Montenegro. No, it was probably the only thing of any beauty at all in Montenegro.

It was now time for lunch, so I found a bar-restaurant on the ground floor of a nearby housing block and ordered a Montenegro pizza and glass of cola for 5.40 euros (£4.00). There were no windows but that didn't bother me: there was nothing of any interest outside. After catching up on social media and checking my route map in the Lonely Planet guidebook, I paid my bill and set-off in the direction of Bulevar Svetog Petra Cetinjskog, heading back in the general direction of the train station.

As I walked along, a fellow on a bike pedalled towards me on the pavement, and whichever way I moved to get out of his way, he changed direction to aim for me. He seemed to be relishing this opportunity to intimidate a Westerner and grinned devilishly at me. At least I got a third smile out of somebody that day – perhaps they were naturally sadistic, I thought.

My next objective was to visit the beach on the east bank of the Morača River. Perhaps I should have known better since after crossing to 13 Jula Avenue and across the wide four-laned Millenium Bridge, the river below had no beach whatsoever. I saw two toddlers far below in the gulley playing on a tennis-court-sized strip of gravel. So this was the beach. Splendid.

There was, according to the unfortunate Montenegro Tourist Authority, a fortress above the beach-cum-gulley. I discovered a mound of worn brickwork, which was collapsing into heaps of rubble, and a galvanised rubbish skip strategically placed in front. I didn't even want to waste my time walking closer to get a look – it was like an industrial area. I would most likely get irritated by the flies around the rubbish skip, or worse still, trip and fall down the steep gulley onto the gravel "beach".

I continued to trudge along, staring back at the menacing eyes watching me, and reached the main crossroads where the road was fenced off by the police with blue-and-white cordon tape. I wondered what it was: a marathon race? A tourist ran over by a steamroller? I turned right towards the town centre and passed ugly low-rise buildings with ground-floor stores with famous branded apparel. Everywhere was closed since it was Sunday. At the town square, *Trg Republike*, stood a fountain.

With nothing to see, and being too early for my 8:05 p.m. train out of this miserable city, I found a bar café to wait. I ordered a Turkish coffee and did some laptop work while listening to the latest music available in Podgorica: The Best of Abba. I was pretty certain it was playing on an audio cassette player.

When it started to turn dusk, I headed back to the train station and took the long route down a narrow lane – where I was nearly run over by a car. Those killer zombies were determined to get me. I fetched my backpack from luggage storage and yomped to platform one, where I waited on a wooden bench with all the other folks wanting to get out of town before dying of boredom.

Two fellows were talking on the next bench.

'Are you going to Belgrade,' I asked the shortest fellow.

'Yes. Belgrade. Waiting,' he held up eight fingers.

'Yes, 8 p.m.,' I replied, 'I will follow you.'

By now, the evening was quite cool and dark – perfect zombie weather. The deathly quiet railway lines, about a half-dozen of them, were illuminated by the orange glow of arc lamps high overhead. After what seemed like an eternity, the station Tannoy announced something in Slavic, and the two men and most other passengers grabbed their possessions and headed across the rail crossing to platform three. It was another 30 minutes of standing in the cold breeze before the train arrived.

It was a red-over-blue JŽ series 461 locomotive

with a white go-faster stripe – a bigger relative of the ex-Yugoslavian railways locomotive which had hauled me to Mostar. The carriages had no numbering on them to my disdain. I headed down the carriage in the wrong direction then doubled back to the second carriage, which was exactly as the ticket lady had told me. Fool me.

After a conductor inspected my ticket, he ushered me on to carriage 463 and took my ticket. I climbed high and squeezed in. It was an ageing, worn carriage just like the ones I had rode in Bosnia. The toilet door was ajar revealing an awful-looking, brown stained toilet. The second cabin had my bunk number, 14, written on it. Inside, the cabin was empty – thankfully there was nobody to bother me yet.

I dumped my bags in the corner to mark my territory and peered about. Three bunks were on the right, a basin was hidden under a hinged wooden tabletop on the left, a fan switch that didn't work, a fluorescent strip light over the sink – which also didn't work – and inside a bathroom cabinet, some old scrunched-up tissues. The beds were quite neatly made up: a rubber-hard pillow covered in a light-green linen case, a matching flat sheet and a folded tartan-designed blanket at the foot of the bed.

Momentarily, an old gent, about 60 years old and wearing a dark jacket and grey pants, entered the cabin. To my surprise he grunted at me – perhaps a zombie greeting? I heard a tap on the window and turned to see that it was his wife in a pink tea-cosy-like knitted hat waving him off. Pleasantries were done, then the train started to grunt and pull away. Since no-one had claimed the top bunk, I stowed my backpack high up there along with my waterproof coat and belt, and the old fellow took the bag rack above the sink.

Quickly getting to work, I went for a pee, took off my boots and put on my sleeping shorts and T-shirt. I folded my jeans with valuables inside and hid them under my pillow. I decided I had to sleep as early as possible – for the train would be arriving early in Belgrade at 6 a.m. – and I locked the cabin door.

That was the last I recall of that awful place, for I rapidly fell asleep in my top bunk to the gentle rocking of the old carriage. My plan to have a decent night's sleep was not meant to be. At the very next station, somebody pushed and pulled the door, flipping the door handle and knocking loudly. Swearing, I reached across and opened it. The train conductor was standing there with a curly-haired, wiry man in his late thirties.

The conductor showed Curly-Hair the top bunk, which caused him to protest in Slavic, but the conductor shrugged his shoulders and fetched down my things to make space. Curly-Hair sighed and quickly scarpered up the steel ladder, shoes and all, where he remained for the rest of the night.

Locking the door again, I foolishly expected a bit of sleep but couldn't rest well because there was a stench of tobacco smoke. The cigarettes they were smoking in the station waiting area and bars in Podgorica were similar to Indonesian ones with a pervasive smell of cloves. The smell wouldn't clear up; perhaps my nose was lined with the smoke? But the odour seemed to be getting stronger, and I wondered if Curly-Hair was smoking in his top bunk. Or maybe he just smelled so strongly of smoke that he was stinking out the cabin?

I eventually managed to doze off but was startled by another round of shaking and banging of the door. I blearily opened it to find the train conductor outside again.

'Passport! Passport!' he bellowed then walked away. I took my jeans from under my rubber-hard pillow and unrolled them. I checked my smartphone; it was 11 p.m. I pulled out my passport then lay with it in hand – trying to rest my eyes – not wanting to fully awake.

After five minutes or so, a customs officer barged in. He chuckled at the sight of me half under my blanket – bare-chested – then thumbed through my passport and grunted 'Okay'. After checking the other two co-habitants, he closed the door and I wearily locked it again.

Wait a minute, I thought, there should also be a Serbian border to cross. I tried to stay awake, cradling my passport on my chest, as I expected to reach the Serbian border within a few minutes. What seemed like forever passed and I dozed off again. Sure enough, at 11:30 p.m. there was another incident of handle-slapping and banging. I unlocked the door again to see a tall border guard.

'Serbia?' I asked.

'Yes.'

'Hooray,' I whooped.

The border guard thumbed through my passport, then holding it in his palm, thunked it with a stainless-less stamp and handed it back. I looked at the stamp:

'DUBELI BRIJEG.26.IX. 15'

I grinned to myself; this was country number 76 – only one behind Andy. I began thinking of where I could travel after my sixth cavale and what kind of excuse I could tell my wife.

Serbia (No. 76)

I was enjoying a fragile sleep on the night train from Podgorica, Montenegro to Belgrade, Serbia. At some hour in my slumber, I was woken again by the old man on the lower bunk who went to urinate. When he came back the stench of urine was overpowering. What had he done? Had the old man pissed all over himself? Or had he tramped through pools of urine and brought it inside the cabin on his shoes? I pulled the faded-green linen sheet over my face to try and mask the smell of Pissy-Git.

That night I woke another couple of times. One occasion was due to a thoughtful intruder who violently hammered away at the door and shook the handle. I shouted at them to no avail. I thudded the door with my fist half a dozen times to frighten them away. Later, I woke-up perspiring like crazy with my chest soaked. The cabin was absolutely roasting and still stank of urine and clove cigarettes.

By 5 a.m., Pissy-Git was up again. What had I done to deserve this? I was not getting any decent sleep. This awful train was like Alcatraz on wheels. I started to wonder if I could dig my way out of the cabin with a dessert spoon and climb through a duct to the roof. In the next cabin, on the other side of the wall next to my right ear, someone was snoring loudly like a pig. I tried to sleep again for a while, then at 5:16 a.m., I realised that my smartphone alarm would be ringing in less than 15 minutes. I surrendered and decided to get ready for the day.

I was going to get another sleeper train the next evening, so there was going to be no opportunity for a decent shower. So, I decided to take my luck in the train bathroom – which was probably a foot deep in urine based on my encounter with Pissy-Git. I padded to the bathroom with my washbag then gingerly washed my face with soap and dried with my microfibre towel. I took the utmost care not to drop any of my belongings lest they touch the urine-dampened lino floor. I brushed my teeth, applied another layer of deodorant to my armpits then carefully re-packed. That would have to do.

I popped back on my T-shirt, yesterday's socks and my boots then lay down again to doze, and as soon as I did, the conductor returned one last time to torment me. He handed back my ticket and cheerfully said goodbye and that there were 20 minutes to go. Thirty minutes later, I heard a scurry of feet and clumping of bags, so I assumed we were at the terminal. I fled, leaving Pissy-Git staring at his shoes and Curly-Man stinking in his bunk.

Belgrade train station was a cluster of dirty-yellow neo-classic buildings. Surprisingly, the station had no arched roof to protect the passengers from the elements. How bitterly cold it would be in the winter? I followed the railway lines past the wheezing locomotive and made a beeline for the ticket office to arrange my ride out of Serbia.

First, I changed my leftover Croatian kuna and Bosnian ka mark, along with 20 euros, into Serbian dinar. The next window was the tourist information counter lady.

'Do you have trains to Sofia?' I enquired.

'Not here. Ticket office,' the lady pointed. Confusingly, I followed her direction back round to another room where there was a line of ticket counters numbered up to 12. I found an empty window and asked the blonde-haired middle-aged lady, who scowled at me in disdain.

'Sofia please,' I requested.

She responded without even lifting her head.

'Not here! International, window 12,' she barked.

At window 12, the lady was much more polite. I paid 30 euros (£22) for a couchette in a 4-bed cabin again – despite my night train from hell the previous night. Armed with my ticket out of town, I searched outside for the luggage storage, which was conveniently located behind a car transporter ramp, past a freight loading bays and through puddles and barriers.

Unburdened of my load, I went in search of breakfast and located a café near platform A – coincidentally called 'Peron A' – translating to 'Station A' in Slavic. I ordered a Turkish coffee and cheese omelette then checked my email.

I was trying to drive up my enthusiasm at country number 76, but the Serbians I had encountered so far were as welcoming as the spear-chucking tribes of North Sentinel Islands. Mind you, Serbia had form given that its bullyboy ex-leader, Slobodan Milošević, had bullied, attacked, ethnic cleansed and tried to annex most of his neighbouring states. He had attempted to fabricate a Greater Serbia from the weaker states of the former Yugoslavian union. But eventually – due to a combination of gritty resistance and patchy intervention from the United Nations and NATO – Slovenia, Croatia, Bosnia and Herzegovina and Macedonia all broke free.

Even the state of Serbia had begun to fracture. The southern province of Kosovo, which was predominantly ethnic Albanian, declared independence in 2008. After bullyboy Milošević got into genocide mode again, NATO and the United Nations undertook the bombing of Belgrade to teach him a damned good lesson. Maybe there were still scars or signs of the bombing campaign? That would be cool to see, I thought. And Milošević thoroughly deserved it.

Andy was getting agitated since my tally was climbing into the seventies. He seemed resolved to the reality that I would match his tally by the end of the week. I emailed him my updated travel plan: I would accomplish 77 by the next day and we would be at parity. Andy had already booked his next holidays to Thailand and Indonesia and would not have any remaining holiday days until late 2016.

The tall waiter in Peron A brought me my Turkish coffee and placed it on the grubby table cloth where a few flies hopped about. I was wondering about the probability of suffering any tummy problems when he served my round omelette floating in a pool of oil with a large bap the size of a half football. I spooned on some ketchup and ate chunks of bread stuffed with lumps of omelette.

At the leisurely time of 9 a.m., I paid my bill of 140 dinars (£0.85) for my oily breakfast then left a small tip. I braved another scowl from the friendly tourist information lady and she told me to take the number two tram to my first stop, the Belgrade Fortress. I drearily stepped out into the drizzle and cold wind and realised it was much cooler than Montenegro: a neon street sign displayed the temperature was 11 Celsius.

I found a small tobacco kiosk to the left side of the main station exit, bought a reloadable tram card with 200 dinars (£1.25) load then waited at the tram platform. A three-carriage, 1960s-looking tram in pine-green pulled up, and I climbed aboard and bagged a single seat on the right. It was a similar layout to the Sarajevo trams with plastic seats, which looked like cheap stackable chairs used in schools. A wonderfully warm current of air rose from the enamelled-steel heater running down the sides of the carriage.

The tram creaked and trundled off, turned left and snaked up the main thoroughfare, Nemanjina Street. I was surprised to notice some bombed-out buildings, about ten storeys high – I figured that these were the Serbian Defence Ministry buildings destroyed by NATO. As I traced my journey on my tourist map, I realised that I was heading in the wrong direction. At the next stop, I alighted, crossed the tram lines and stood shivering for ten minutes until a red number two tram came to relieve me. Ah, warmth again.

The tram trundled along in abject misery down Karadordeva Street and stopped at a turn-around point near the fortress. Everyone alighted in silence and hopped into another red tram in front, so I followed suit. Minutes later it trundled off and stopped right in front of the park and fortress.

The park was pleasant-looking given the cold and continuous drizzle, and I followed the path through a gate to the entrance to the fortress. It was a wooden castle keep with a line of various small tanks and artillery guns parked on a grass lawn in front of the fortress walls. By the time I had found the entrance to the military museum, it dawned on me that it was Monday – which was a closed day for the Slav government for some bizarre reason. I set up my tripod to take a photograph.

Stupidly, probably in ire at the rain which was soaking my camera, I unlatched the base clamp of my tripod, and my Nikon camera dropped like a brick onto the rocky path. Swearing like a trooper, I found the lens hood had broken off, and the casing around the exposure thumb-wheel was cracked.

'Damn it,' I cursed myself.

Angrily, I stuffed the camera under my jacket for protection and marched through the castle keep into the fortress proper. By now, the drizzle had worsened, and at the rear of the fortress, the thick grey cloud hung close the ground and I was getting drenched. There was a cracking view down to the confluence of the Danube and Sava rivers below and no barriers to protect against tumbling down over the fortress wall. A subtle sign warned visitors.

'FALLING RISK YOU WILL DIE'.

The Danube, the second-longest river in Europe, was once the eastern frontier of the Roman Empire. Eighteen centuries earlier, I would have been facing an empire which stretched over 2,500 kilometres to Hadrian's Wall on the northern border of England.

If the weather was fine, then I would have sat on the grassy bank and contemplated the geographical and historical importance of the location. As it was, I was soggy, cold and thoroughly annoyed with myself for cracking my camera case. It was time to go, so I marched back towards the city centre to find the infamous Hotel Moskva. It was a grand-old-dame establishment – all proper with doormen and waiters like the Peninsula Hotel in Hong Kong.

I tramped along Knez Mihailova for ten blocks, and after a stop along the way for an espresso to dry off a bit and clean my camera, I located the Moskva. The building was beautifully renovated, five storeys high with the upper floors painted hazelwood-brown with green accents. The ground floor was walnut brown with a flight of stairs from the pavement to brass revolving doors. Despite my variable knowledge of Cyrillic, the proud sign on the roof was unmistakable, 'хотел Москва'. Although, it seemed to be neither a translation of Serbian or even Russian.

I tramped up the red carpet and through a lounge lobby graced with four huge bronze-and-brass chandeliers like the Hall of Mirrors in Versailles. The walls were newly painted white over burgundy and the ornate ceiling accented with gold leaf. Clusters of armchairs and sofas with rose-red-and-beige-striped fabric were clustered on red Turkish rugs and occupied by dozens of middle-aged guests.

Without batting an eyelid at my hiking boots and unshaven face, a bow-tied waiter with a starched white shirt and black apron showed me to a coffee table graced by two ornate Italian sofas. This would be a perfect spot to have a coffee and something to eat while I dried out and checked my social media.

The Moskva was a majestic Russian Art Nouveau building opened in 1908 by King Petar I Karađorđević and was a hangout with poets and politicos. The venerable guest list including Albert Einstein, Indira Gandhi, Robert de Niro, Pavarotti and Alfred Hitchcock. It was proper posh. And it accepted riff-raff travellers like me.

The lobby café menu was dominated by sandwiches, cakes and drinks. I scanned the menu for raspberry cakes since, staggeringly, Serbia produced 95% of the world's raspberries – so I figured they ought to be cheap and tasty. I settled for a club sandwich at a very reasonable 390 dinar (£2.50) and a pot of Russian leaf tea at 140 dinars a pot (£0.85). What a bargain for a five-star hotel.

After a while, I was joined by two Australian ladies who were on a business trip. We exchanged some stories, then after they departed, a gaggle of Serbian couples milled about the opposite sofa. A miserable-looking Serbian lady glared at me in the hope that I would leave so they could claim both sofas. As I glared back at her, the shirty old bat hurriedly looked away in a thinly disguised disgust. Perhaps she was jealous of my grubby Columbia hiking boots.

I spent a good couple of hours in the hotel in the hope that the rain would subside. When it did a little, I paid the waiter and gave a generous 100 dinar (£0.62) tip. After using their five-star toilet in the basement for a number two, I headed back into the drizzle.

My next target was Republique Square, which promised to be a ten-second wonder, then locate the Automobile Museum where my guidebook claimed Marshal Tito's limousine was on display. I returned along Knez Mihailova then turned right into the square, where I stumbled across another horse-riding dude statue, Mihailo Obrenović III, Prince of Serbia. The statue was in front of the neo-classical National Museum, which would not look out of place in Paris. After ten seconds, which seemed far too long, I pressed on across the square and up Makedonska Street.

After getting a bit lost with the map, I turned left down Majke Jevrosime Kondina and located the museum. Inside, I paid the 200 dinars (£1.25) entrance fee and received a lecture from the curator. Because I was the only visitor, he took a deck chair inside the display hall to keep a beady eye on me – just in case I had a fetish for stealing Marshal Tito memorabilia.

I was somehow expecting to see samples of Eastern European or Russian cars, such as the Yugo, Trabant or even a Zil limousine. Disappointingly, there was not even one communist-era car, and I was rather surprised to find a yellow Robin Reliant with Trotter and Company logos and tiger-seat covers: the car from the television series Only Fools and Horses. I did, however, find Marshall Tito's black 1957 Cadillac Eldorado DeVille and stretched Mercedes limousine on display, which was some compensation.

My final task was to head back to the buildings bombed by NATO, which I had spied near the train station. I walked south then took a left down Kralja Milana, passing the City Assembly and National Palace, until I reached Slavija Square. I recognised the roundabout where I had jumped off the number two tram earlier.

I walked back down Nemanjina Street but couldn't find any bombed buildings along the way. Where were they? As I neared the train station, I found the Yugoslavia Ministry of Defence Buildings. There was a gaping hole in the third and fourth storey of building Block A on the right – it looked like a missile had pierced the fifth-floor side and exited the front facade on the third floor. It had been bombed in 1999 by NATO, and the Serbian government had left it like an open war-wound to try and gain sympathy over claims of bullying from the West. They had to be joking – it was like Adolf Hitler showing off his war wound in a pub.

Then it was back to the train station, where I recovered my backpack, charged my devices and dried off in Peron A Café. I dined on a beefburger for dinner and washed it down with several cups of Turkish coffee – which in hindsight wasn't a smart way to get a decent sleep on the train. The sleeper was due at 10:05 p.m. – a long and boring wait – but anyhow, I did my write-ups and found myself a hostel in Sofia on the Booking.com website. I made a reservation for two nights and sketched the direction map on the back of an old receipt I found in my pocket.

It was now 9:30 p.m., and I hadn't heard any announcements for the Sofia train nor seen any signs of carriages being shunted to the platform. All I could see were a few forlorn carriages lounging at platform one. I decided it would be prudent to scout about, so I asked the waiter for my bill. It was 680 dinar Serbia (£4.20), but when I opened my wallet, I had only 600 in notes.

'Can I pay part in euro?' I asked.

'Sure. Add euro 60 cents,' the waiter replied.

I rummaged around in my wallet. I hadn't any local Serbian coins left and wanted to give a decent tip to the waiter since he had been kind and attentive. I gave him a couple of two-euro coins, and he thanked me profusely – which I assumed meant I had over-tipped. He clicked his heels and dashed around the restaurant singing to himself. That was just way too happy, so besieged with tipper's remorse, I calculated the tip in my head. It was around a 500 dinar tip (£3.00), which was a lot, since a typical bill seemed to be 200 to 300. Never mind, I thought to myself.

Outside, I approached three carriages at platform one where a few-dozen passengers and a couple of conductors milled about. The other platforms were like a deserted steel mill in a Hollywood movie. I approached a conductor.

'Belgrade?' I asked.

'*Da, da,*' he answered.

I showed him my ticket and pointed to the carriage number.

'4-6-3. 4-6-3.' I pointed to him. He grabbed my ticket

'Here. Follow,' he beckoned.

The metal stairs were as steep as the Mayan temple steps of the Bosnian railway carriages, and inside it looked precisely the same – but way more decrepit and dilapidated. It was essentially a notch above an Indian cattle train smeared in animal excrement. I peeked into the toilet, which had an enamelled toilet bowl and a steel foot-pedal which allowed your deposit to slide into a sluice box. Or the railway gravel underneath – who knows.

There was a washroom next door. I anxiously peered in and noticed a rusted and badly painted paper towel dispenser – rancid looking and empty of towels. The floor was dirty hospital-green with a rusted floor drain and stainless steel sink. This was patently not the Orient Express.

I continued to follow the guard who led me to a six-berth cabin in the middle of the carriage. I poked my head inside where a short blonde-haired woman was milling about with her wheelie suitcase.

'Here. 61. Here,' he prompted.

'But this is six-berth. I paid for a four-berth,' I grumbled in futility.

The conductor looked at me and shrugged his shoulders – he couldn't understand my English. The lady piped-up in perfect English but with a Russian-sounding accent.

'I also complained. I just went to the ticket office to protest that I had paid for a four-berth. They said sorry but only four people are allowed inside. It's not the same, I told them,' she grumbled.

The conductor slipped away to get ready for the journey, and I decided to inspect my abode for the night. The cabin was absolutely falling apart: the main light was no brighter than a birthday-cake candle – the fluorescent tube shone grey through the cracked and grubby diffuser; there were three chocolate-brown material-covered couchettes on each side with heavily-painted steel frames with rust poking through; and the floor was shabby blue carpet, which looked like it had been salvaged from a council tip. The knobs had fallen off all the instruments for ventilation, heating and the

Tannoy volume. I tried closing the light-blue curtains which covered the aisle windows, but they were rotten – half the hooks were ripped off the hem. I had paid to sleep in this dump; at least squatters didn't need to pay for their room, I thought.

'I want to take the middle bunk,' I told the lady.

'Me too, the lower bunks are near the carpet – it's dirty and dusty,' she quipped.

She was quite organised and pottered around the cabin preparing things. We agreed to stow our baggage on the lower bunks, and presently, the conductor returned with a pile of dirty-white linen folded into newspaper-sized piles. He placed a pillowcase and two sheets in four piles on the middle bunks.

'Looks like we are expecting guests,' I said assumingly, shortly after which the conductor returned with two young men with shaven heads. He led them into the cabin, so I decided to step back into the aisle. They looked Balkan, and they smiled in silence and stowed their bags in the lower bunks after talking in *Balkanese* to the lady.

'I told them they can take the top two bunks,' said the lady, 'I am from Serbia. I work on the cruise ships and travelling to see a friend in Eastern Bulgaria.'

Cruise-Lady busied herself making the beds, while I helped to put pillowcases on the stained pillows, which were placed at the cabin-door end. The conductor returned with four red blankets, which had a tartan design. I finished setting up my couchette then took off my boots and lay down to make space.

I looked at the underside of the couchette above me, where a long mirror was affixed to it. The end closest to my head had been broken into a large dagger shape and was hanging down enough to insert my finger behind it. If I sat upright in the night, the giant shard would be level with my scalp. I shuddered. I couldn't sleep there – even thinking about it scared me.

'Why don't you turn around?' suggested Cruise-Lady.

'Great idea. Why didn't I think of that?' I replied in appreciation and rearranged my pillow to the window end.

The station guard blew his whistle, and the locomotive blew its horn and gave an initial tug of the three carriages, which rattled angrily back and forth on their couplings. Then we were away. I walked down the aisle to stretch my legs and came across an Australian couple just two cabins down. They were staring at their cabin in disbelief – probably wondering what they had let themselves in for.

'Wonderful cabin, huh?' I told them.

They laughed feebly and continued to stare at their squatter's bedroom on wheels.

Back at the cabin, the two Balkanese were already perched on their upper bunks, and Cruise-Lady was also getting tucked-in. There was no point in trying to brush my teeth or wash in the washroom: it was an utterly lost hope. It's not even worth to change into my shorts and tee-Shirt, I thought, so I decided to just sleep in my jeans and shirt. I lay down under the handkerchief-sized bedsheet and stared at the great shard of broken glass above the foot of the bed.

The Balkanese contingency were having a good banter going and laughing amongst themselves.

'Where are the guys from?' I asked Cruise-Lady.

'They say they are from Bosnia. I'm not sure what ethnic group they are, though.'

I set my smartphone for 8 a.m. and dozed off. I slept rather soundly on the sleeper train despite the bedding sized for a gnome and the giant shard-of-death suspended above me. I awoke at 7 a.m. to someone tapping on the cabin window.

'Are we at the border?' I asked Cruise-Lady.

'Yes, we are at the Serbian border,' she answered.

Ace. Another tick, I was about to catch up with Andy.

I thought it best to take a quick wee before the border guards turned-up. The toilet was a bit creepy because there was no working light, and I stood my distance at the entrance urinating on the rusty flap in the bottom of the toilet bowl. I stepped on the enormous pedal, but no water flushed into the bowl. My urine just tipped into the void below, and some used toilet paper in the bowl slithered downhill a little, a glob of it sliding off the end of the flap into the darkness – presumably landing in a heap at the Serbian border.

Later, back in my bunk, the Serbian border guard returned. The Bosnian above me, who had been designated the official door opener and closer, unhooked the door latch. I reached for my eyeglasses, which were scorching hot on the heater, and pulled my passport out of my pocket to present to the border guard.

He took my passport, looked at me lying down then shook his head disapprovingly. I propped myself up on my elbows to make a better impression, and he studied my face and compared it with my passport. Momentarily, he shrugged his shoulders and slinked away, clutching a thick wedge of various red and blue passports.

Another intrusion later at the Bulgarian border, and following the usual bated breath that my passport would be returned safely, we were rolling on our way again. I snoozed a little more until I awoke to a tap on the cabin door again, and the conductor advised that we were reaching Sofia in ten minutes.

There ended my visit to Serbia. I was a little apprehensive about this visit since, according to other Balkan people I had spoken with, the Serbs were somewhat boastful and felt they were superior to the other folk in that region. Despite the rotten weather, I found the communist past and military escapades were interesting, and it was a neat little tick on the step to matching Andy's tally.

Country number 77 beckoned, and I would match Andy's tally that day. That was worth suffering a nasty train journey.

Bulgaria (No. 77)

I was completely surprised to discover that the platforms in Sofia Central Station were all brand spanking new. Unfinished cement – yes – but certainly not the typically decrepit Cold-War-era stations of Eastern Europe. A throng of uniformed porters deluged the limited passengers to fight over the slim pickings.

'Where you go? You need taxi? You need help?'

'Sorry, I don't need anything,' I replied

The Serbian Cruise-Lady looked like she needed help with her unnecessarily large suitcase, and a frenzy of pushing and shoving porters ensued – allowing me to make my getaway. The station was still under construction, and the underpasses were granite-tiled halfway up the wall and the exit to the concourse was bare concrete. Still, it was impressive that they were investing in the future, or to be more precise – according to the boastful boilerplates – it was the European Union that was investing.

I changed 50 euros into 95 Bulgarian lev, had a

breakfast of goats-cheese börek pastry and Turkish coffee then took the Metro to Dan Lukha station. I exited to a shabby residential street. Navigating was a bit awkward since my improvised map had Roman-alphabet street names but all the street signs were in Cyrillic. I scrutinised the signs intently. I usually found that if I stared at Cyrillic words for a few minutes, the name seemed to pop right out at me – just like staring at one of those 3D pictures that jump out of a pattern of dots when you stare at it.

It was claimed that Cyrillic originated in Bulgaria. Saint Cyril developed the forerunner of Cyrillic to translate the Greek alphabet into one that could support the wider number of 43 letters needed for the richer sounds of the Slavic languages. It was all double Dutch to me.

I eventually located The Ten Coins Hostel and was checked in by the owner who was a portly man in his thirties. He was a traveller and told me half his life story. After he had showed me my four-bed dormitory with kiddie beds and his collection of foreign coins and banknotes, I showered then took the Metro to Serdica in Sofia's city centre.

Bulgaria was not a huge country: at the end of the communist era, its entire population of 8.8 million was about the size of modern London. It was facing a demographic timebomb – only six babies were being born for every ten citizens dying. Within a decade of the end of communism, the population had dropped by the size of Glasgow. Another decade later, in 2010, it had dropped again by size of the population of Liverpool. It had dropped a staggering 50 places in the world population ranking from number 51 in 1950 to 105 in 2015. Would there be anyone in the city centre, I wondered.

Sofia was not an unpretty city: there had been a lot of investment in renovating the buildings and streets. In the open concourse of Serdica, I bought a fresh tourist T-shirt of Vladimir Putin and underneath it read 'НАС НЕ Д ОГОНЯ Т'. Which according to the vendor was a reference to the girl pop group t.A.T.u and their hit song, 'Not gonna get us'.

Up the Metro station exit stairs, I appeared right in the centre of Sofia City. It was claimed that the city was founded 7,000 years ago, which made it the second-oldest city on the continent. Getting my orientation with the Lonely Planet map, I was on the main crossroads with the Communist Party Building ahead of me, and the Sofia Balkan Hotel to my right was shrouded with construction works.

Right in front of me stood the gold Saint Sofia Statue. The woman stood on a column in an "I'm flying" pose from the *Titanic* movie and wore a blocky mural crown and with her pet owl on her outstretched arm. Curiously, she was facing the Communist Party building. Was this a signal? Or maybe she was facing Mecca?

I looked around for somewhere to eat and passed a building painted in red, white and green stripes. I discovered it was the headquarters of the Socialist Party of Bulgaria. The front had an impressive collection of socialist statues of workers and fighters. One statue was of a man with a rifle; how on earth was that a worker's statue? Did Bulgarian steelworkers run around shooting people?

Bewildered and now hungry, I looped-back up Todor Alexandrov and found a café, which miraculously served hot food. Surnames with suffixes of '-ov' were common in Bulgaria. Traditionally, they took their father's first name and added an -ov for their surname. Then they adopted their grandfather's first name. If I had been a Bulgarian then perhaps my name would have been Albert Kennov.

I did some city sightseeing of the Communist Party Building, National Art Gallery and the Russian church of St. Nicholas of Myra the Wonderworker, which sounded like it was dedicated to a Russian version of Batwoman.

Generally heading in the direction of the Monument to the Russian Army, I was drawn to Sofia's largest and most iconic sight – the Orthodox St. Alexsander Nevski Cathedral. Its huge gold domes were visible from a distance and made it easy to locate. By now, I was being tailed by an inquisitive Sofian who took a liking to my DSLR camera. He avidly asked questions and told me how expensive cameras were in Bulgaria. He hoped to be able to travel to Germany to buy one, which I thought was a bit unambitious as a life goal.

It started to dawn on me that the Bulgarians were a wee bit eccentric. They agree or approve by shaking their head. Along with the Scots and Irish, they are one of only three nations that play bagpipes in their traditional music. They also had the bright idea of backing the Germans in the Second World War – despite doing so in the First World War and being heavily punished for it under the Treaty of Neuilly – which included the handover of all its territories and payment of heavy reparations. Not a clever idea.

Turning left down Noemvri, the cobbled street led uphill to the spectacular cathedral. I took a position on a pedestrian zone to the left and watched in amazement at its beauty. Built as a tribute to the Russian army who liberated Bulgaria from the Ottoman Empire in 1878, it was built in Neo-Byzantine style and was the second-largest cathedral in the Balkans. It was a based on typical Orthodox Christian central-plan design, with a long nave, gold-leafed domes and two-level basilica roof with two layers of clerestory. Huge apses with copper domes were appended to the transepts.

I ventured inside and found it unusually dark with brass chandeliers with dim bulbs. Brass stands for offering candles stood to the right, and I observed here were no pews. Maybe they brought out plastic fold-away chairs on Sundays? Or maybe they preferred standing like in the pubs in Britain? Who knows? I wondered why it was so basic for such a glorious cathedral: it was the opposite of the unfinished Cathedral in Podgorica, which had a dull exterior and beautiful interior.

Back to Tsar Osvoboditel, my main target of the day was the Monument to the Soviet Army. I am a massive fan of communist monuments: Stalinist designs, socialist themes and Cold-War patriotic statues. At the corner of Vasil Levsky, I found the compact Knyazheska Park that housed the monument.

The monument was built in 1954 on the 10th anniversary of the liberation by the Soviet Army and looked as jaded as a Serbian Railway carriage. I passed a huge plinth with the Balkan's favourite statue, a bloke-hero on a horse, and further along was a stone pathway leading up to the monument lined with cast-iron wreathes. The entrance to the main pathway was flanked by two plinths with fantastic communist cast-iron statues.

The cenrepiece of one statue was a Soviet soldier on an army motorbike being welcomed by the Bulgarian peasants and uniformed busty ladies patriotically holding a toddler aloft. I think the sculptor copied a scene of Steve McQueen in the Hollywood movie *The Great Escape*. The characters were all dressed in flat caps and shawls, and they were embracing and kissing each other as one does in liberation. What a wonderful sight – full of messages. And full of exaggeration.

The liberation statue itself was about three storeys high. Its central figure was a Russian soldier holding a rifle aloft and hugging a Bulgarian peasant-dude who, of course, was shorter and looked pretty chuffed at being liberated. The peasant probably changed his mind a decade later when he had to live in a pre-fabricated socialist apartment block and would be shipped to a gulag in Siberia if he complained. Naturally, the woman and baby were there for the photo-taking as well.

Some teenagers were noisily skateboarding up and down the monument ramps. If their fathers had dared to skateboard over a Soviet war memorial in the Communist era they would have been shipped off to Siberia on the charge of desecration. But at least the statues weren't graffiti-covered or vandalised. I took some funny photos together with the cast-iron peasant celebrants then headed back to the small café at the park's edge of Vasil Levski.

I decided to take a short rest and a celebratory Shumensko beer for reaching 77 countries – level with Andy. A club cigar went down well too, and despite interruptions from a Romanian beggar girl, I enjoyed a smug satisfaction that I had got this far. I decided to post an update on Facebook at my achievement and tagged Andy in the posting.

There were warnings in my travel guidebook to take care in quiet areas around parks and abandoned areas at night. So since it was starting to get late, I decided it wise to return to the pedestrianised Vitosha Boulevard where I dined alfresco on chicken and broccoli fettuccine and a pint of Zagorka draft beer, which came to the princely sum of 13 lev (£5).

Back at the hostel, one of the Japanese guys from the large dormitory was cooking a sort of omelette in the kitchen and another was still huddled over his Apple Macbook. I think he must have been rooted there the entire day, and he avidly tapped away on his keyboard. It was still too early to sleep, so I broke out my laptop to catch-up with some travel notes on the kitchen table and refreshed myself with some glasses of water.

An hour later, two of my dormitory-mates arrived: a Russian girl who had been visiting a conference and a Dutch guy who checked in and milled back and forth to our four-bed dormitory. The Russian girl returned after changing, and we chatted for a while. She looked like I imagined a Russian librarian would. It transpired she was living in Prague, which was a lovely city, but she had become bored. She wanted to travel.

'Where do you want to travel to?' I asked.

'Spain. I want to visit Catalonia. They have a different language from the Spanish,' she joyfully replied.

'They are voting for independence,' I noted, 'Soon Europe will be made up of a hundred small states. Not unlike the Ukraine situation.'

She perked-up. I wanted to understand what she thought about the Russian invasion of Crimea and Eastern Ukraine.

'Crimea belonged to Russia, anyway,' she calmly replied, 'and so we are just getting it back again.'

'But you have to go about it the right way,' I replied, 'you can't just invade. How about the Roman Empire? They ruled much of Europe in their day, including England. The Italians can't just invade

England then say it used to belong to them.'

Russian-Librarian-Girl thought for a moment calmly.

'But the Eastern Ukrainians want to be together with Russia,' she retorted.

Well, I wasn't going to convince her, but at least, it confirmed my suspicions that the Russians thought nothing of invading other countries arbitrarily based on their opinion of what was right. Or not.

That night I slept bloody awfully. The Bulgarian mattress crunched and grated under my body, and our new dorm-mate, the Dutchman in the corner, was regularly tossing and turning too. Russian-Librarian-Girl made funny noises in her sleep: sort of a cross between a sigh and a moan. But I was determined to sleep as much as possible to save my energy for the long flight home to Manila. I ignored the others getting ready one-by-one, and by the time I arose, it was just the Dutchman and myself.

I washed and paid my 36 lev (£13.50) to the hostel owner. He asked what I would do today.

'I plan to search for interesting communist-era housing,' I told him.

'The tourists like the Cold War thing. I had some Japanese guests asking where they could see Communist-era architecture. I told them to walk about this area.'

He pointed to the area around the hostel on a map above his head.

'Sounds interesting, I'd love to see that too. Where exactly?' I pushed him.

So, he pointed out some local areas of interest, including the local produce market, and I thanked him and left the hostel into the glorious sun.

I passed market stalls selling pumpkins piled up in

enormous waist-high heaps the area of a squash court, ate some awful food in a cafeteria and wandered the 1970s-style Socialist housing blocks. They were certainly ugly enough – quite forlorn with rusting balconies – but nothing like their utterly awful counterparts in Podgorica.

A jolly Iranian guy at the hostel had told me that the cultural centre was worth a visit, so I took the Metro to NDK Station. I visited the centre and by evening returned to Vitosha again to eat. I passed Sofians at their usual business of supping espressos and puffing on cigarettes outside the shop fronts and soon arrived at the affable Raffy's. I chose a small table at the alfresco dining area right under a patio heater, which was toasting warm.

I ordered a dish of pork steak and a local Bulgarian wine, a demi-bottle of Tricycle Cabernet Syrah Merlot. The wine was most excellent, and soon enough, my dinner was consumed. I enjoyed some social media while smoking my remaining Goldfoot cigarillos washed down by Tricycle until it was time to head back to the Ten Coins. Back at the common room, I greeted my fellow travellers, who were peeling vegetables, and pretended I hadn't been dining on pork steak and wine while puffing on cigars.

Today was 1 October 2015 and the last day of my sixth cavale. I had been woken at 3 a.m. by my daughter accidentally calling me from her mobile, and I spent an hour panicking and trying to call her and my wife to see if everything was alright. I couldn't sleep properly after that, and my bunkmates, the bearded Dutch guy and the Russian-Librarian-Girl, tossed and turned on the *cheapo* Bulgarian mattresses, which made loud crunching noises again as the springs twisted and grated against each other.

I fell asleep again for a good while and awoke with a startle at 10:23 a.m.; it was well past my wake-up time, but anyway, my flight was an evening one. I took a final hot shower and realised inside the bathroom that I had forgotten to take my towel with me. So I had to drip dry and walk through the hostel common room in wet shorts. After goodbyes to the kindly hostel owner, I strode out into the Bulgarian autumn sun like the prisoner Billy Hayes in the movie Midnight Express.

I took the squeaky-clean Metro line to Sofia airport. And wow, the stations were all new, the terminal station was brand spanking new and the Sofia Airport Terminal Two was a modern design with an arched skylighted roof like Hong Kong airport. All those European Union funds were going somewhere useful – I couldn't help but feel that the Bulgarian people were feeling upbeat with all these on-going works to drag it out of the sad, decaying socialism to European Union standards, whatever that may be.

Overall, Cavale Six was a success: I had covered the bulk of the Balkans. Was Slovenia the Balkans? A Japanese guy last night had told me that it wasn't. Anyhow, my tally was now 77, which equalled Andy. I was now positioned to overtake him on the home stretch.

My mind was already thinking about how, and where, I would reach country number 78. My next target on my goal to reach 100 countries.

OVERTAKING ANDY

3: Backbreaking Bangladesh

So there I was, gloating after my Balkan trip and back at home in The Philippines. I was exchanging emails with Andy who was not certain that he was going to get any new ticks in the next 12 months. He had already booked a holiday to Laos and a ski trip to Austria, but they were not new countries for him. So, I had a window of opportunity to pole-vault over his tally, which was a milestone on the road to reach the century.

I needed to make a short visit to England ahead of my repatriation in December. Aha! That would be a perfect opportunity to hit a tick or two on the way there and back from Manila. I was salivating at the prospect of hopping through some interesting destinations, but my wife was already firing warning shots about dilly-dallying along the way.

'You just go straight there and back, huh?' she warned.

'Sure, I will go in a straight line,' I writhed, 'but those direct flights are *so* expensive. I might need to buy cheap one-way flights...'

She knew I wouldn't get a direct flight, yet I got the message to keep my itinerary tight. My first act was to buy a one-way flight from Manila to Bangladesh. It was a bargain flight and would boost my miserable tally for Asia. And I was flying west so it was heading loosely in the right direction. Since Bangladesh was a dirt-poor and seriously overcrowded country, I had no interest in spending much time there or touring about. I just wanted to see the capital and get a brief taste of the people.

Where could my next hop be? I kept thinking about those hard-to-get-reach places in Europe. Those countries that Andy hadn't visited or were off the beaten track. Or a bit dodgy to visit? And then the owner of the Ten Coins Hostel came to mind – he was a Ukrainian. He had told me he had been desperate to get his family out of Ukraine due to the fighting. Also, I had met a young Ukrainian guy in a hostel in Stockholm – he was hiding there to avoid conscription.

Both these Ukrainians were worried about the state of their country due to Russia annexing the Crimean Peninsula in 2015 and the on-going conflict in the eastern part of the country. And then I recalled the Russian lady in the Ten Coins who believed that Russia had the right to garner swathes of ex-Soviet Socialist Republics at will. These must have been divine messages. Yes, how about visiting Ukraine? Devilish – a bit bold – and Andy hadn't been there. Well, not exactly true. Both of us had travelled through Ukraine on the train from Budapest to Moscow 25 years earlier – but that didn't score.

So, I hunted on Skyscanner and Expedia to check flights to Ukraine. Perfect, there were reasonably priced flights from Manchester to Kiev on KLM and Ukrainian Airlines. And then I began to think what I would do there. Of course. There was Chernobyl. Magic, truly a top-ten dark tourist site. I trawled the internet for day tours to Chernobyl. Brilliant – 100 US dollars and it was locked in. Option for a Geiger counter? Yes, I will take one of those, please. Sorted.

So, I firmed up my flights to Dhaka, Manchester and Kiev then booked myself a cheap hotel in Dhaka and a hostel in Kiev. Then I informed Andy that I would be getting two more ticks.

Bangladesh (No. 78)

This was going to be it. Unless Andy announced he had taken a day flight to Guernsey the previous night, I was going to overtake his tally of 77 countries that very day. I was excited at the prospect of finally overtaking him after many years.

I took a ridiculously early – but satisfyingly cheap – Tigerair flight at 6:05 a.m. from Manila then suffered a gruelling and utterly boring eight hours in Changi Airport in Singapore. I surfed the internet, inspected chocolate bars in the duty-free shops, drank as much water as possible from the water fountains and urinated in every bathroom in the terminal. Tigerair flight 2729 boarded at 4:45 p.m., and I had never been so desperate to board an aircraft.

The flight to Dhaka was pleasant enough, although it was a budget airline with no food. Or drinks. Or pillows – or blankets. And enough leg-room for a pygmy. Still, it departed promptly on schedule and landed just ahead of time shortly before 8 p.m., and I disembarked. The majority of the passengers were Bangladeshis, but there were a handful of Westerners. I noticed a European-looking businessman who strode past at a fair rate of knots, so I decided to strut after him to see where the visa-on-arrival kiosk was.

Euro-Strider marched to the end of the gate area, down some steps then joined a short queue of foreigners in front of two wooden desks. I peeked around the queue to see it was manned by officers dressed in khaki green uniforms with 'Police' marked on their lapels.

'Is this the visa-on-arrival?' I asked Euro-Strider.

'Yes,' he answered in a Nordic accent, 'you present your passport here then pay over there,' he nodded at a bank kiosk nearby, 'then head to the immigration queue.'

'How much does it cost?' I enquired.

'Oh, it depends. Sometimes more, sometimes less. I think it's 51 US dollars, but I met someone who negotiated the price down to 17 dollars – I also know an American who paid 174 dollars,' he advised.

After Euro-Strider's turn, I presented my passport to the Police-cum-immigration-officer

'Is this your first time in Bangladesh?' he asked me.

'Yes.'

Police-cum-immigration-officer crouched over a giant ledger on his old wooden desk. It was inches thick with oversized pages much like an accountants ledger from Samuel Pepy's days. He slowly wrote an entry in the log copying from my passport then handed me a slip of paper.

'Pay 51 US dollars,' he sternly informed me.

After paying at a counter of the Sonali Bank, I followed Euro-Strider back to the second Police-cum-immigration-officer.

'They have changed the procedure again,' he sighed, 'we now need to queue here as well.

After the second officer zealously thumbed through my passport, I joined the real immigration counter queue where another officer meticulously inspected my hundreds of passport stamps before asking me to stand for a photo.

'Where are you from?' he asked me.

'England,' I replied wondering why he hadn't noticed 'United Kingdom' printed on the front of my passport.

'Please, down. You are very tall for my camera,' he instructed.

I stooped down while he took a photo, then with a *whump* of his stamp, I was though. Woohoo. I walked to the luggage carousel area, which was thronged by passengers. To the right of the hatch, where baggage emerged on the carousel, was a window two-metres high by about five wide. I heard gasps from some of the passengers closer to the window, so I grabbed a trolley and headed to the front of the queue.

There were three airport workers behind the window, and one of them grabbed a suitcase off a truck bed and threw it down two metres on to the carousel with all his might. The suitcase made an almighty crunching sound

'What the fuck!' shouted a big fat American.

A Bangladeshi was fetching his suitcase off the carousel.

'I am sorry you have to see that. I am ashamed of my fellow countrymen,' he waggled his head in shame.

The last dozen of us remaining passengers watched in shock as the airport workers hurled our baggage onto the carousel with all their strength. The workers didn't bat an eyelid; it was unimaginable that they were boldly trying to damage our baggage right in front of our eyes.

My suitcase was the last one and fortunately wasn't split open. I was waved through the customs green channel then entered the arrivals hall to look for a burean de change. I exchanged 120 US dollars and some left-over Singapore dollars into Bangladeshi taka then headed to the service car kiosks. There were three kiosks in a row, and their occupants all waved furiously at me.

'Sir! Sir! Here. Where are you from?' asked one of them excitedly.

'England.'

'Oh yes. Manchester United. Chelsea. Where are you going?' he asked.

I showed him the hotel address I was clutching.

'Service car is 650 taka – standard rates,' he advised me.

That was only £5.60, which was not unreasonable for an airport taxi. I paid the man in the kiosk, and his colleague beckoned me to follow him outside. He walked ten metres to the kerbside then held his hand aloft to stop a small black Kia car. It was not even labelled as a service car or taxi and was absolutely rotten. The Kia looked like it had endured a long hard life getting battered in Dhaka.

The driver got out and opened the boot, then the kiosk-guy handed him two 100 taka notes (£1.70).

'What the hell?' I protested, 'I just paid you 650 taka – then you just hailed a wrecked car and paid him 200. This piece of junk is not even a real service car!'

'This real,' Kiosk-Conman said, 'don't worry – see my identity card.' He proudly presented his lanyard.

'Your identity card doesn't prove this is a real service car,' I complained.

I remonstrated a little but decided to concede and trust the taxi driver. But I was not going to give even one taka tip to Kiosk-Conman. The driver, who was slight and skinny, waggled his head then helped me in and set-off. The car had rotten upholstery, but at least the air conditioning worked. Waggly-Driver trundled a few blocks out of the airport area then along a dimly lit wide avenue choked with speeding buses sounding their horns.

'Look left. Look [for] your hotel,' asked Waggly-Driver.

'Erm. Aren't you supposed to know where the hotel is?'

'Yes. Where [are] you from?' he rapidly changed the conversation.

'England?'

'I love England. Wayne Rooney. Beckham. Manchester United,' he excitedly told me as he continued to waggle his head.

We reached a junction, U-turned into the service road and drove at about two kilometres per hour.

'Where you hotel?' he asked in awful English,

'I don't know. I thought you were the taxi driver,' I retorted.

A lorry was angrily horning behind us.

'Why don't you ask someone?' I asked.

'Cannot. No good. You have [the] hotel telephone?' the driver politely answered.

I pulled out my boarding pass, which I had scribbled the hotel details, and read it to him. He called them and discovered we were only 20 metres away. He turned back to road 10 then stopped outside the hotel.

Waggly-Driver turned towards me, 'Give present.'

Cheeky swine, I thought.

'You have to help me get out first,' I instructed.

Waggly-Driver leapt out and loitered around me. I gave him 50 taka (£0.43), and he frowned back at me.

'This [is] only change,' he moaned.

I grumbled then exchanged it for a 100 taka note, and he muttered and got back in his taxi.

The bellboy assisted me inside the Redwood Hotel & Suites, which sounded way too upmarket for a grubby one-star hotel. I checked in at the simple reception, paid 2,750 taka (£23.70) for two nights then took the lift to the third floor. Inside the lift, the bellboy smiled intently at me.

'Where are you from, Sir?' he enquired.

'England,' I replied.

'Oh, London. Me, I love London,' he beamed.

The room was acceptable, but tatty, and continued the grubby theme. I gave the bellboy a 50 taka tip (£0.43) then went down to the William Café on the ground floor. A waiter assisted me to a free table.

'Where are you from, Sir?' he eagerly asked.

'England.'

'Oh,' he beamed, 'I love Sherlock Holmes. I have read his every book. I like London.'

I was pretty sure that nineteenth-century London was not exactly a likeable place. This whole England thing was going to get tiresome, I thought to myself. Maybe I should say I am from somewhere obscure such as Azerbaijan? Or the Faroe Islands? That should get them puzzled.

There seemed to be no Asian food on the menu, so I settled for a hot-dog and an Americano coffee then retired to my room. The traffic noise was unimaginable, and even at three floors up and being a heavy sleeper, I felt like I was trying to sleep on the central reservation of the M1 Motorway.

Morning came, and I had set my alarm for 6 a.m. to hit the city early. Interestingly, the bathtub had no shower curtain. I stepped in the shower and discovered, after fuming for ten minutes, that there was no hot water. Seething, I dressed and went down to reception.

'I seem to be having trouble with my hot water,' I complained.

The receptionist-boy smiled cheerfully, 'Sorry Sir, you need to let the water run for 15 to 20 minutes first.'

'What!'

I decided to take breakfast first, so I took the lift to the roof-top café on the fifth floor. There was just myself and an East Asian guy. The breakfast spread was composed of bland omelette, vegetable rice, unspiced dhal, vegetables in sauce and nan bread. There was sliced bread, but the toaster was cracked and heavily rusted – it looked like it had been found on a rubbish tip!

After drinking coffee and forcing myself to eat a sample of each dish, I stepped out the sliding glass door to take a look at the street. It was noisier than any I had ever experienced with car and bus horns blaring incessantly.

After the disappointing breakfast and a successful shower, I asked the duty manager to arrange transportation to the parliament building for me.

'You want a service car? It's four thousand for a day.'

'What? That's too much,' I moaned.

Duty-Manager scratched his chin, 'You like CNG? It is three-wheel – maybe 300 to 400 taka.'

'Fine, let's go,' I agreed. It was no more than £3.50.

After a short wait, the bellboy called me outside where a driver aged about 40 years old was leaning on his green tuk-tuk. The vehicle was completely enclosed with a mesh cage, and he opened the passenger cage door and beckoned me to climb in. The engine screamed into life, and it roared off down the service road weaving in and out of the hand-pulled rickshaws.

The rickshaws were gaily decorated and more numerous than the pedestrians – the streets were choked with them. Over 400,000 rickshaws were cluttering the streets of Dhaka, but I had read in the newspaper over breakfast that there could be an additional 600,000 illegal rickshaws. Based on the Bangladesh Bureau of Statistics, rickshaw pullers earned about 450 taka (£3.90) per day. They would ply an average of 42 kilometres every day – which was the equivalent of a running a marathon while pulling a heavy cart through polluted traffic – for just 10 pence a kilometre.

The tuk-tuk was like a rat-cage on three wheels, and although I felt safe from pick-pockets at road junctions, I was roundly confident I was going to be crushed like a tin can if we crashed. The traffic was worse than Manila: the buses were scraped and battered with all their lights smashed-out, the tuk-tuks raced to squeeze in every available gap and the cars angrily chastised anyone and everyone with their horns. Conspicuous with their absence were motorbikes, and I wondered why there were almost none to be seen.

It took an hour to travel just 19 kilometres. Every few hundred metres our tuk-tuk would get stuck in horrendous junctions snarled with traffic facing each other with no way to go. The junctions were controlled by stern-looking policemen wearing green uniforms and jack-boots, and they brandished truncheons which they waved and pointed in a surly manner at the melee.

After a rough and ear-splitting ride, we eventually arrived at the national Parliament of Bangladesh, which was one of the largest legislative centres in the world. I was directed to the side entrance where I was surprised to find open fields surrounding the huge concrete building. A half-dozen workers were picking at rubbish around the grounds – it looked like they were planting rice in paddy fields. It was a surreal scene in the middle of such a hectic and crowded city. Astonishingly, the grounds covered a phenomenal 0.8 million square metres. The tuk-tuk driver parked in a layby, and I alighted and strolled about under the watchful eye of a few vendors.

Tourists weren't allowed inside the building, so I instructed the driver to take me to the Liberation War Museum next. Another perilous 40-minute journey later, we arrived at a narrow back street outside the museum. It was a two-storey building, which looked more like a house. I paid a wallet-busting 5 taka (£0.04) at the entrance and shuffled through a mass of schoolchildren inside the building.

The museum was a series of small rooms surrounding a courtyard, and I followed the yellow-and-red lines painted on the floor to navigate the exhibits. They were predominantly picture-framed articles mounted on the walls and personal items from the war arranged on cabinets and tables. The independence struggle stemmed from the Bangladeshi's desire for their Bangla language and culture to be recognised and protected within the Pakistan state, which was dominated by West Pakistan. By 1971, the struggle had escalated into mass protests and non-cooperation with the Paki-dominated government – then atrocities mounted.

'Where are you from?' asked a jolly-looking young man who was shuffling along the exhibits next to me.

'England,' I replied. I decided to steer him away from football and Sherlock Holmes discussions and ask about the Liberation War.

'Are you angry at the Pakistanis – with what they did to the Bangla people?' I asked.

'No, we are friends with Pakistan. We are friends with India. With everyone,' he answered.

I supposed he was too young to be linked to the events. We passed news stories of mass graves of Bengalis killed by the Pakistan military; of 200,000 women being raped and killed; and the Bengali intelligentsia being systematically murdered to hobble the Bangladesh new statehood – just as West Pakistan realised they were going to lose. Human skulls from a killing field were lined-up in a glass display case along with gruesome photos of women and children who were shot and killed – they were shocking eye-openers.

At the conclusion of the exhibition, I went to the courtyard and ordered a cup of tea from the museum café. As I looked for somewhere to sit, I was invited by an elderly man to sit at a dirty plastic patio table with his family. He was dressed in traditional white linen clothes and had his hair and beard dyed in orangutan orange.

'Where from you?' he asked in terrible English.

'England,' I drearily replied. I spoke in simple English to make it easier for him to understand.

'Were you here in the war?' I asked him.

'Yes. I was 14 years old. My family...we hide in [the] house.'

'Are you still angry with the Pakistanis?' I asked innocently.

'Yes,' he growled through gritted teeth, 'we hate them. They kill my family,' he swept his arm about the table to point at his family members, 'they kill. We cannot forget.'

'Do you like India?' I asked.

The Pakistanis had foolishly tried to invade India in December 1971 triggering New Delhi to join hands with the Bengali militia. That sealed the fate of the Pakistani army in East Pakistan.

Orange-beard waggled his head, 'Yes. They help us.'

He tousled his beard and stared in deep thought. He seemed alarmed about what had happened over 40 years ago, and we were struggling with his lack of

English and my total absence of Bangla language skills. I excused myself and took my empty cup away. At least I didn't get asked about Manchester United or Sherlock Holmes.

I collecting my rucksack from the museum administration office and was reunited with my tuk-tuk driver outside the main gates. He was patiently waiting like a faithful collie dog. Tuk-Tuk-Man held open the passenger door of the green rat-cage-on-three-wheels like a Peninsula Hotel doorman holding open the door of a Rolls Royce for a celebrity. Then he revved up his engine to head back to the hotel.

The journey back to the hotel took over an hour, and my back was bumping and grinding on the bony seat of the rat cage all the way. By the time I arrived at the hotel, my lower back was in agony and I could barely walk.

The friendly face of the waiter in the hotel's café was lit-up by his white piano teeth as I walked awkwardly to a table and asked for a menu. I ordered a traditional Bangla meal of fish and chips and retired early for the 4 a.m. wake-up call to head back to the airport in the morning. I was looking forward for my Turkish Airlines flight to Istanbul and onwards to Manchester.

To the chagrin of the tourist authority, Dhaka does not offer much to see – a view of the monolithic parliament building and a ramshackle museum being the highlight of a visit. I had the distinct feeling I would rapidly tire of the country by having to constantly talk about fictional characters of English literature with every Tom, Dick and Mohammed. Yet, I was pleased to have had a short oppportunity to learn more about this desperately poor country and cheerful folk.

I would have to carefully contemplate a return to

this crowded and noisy country. Anyhow, it was a milestone: broken spine or not, I had overtaken Andy's tally and was now at 78 countries.

4: Glowing Report From Chernobyl

Ukraine (No. 79)

I had travelled through Ukraine before, on the Budapest to Moscow train, but only had the opportunity to peer through the grimy Soviet train windows. No getting off the train – sorry. That was in 1990 before the disintegration of the Soviet Union when Ukraine was known as "Little Russia".

This time was for real; I would be staying there to earn a full tick. Not that tourists were clamouring to pack their suntan cream and flip-flops for a package holiday in Ukraine. Russian paramilitary organizations, arguably under the control of the Kremlin, had been fighting in East Ukraine. The Ruskies had also annexed the Ukrainian autonomous region of Crimea in March 2014, and fighting had raged in Donetsk and Luhansk until the signing of the Minsk Protocol in September 2014.

To make matters worse, we also had witnessed on world television the shooting down of the Malaysia Airlines flight MH17 on 17 July 2014 while flying over Eastern Ukraine – killing all 283 passengers and 15 crew onboard – by the Donbass People's Militia. It was not a shock to learn that I was the only Western tourist on the flight.

Yet, Ukraine wanted to open to the West, and a political tug-of-war raged between Moscow and

Brussels. The Ukrainians wanted to be more like their Euro-cousins – sipping Bordeaux and driving Peugeots and Mercedes saloons – than the "Great Russians" who drank themselves unconscious with vodka and chugged about in their Lada and Volgas.

This fight for the mind and soul of Ukrainians had an obvious winner in the European Union, however, it had potentially catastrophic consequences of upsetting their former masters in the ever-more unpredictable regime of Vladimir Putin. With such bullyboy next-door neighbours, Ukraine had to protect itself, and they had the second-largest standing army in Europe.

I had absolutely no idea what to expect in Ukraine and had invested little time in research. I knew that Ukraine was sympathetic to Europe and was accepting visitors with European Union passports with no hassle. According to the British Foreign and Commonwealth Office, visas were unnecessary.

My Ukraine International Airlines Flight 9383 from Manchester landed promptly at 7 p.m. after a short stopover in Amsterdam, and I entered the immigration area with minimal fuss. Kiev Borispol Airport was brand new: a modest atrium-roofed terminal similar to what I had seen in Sofia. Half the immigration counters were closed with their aluminium shutters pulled down.

After clearing the foreign passport queue, I collected my near-empty suitcase from the luggage carousel, passed through the customs green channel with no hassle and exited into a sea of faces in the arrivals lounge. As I turned right, a young man, perhaps in his early twenties, caught my eye holding a card with 'Colin Rice' written on it. Since my name is hardly common and we were in Ukraine, I assumed he was looking for me.

But I couldn't remember requesting airport pick-up: I normally figured things out on landing. Perhaps he was a scam artist or kidnapper? Despite being quite concerned and puzzled, I approached him.

The mysterious greeter was a formidable size – taller than me – so I estimated that he must have been six-foot-five tall. He sported a blonde military hairstyle and a three-quarter-length black leather jacket. He looked like Vladimir Putin's giant nephew. I approached him cautiously.

'I am Colin Rice,' I announced.

'Follow,' Putin-nephew boomed as he turned on his heels.

'Erm. You are from?' I enquired.

'Hostel.'

Well, the balance of probability was that he was kosher, so I followed him outside the terminal pushing my suitcase along on all four wheels. Outside it was chilly, perhaps a few degrees above zero, and he led me along the terminal car park to a small sedan, which must have been over a decade old. He put my suitcase in the boot, and I climbed in the front passenger seat. Then we took off with the engine straining away.

The highway to Kiev city centre was quite impressive, metalled and with eight lanes, and we passed a few-dozen new car showrooms with mostly European brands. Every kilometre or so, we passed an overhead gantry where an LED sign flashed that the temperature was 3 degrees Celsius. The outer lanes were marked a surprising 130-kilometres-per-hour speed limit, which Putin-nephew was determined to challenge by screaming along the fast lane with his giant foot to the metal. After 30 minutes, we reached the city, jiggled down the cobbled Andriivs'kyi Descent then turned into a narrow courtyard, which was the hostel car park.

The front desk of the Dream House Hostel was manned by several pretty *receptionistas*, one of whom checked me in. I paid her 330 hryvnia (£9.80) and she assigned me a bunk in a four-bed dormitory in the basement. I decided that I should eat first before heading down to my bed, so I visited the next door restaurant and ordered what everyone should order in Kiev: chicken Kiev – along with a 30cl of local Lvivske lager. Although, chicken Kiev reputedly didn't originate from Kiev – it was a nineteenth-century French dish introduced by the Russians to Belarus.

My back was in excruciating pain, and I struggled to drag my suitcase down the tiled steps to the basement. The dormitory was modern but quite cramped with four bunk beds, a bank of lockers and two small tables crammed in. Under the watchful eye of a young Ukranian woman, who was studying at one of the tables, I struggled to make up my upper bunk.

I looked for somewhere to put my things, but the dormitory was as cluttered as a Hong Kong cage hostel. The lockers had all been garnered, the window alcove next to my bunk was littered with plastic bags of stuff, the minuscule pinewood table was covered in snacks and stationery and some cheeky bugger had even hung his wet towel on the side of my bunk. I found by luck that a tiny stool was unclaimed, so I took off my jacket and outer clothes, perching them precariously on the stool and kicked off my boots.

At that moment a slim guy, maybe 30 years old, entered the dormitory with a toothbrush hanging from his mouth. He was Middle Eastern-looking with a shaved head and resembled an Israeli conscript. Upon seeing me, his eyes widened in mild shock.

'Are you going to sleep *there* ?' he nodded to the bunk.

'Erm. Yes. Why not?' I replied.

Conscript-Man stooped and inspected the underside of my bunk.

'These wooden slats are only thin. I think they will break,' he grumbled as he poked around and tugged on a few slats.

'It's not my problem,' I shrugged, 'I requested a lower bunk – it's their fault if it breaks.'

Conscript-Man studied me gingerly climbing the bunk ladder with my stiff back, and then I sprawled myself onto the bed while holding on to the bedframe to take the weight off a bit. I was determined to prove there was no problem.

'I think that you will collapse on me in the night,' Conscript-Man withered on with his point.

'No. I've stayed in hundreds of hostels – no problem,' I rebutted.

'Do you snore?' he laboured on.

'Well, I never heard myself snore,' I retorted, 'do you snore?'

Conscript-Man man grunted, shrugged his shoulders and left the room as I lay in excruciating pain with my back. That night I tossed and turned in pain and only slept for maybe a couple of hours. However, the bed slats survived their ultimate test. At one point in the early hours, I awoke to see Conscript-Man's drunken red eyes staring at me from only a foot away.

'You okay?' he asked. I grunted back.

The next morning, I awoke early for my much-awaited tour to Chernobyl. I washed as best as I could then headed upstairs to book a taxi from reception. Soon enough, I was on my way to the tour rendezvous point with the small saloon hurtling itself around the cobbled streets. Within 15 minutes, I was dropped outside Central Train Station.

I located the tour's white minibus, which had a radioactivity warning sign on it. I showed my receipt and soon we were on our way. After a 90-minute drive, we arrived at the 30-kilometre checkpoint and, after a passport check, entered the exclusion zone. There was a warning sign on the checkpoint:

'CARE! Radiation affected area. Chernobyl zone. Restricted territory. Unauthorized entry BANNED.'

We visited the abandoned village of Zalissya, which had been abandoned in April 1986 following the disaster. We visited long-abandoned houses, one of which was occupied by an old lady who had returned after the Soviet clean-up operation. She had an orchard and offered me an apple – which I ate with careless abandon.

After a further drive, we arrived at the actual town of Chernobyl, and I disembarked to wander the town. I was surprised to learn that there were scientists, plant workers and government officials still living and working in Chernobyl. Logically, they had to remain to prevent the damaged plant from having another meltdown. A whole community was sitting at the edge of the site of the world's worst-ever nuclear incident.

Back on the minibus, we continued to the nuclear power plant and passed the ten-kilometre Leviv exclusion zone checkpoint. After stopping at the fire station and an abandoned school, the plant's reactors appeared to my left. We turned left a couple of times around the plant, and then the famous reactor four came into view.

My heart missed a beat. Okay, I thought to myself, we are really, *really* close here. Maybe *too* close for comfort. The minibus stopped at a car park right outside the reactor perimeter wall. A four-meter-high granite monument of cupped hands stood in front of the carpark. There was only a grassy strip and a five-meter-wide road between me and the concrete-block perimeter wall. The wall was about two metres high and topped with razor wire, and I wondered what was point of the such security – why would you scale the wall to risk acute radiation sickness?

'Please only take photos of reactor four and the new sarcophagus,' warned Anatoly as he nodded towards the guard, 'not the other buildings or perimeter walls – they don't like that.'

Excited, I grabbed my camera and trotted to the monument. I was frighteningly close to the concrete and steel-shrouded reactor four – just around 200 meters from me. The sides of the reactor were stepped and shrouded in light-grey painted steel with streaks of rust, and the top was capped with scaffolding works from a construction project to improve the rotting shielding. The front of the reactor was also covered in a steel-girder framework and a stacked wall of concrete beams, and on the roof was the infamous yellow-and-white-striped chimney like a birthday candle.

I took the Geiger counter out of my pocket, and the reading was now showing 3.00 microSieverts – about fifteen times higher than Zalissya village. The uniformed guard had returned to his post, so perhaps foolishly, I decided to try and approach the perimeter wall. With each stride, the Geiger counter climbed another 0.2 microSieverts until I reached the other side of the road, and it beeped angrily at me as the safety threshold of 3.33 microSieverts was breached.

A cumulative 1,000 microSieverts is recognised as the exposure that would probably cause a fatal cancer many years later in life. If you spent 12.5 days here then you would reach that level. I wondered how long the security guard had been working here – perhaps he glowed in the dark.

Just walking eight meters, the radiation level had increased one microSievert. If it was another 200 meters to the reactor four shroud, would that mean the radiation would climb another 25 or so? Whichever way, I was pretty certain that approaching one of the most contaminated chunks of planet earth would not be a safe proposition. The most contaminated areas of the plant, including the control room, had been estimated at 300 microSieverts – which would be a fatal dose in just over a minute.

After lunch at the nuclear plant workers canteen, which amazingly had remained open to serve the thousands of workers still maintaining the plant, the bus continued to the city of Pripyat. This was a Soviet Union model city built just 3.5 kilometres to the northwest of the nuclear plant to house the engineers, scientists and workers operating the plant. Built in 1970, it was slated as one of the best cities in the Soviet Union and was only inhabited for 16 years before it was permanently evacuated.

The city was like an apocalypse movie set – especially as dusk was now falling. At the city centre, the bus stopped facing the Pripyat Entertainment Centre, and I was excited and frightened as I stepped into this real-life disaster zone.

The main square was paved in crumbling concrete with the steps breaking off into small lumps like Cheshire cheese, which exposed the metal reinforcement bars inside. Shattered glass littered the pathways, desiccated young trees blocked the way and debris lay in every direction.

Across the main square was a derelict supermarket, and I stepped through what was once the main front window. Inside were a dozen checkout lanes. Looters had sneaked into Pripyat after the initial nuclear cleanup operation. Destitute after the fall of the Soviet empire, the Ukrainians were willing to risk radioactive poisoning to loot the houses and shops to scavenge a meagre living.

At the rear of the entertainment centre was the centrepiece of dark tourism photos – the funfair that had never operated. A dodgem ride had been piled with leaves and most of the cars presumably taken by looters for scrap metal. The seats had rotted completely through. Across the funfair was a Skyride, which they used to call the Paratrooper in my days, with the wooden steps rotted away and a red-and-rust frame. The centrepiece was the infamous Ferris wheel, which was also similarly rotted, and I sat in a carriage for full apocalyptic effect.

After we visited some apartment blocks, the minibus returned to Kiev in the dark. I thought about taking the Metro from Central Station, but my back was still stiff – and it was late – so I took a taxi back to the hostel. Exhausted after the long day, I slinked into the restaurant for a meal of pork and mashed potatoes washed down with a 50cl glass of lager.

I went back downstairs to my dormitory at 10 p.m. where Conscript-Man was pottering about.

'How's your day?' he enquired.

I told him about the Chernobyl tour.

'I've never even been there,' he answered in a disbelieving tone, 'was it worth it?'

'Absolutely,' I replied, 'it was brilliant.'

Conscript-Man shook his head in self-disgust as he shuffled out of the dormitory.

I slept much better that night and awoke at 8 a.m. I was planning a lazy day – it was going to be a very long one. My flight to Dubai was at 7 p.m. and I was going to sit overnight in the airport terminal for eight hours until my onward flight to Manila. I ordered an airport car from one of the cute *receptionistas* and took breakfast next door.

My plan for the day was to do a walking tour of the city around the hostel area. I deposited my backpack in the hostel storage, checked out then headed right up the cobbled Andriivs'kyi Descent towards the direction of Independence Square.

The hostel was at the bottom of the descent, and I walked up the winding road swishing through corn-yellow autumn leaves. It was a bracing five degrees Celsius, and the sky was filled with gloomy clouds. Grand late-1800s buildings lined the street and were gaily painted in pastel colours – mostly shades of yellow with white accents. It appeared like they had only been renovated in recent years, and some were still under renovation. Others were artificially boarded up and painted like a movie set to look pleasant to the tourists.

I wondered what this street looked like in the 1990s. It must have been in a severely dilapidated state with old Soviet-era buildings housing various government agencies and quangos – decrepit and underfunded.

Souvenir sellers were setting up shop at the edge of the pavements; mostly tables with various trinkets laid out. As I neared the top of the hill, the pitches were larger and similar to market stalls. I shopped at one and bought some Chernobyl souvenir T-shirts. Some stalls were selling communist memorabilia such as MIG21 fighter instrument displays, Soviet commander wind-up watches and military-fatigue paraphernalia. Russian President Vladimir Putin seemed to be a much-scorned figure, and his face appeared on mugs and even toilet paper.

Further up the steep hill, I reached St. Andrew's Church. It was an eighteenth-century Baroque building painted sapphire blue with peacock-blue onion domes gilded with gold leaf. At the top of the hill, I turned left down Desyatynna Street then into the magnificent St. Michael's Square.

The Ukrainians marched about on their way – quite strident as if they had somewhere very important to be. They wore woollen three-quarter coats or ski jackets, jeans and casual shoes. They looked less Russian than the Russians – much more Western European in dress and appearance.

I continued past the Monument to Famine Victims, and right in front of me was St. Michaels Monastery. It was 1 p.m., and the church bells chimed to a musical fanfare as the churchgoers were just departing. The main entrance was through a great Baroque-style square tower, the Economic Gates. It had three tiers like a cake and was painted pale-blue and white with a bulbous gold-leaf dome on the top. It must have been around 30 metres in height without the cross.

I passed through the tower gate into another square where the cathedral itself stood. It was a predictable sapphire blue with lots of gold-leaf domes and plenty of crosses, white columns and ornate arched windows to embellish it. The original cathedral had been demolished by the Soviets in the 1930s, and after independence, the Ukrainians had rebuilt it. Small wonder there was animosity between the Ukrainians and their former Soviet Union masters.

I studied more of the pretty period buildings and statues of sad and frowning saints in and around the square then decided it was time to eat. So amid the throngs, I headed back towards the hostel. I found a basement beer house on the corner of Velyka Zhytomyrska and Andriivs'kyi Descent named The Black Piglet. I ordered a large glass of beer, bread spread with flavoured lard and a typical Eastern European pork and potato dinner. What a pleasant end to my fascinating trip.

Later that afternoon, I reached the hostel – full of lard and beer – and probably mildly radioactive. I dozed in an armchair in reception until I was woken by the same pretty *receptionista* for the service car back to the airport.

I wondered on the way to the airport if my flight to Dubai would be flying out of reach of the surface-to-air missiles of the pro-Soviet occupation forces of Donbass.

ODDS AND SODS OF EUROPE

5: Tobacco Mountain

By December 2015, I had relocated back to England, and my country ticks had ballooned to 79. I was confident that I could quickly ratchet up some new countries since I now had a new base to work from. I was on the doorstep of Europe – a continent which I had broken the back of – but there were still plenty of pockets to explore. According to Andy's country tracker, his elaborate spreadsheet which catalogued the countries and territories we had and hadn't visited, I still had 20 countries left to conquer in Europe.

Embarrassingly, I had visited countries in every continent on earth – but not Ireland – which was inexcusable considering that it was a ferry ride away from the Port of Liverpool. I had a dumb idea: I had to travel down to London for a business meeting. Maybe I could fly from Manchester to London via Dublin and tick-off that pesky Ireland?

Of course, it was a preposterous idea. Yet, the cost of a flight to London via Dublin was the same price as a rush-hour express train. My wife did not buy that story one bit, but she somehow glossed over my feeble excuse and allowed me to buy my ticket via Dublin. Sort of.

So, I visited the city of Dublin taking in Kilmainham Gaol and sampling the wonderful

Guinness in the pubs – and Ireland became country tick number 80.

I then analysed Andy's country-tracker spreadsheet to search for other easy ticks from the UK. There it was – The Isle of Man. It was a Crown Dependency: in other words, it belonged to the Queen – not the UK. I bought a day-return flight for a mere £55 from Liverpool's John Lennon Airport, visited the quirky town of Douglas and the Great Laxey Wheel – and that was tick number 81.

I scoured Andy's country-tracker spreadsheet again after my wife had simmered down from my Isle of Man jaunt. She had been running lower and lower on cigarettes. We had bought several cartons from Doha airport's duty-free shop, but she was now breaking open her last carton. The cost of Marlboro in England was a wallet-busting £92 per carton.

'Honey. How about I fly to Spain and pick up some duty-free on the way home?' I chanced my luck.

No response.

'And I heard that Andorra has even cheaper cigarettes. Only a pound a pack,' I continued.

Still no response.

I checked her cigarette stock daily and waited for her to be in a good mood. Who would blink first? Nine packs left. Eight. Seven. Six. Five packs left. When she was down to 4 packs, I got a response.

'How much are cigarettes in Andorra?' she enquired while studiously watching a television show.

'I read on the internet that it was only a pound a pack. Do you want me to go and get you some?'

I was delighted to get a grunt in response. That was good enough for me: it was a faint amber light. So I got straight on to the flight websites to search for cheap flights to Barcelona and researched onward buses to

Andorra.

By her last three packets, I had an itinerary in place.

'Honey. It will take me three days to get there and back,' I spoke gently. She gave me a furrowed scowl. I was ready for her question.

'The flight is two and a half hours then there's a three-hour bus journey to Andorra. It's high in the mountains you know…'

Another scowl, a pause, a grunt. Then a 'hmmm.'

'So maybe I will arrange it for next week?' I continued, undeterred, 'maybe I will fly on Sunday?'

After a flurry of positive signals, I firmed up my bookings that evening. I booked my return flights on Ryanair from Liverpool airport, an express bus ticket to Andorra and a cheap guesthouse room at €29 (£21) per night. Done!

Andorra (No. 82)

My flight departed from Liverpool's John Lennon airport. I had visited the airport as a child to watch the planes take-off and land but never thought I would set foot in it. It seemed too small for jet planes: I thought it was only used for turboprop flights to the Isle of Man and Ireland. The budget airline phenomenon had reinvigorated the airport – providing flights for the price of a bottle of whisky had resulted in a transformation of the white elephant.

Arriving by a radio cab, I entered the terminal, passed through to departures with my pre-printed boarding pass and sat in Starbucks reading a free copy of the Liverpool Echo nursing a £1.80 brewed coffee, which I had specially selected from the remaining shrapnel in my wallet. This was all too good to be true – I was saving money by the fistful. I then dutifully lined up at the gate.

And I waited and waited. Twenty minutes before take-off, there was no sign of boarding and the queue snaked right down the terminal.

'Ladies and gentlemen. We regret to inform you...' announced the groundcrew. Crap. There was a French air traffic controllers strike pending - and it had just started. Flights at the other gates had been taking off for Europe as scheduled, and I had been desperately unlucky. I wanted to give the ground-crew lady a piece of my mind but realised that I would just be wasting my saliva: it was a budget airline. With my tail between my legs, I took a train back home.

I was even more determined to reach Andorra, so that very night I bought new flights. Then 1 April arrived, and I was hoping that I wouldn't be subject to an April Fool's joke by those bird-brained jokers – the French air traffic controllers. At least, I had had a dry run a fortnight earlier, so I now knew how to get to Liverpool's John Lennon airport using public transport via Liverpool South Parkway. I had succeeded in getting a refund on my Ryanair flights from the abandoned trip, and my new budget outbound flight was on Vueling Airlines, which I had never heard of before. Was it a wordplay on fueling?

Flight VY 8783 was scheduled for 2:25 p.m., and if it wasn't delayed by more than 90 minutes, I calculated that I could catch the 8 p.m. shuttle bus to Andorra. Any delay of more than five hours, and I would be marooned in Barcelona's wonderfully named El Prat airport overnight – too late to catch the last bus to Andorra. Given the success of my first attempted trip, I was on tenterhooks. Thankfully, the flight was only 10 minutes delayed, and despite Vueling having seat legroom which would challenge an infant, I landed more or less on schedule at 6 p.m. Spanish local time.

Unfortunately, I had narrowly missed the 6 p.m. bus to Andorra so needed to wait for the 8 p.m. one. Never mind. I chilled out with a snack-sized paella and a 200ml glass of San Miguel in an arrival's hall cafe. I then wasted a good half-hour locating the bus bay for the Novatel bus to Andorra based upon the horrendously wrong advice from three different tourist information counters who all pointed me in entirely different directions.

The 200-kilometre bus ride to Andorra was rather uneventful. There were only five of us, including a British Airways pilot who was going home to his winter base, and a young British bloke whose mate had been bumped off a flight from Newcastle. The roads were exceptionally maintained: not what I remember from visiting Spain in the 1970s as a kid. Back then, there were potholes everywhere and half-finished roads to nowhere marred with wandering mongrels and heaps of builder's waste. There's progress for you!

The border at Andorra was a non-event. We trundled through a customs post with an unmanned sentry box then past the *policia* border point – which was indeed manned – however, the officer was reading his newspaper and was not even paying attention to the passing traffic. After a few suburban drop-offs, the bus trundled into Andorra La Vella *Estacio Centrale*, and I was deposited in the chilly mountain air just after 11 p.m.

Andorra was one of those weirdy European microstates. The mountainous principality was wedged in the Pyrenees between Spain and France and had a land area

18% smaller than the Isle of Man. Andorra's population, at 78,000, was over 10% smaller too. It had somehow survived being absorbed by the various invaders and empires since its independence, which was granted by Charlemagne, King of the Franks, who booted out the Moors in the ninth century and established it as a buffer state between the French and Moors.

Andorra had been trying to become a *real* country since the 1990s when it had been ruled by the Co-Princes: the President of France and a Spanish bishop. It had established a mission to the United Nations, Embassies in six countries and even fielded an Olympic team. But Andorra remained in the Little League in several areas: it had no standing army to defend itself, was not a member of the European Union, had no airport and no sea access. But hey what, it had tons of cigarettes.

I clutched my printout of a Google map and attempted to orient myself. Failing to locate any useful signs, I crossed the road to a McDonalds to buy a fillet-of-fish and asked the staff for help. A boy with two McDonald's stars pointed me in the right direction – it was only a kilometre to my hotel. So I yomped along the main road from Spain and turned right into *Parc Central*. I followed a woman, who I suspected was heading in the same direction, since she looked far too old for playing on the swings and roundabouts.

I crossed the River Gran Valira, which was a wide, clear babbling river, down Carrer Prat de la Creu to the Andorra government building. Then I yomped a steep 45 degrees up the mountain to the old town square of Plaça Príncep Benlloch.

Mother luck was with me: despite not having minor street names on my map, I weaved down rock-cobbled streets too narrow to accommodate a Fiat 500 and arrived at the Barri Antic Hostel and Pub – a sort of bikers-bar-cum-guesthouse. It was cosy and full of folk who didn't appear to be Harley Davidson owners. I was dutifully checked in by the barman who told me to pay in the morning.

It was now 11:30 p.m., but I was still not tired because I had taken naps on the bus. So I deposited my bag in the simply furnished room and wandered about the atmospheric streets of Andorra for somewhere to get a beer. Sadly, they were all shutting for the night, so I bought a pack of Camel cigarettes and returned to the bikers-bar for non-bikers. I ordered a 50cl San Miguel and smoked two Camels, which tasted acceptable but seemed to make my throat sore. It was chilly outside in the mountain air, so I retreated inside when my hands turned blue then supped up and retired for the night at 2 a.m.

After paying for my room and taking a *café con leche* and croissant for breakfast in the bikers-bar, I wandered off to see the city. The 1500's Casa de la Vall was just 50 metres past the hostel, so I walked there first. It was the historic headquarters of the General Council and the original parliament building, and it stood in a granite square as flat as a billiard table. Roughly built from angular rocks, the three-storey building had shuttered windows and was in a magnificent condition.

I climbed the rock formation to the left, where rough steps led up to a flagpole where the Andorra flag fluttered. There were magnificent yet misty views of the melting snowfields atop the Pyrenees mountains, which loomed ominously over the principality. To the left, the town clothed and hugged the mountain halfway up the to the peaks. I felt compelled to spend some time there and admire the view, however it was drizzling and a chilly few degrees – I didn't fancy getting hypothermic.

Tramping past Sant Esteve Church, the only other historic building of significance in this modern Pyrenean capital, I decided I would have a love hate relationship with this perishing building. Its bell tower was only a stone's throw from my room and had deafeningly chimed every 15 minutes through the night.

I was becoming charmed by the capital of this endearing, tiny principality lodged high up in the Pyrenees. Andorra La Vella was the highest capital city in Europe at 3356 feet – just 200 feet lower than Mount Snowdon. I was also struggling to get a feel for its cultural identity. Unless the Catalonia region of Spain gained independence, Andorra held the conspicuous title of the only country in the world with Catalonian as its official language. Was this territory pro-French, I wondered? Was it pro-Spanish? Or anti-Spanish?

I had to remind myself that my mission was to buy cigarettes, and the duty-free shopping was Andorra's raison d'etre – plus a bit of skiing. If I spent too much time wandering the intensely interesting alleys of Andorra La Velle, and heaven forbid the shops closed before I could buy my wife's cigarettes, she would give me a complete toasting on my return to England.

Priorities in mind, I hit the main touristy shopping street, Avenido Meritxell. The narrow avenue was lined with attractive five-storey buildings, which crowded right up to the edge of the pavement. Some building had their upper floors extending over the pavement, making the road look even narrower. The ground floors were packed with perfumeries, camera shops, McDonalds restaurants and tobacconists.

I stumbled upon a reasonably-priced, well-stocked tobacconist. I was delighted to find 400-stick cartons of Malboro Lights at only 61 euros (£45.00), which was only £2.25 per packet. Compared with £9.35 in the supermarkets in England, I contemplated hiring an articulated lorry to haul enough back to England so that I could retire. I calculated in my head that it was a saving of £70 per carton – one carton alone would pay for my flight.

I wasn't the only one on a ciggy run. With over 7.8 million visitors per year and a population of only 78,000, Andorra had the most visitors in the world per capita – over 100 times the population piled in for cheap cigarettes, spirits and fuel every year.

Delighted with the savings, I bought a packet of Montecristo Clubs with a free cigarette lighter for only 9.90 euros (£7.30) then smugly headed off down the street to admire the other duty-free emporiums stuffed full of Johnny Walker, Camel cigarettes and Toblerones the size of railway sleepers.

My croissant breakfast wasn't much to sustain my marching about, so I found a delightful street café at the Hotel De L'Isard, which was graced with outdoor seating warmed by overhead electric heaters. I took a set lunch of salmon, Belgium fries and pea soup. It was time for a little celebration at reaching country number 82, so I lounged for a while with a glass of Mahou pale lager and sampled three of my newly acquired Montecristo clubs.

The café started playing 'Ferry Cross the Mersey', which seemed totally inappropriate for the Pyrenees, and a bit of a coincidence since I would fly back to John Lennon airport at the banks of the River Mersey. Maybe this was a subliminal message to go home?

I decided that while it was still dry weather, I

would return to the Parc Central for a daytime view of the river and cherry blossom. I headed down Callissa Ciutat Valira, a narrow alley reputedly leading down to the park. I followed a posh lady in an enormous brown fur coat and black stiletto boots. She was walking a dapper whippet-like hound, which was highly suspicious of me.

I assumed this was the shortcut for dog-owners in the posh upper suburbs of Andorra La Vella to reach the park, for the steep path was strewn with streams of dog urine. Fur-lady's hound took a sniff at each urine stream on the way down and added to it. They should have renamed it Callissa de Mutt-Piss. After zig-zagging down a steel ramp, I reached the lower levels and managed to find my way back to the park.

The cherry blossom was incredible, and I had fortuitously visited at precisely the right time. The banks of the River Gran Valira were hemmed-in by concrete banks, which snaked into the distance. Lining both riverbanks were the blush-pink cherry blossom in full bloom with the occasional petals raining on me from the canopy they formed above the footpath. The view at the footbridge was magnificent with the backdrop of steep mountains looming over the valley. The peaks facing the old town had rapidly melting snowfields shrouded in mist, and Alpine houses dotted the lower reaches.

I decided it opportune to check out the bus times for my return to Spain the next morning. I continued onwards past dog-owners with their loveable urinators and the odd toddler playing on the playground, and I reached the station through a scrappy car park and a tyre workshop. The bus depot lady told me that I could buy tickets on the day – it was 28.25 euros (£20.80) for the Alsa Express back to Barcelona at 11 a.m. Satisfied

I was going to get a ride home, I re-traced my exact steps, across the bridge and back up Callissa de Mutt-Piss to Avenido Merixell.

Time to be a tourist again, for I needed a couple of gifts for the family – perhaps some of those enormous slabs of Toblerone. I continued downhill and admired the shop windows full of lethal-looking Swiss Army pen-knives, catapults with packets of steel ball-bearings, Tasers and Rambo-knives which would come in handy for gutting a grizzly bear. There was no way to get these on an aircraft, so I guessed that the Spaniards or French must have been preparing for an invasion of football hooligans.

At the bend on Avenido Merixell, where it crossed the river, stood a statue which I recognised well: Salvador Dali's *La Noblesse du Temps* with its droopy clock. It was a unique backdrop for the mountains behind. Further down Merixell, the stores continued unabashed. I needed a few minutes break so took an hour at the Caféteria Fontverd where I lounged on a 50cl Estrella and a couple of my Cuban clubs.

Rambling further down the street, Andorra reminded me of Hong Kong. Duty-free shopping, handbag stores, fashion stores, Rolex watches, cigar stores and thousands of eager shoppers. I reminded myself this was a place my wife would enjoy but my credit card would not.

I ambled back, taking a Subway sandwich to save a few calories for more beer, and stopped at a tobacco store to admire the stocks of Cuban cigars. I enjoyed another 50cl San Miguel at the Mama Maria restaurant near Callissa de Mutt-Piss and enjoyed one of my cheap Montecristo Number 4s. The evening was chilly, but I felt a bit warm since I put on my beanie hat. Oops, I nearly forgot to check in for my Ryanair flight back to

Liverpool, so I checked in on my mobile then watched the crowds milling past.

Back at the biker-bar, I decided to do a bit of laptop work while basking in the warmth. I grabbed a 50cl beer and a slice of tortilla then took a table in the crowded bar. No sooner had I sat down, then the giant barman began setting things up for the soccer match. He dragged tables in front of the large flat television hanging on the wall, turned on a ceiling sound system and tuned into the football match. Before I knew it, I was surrounded by several dozen Andorrans laughing and shouting as the match started. I had no idea of who was playing so thought it best to ask

'Excuse me, who is playing?' I asked a fit young man just next to me.

'*Ees* Barcelona and *Madreed*,' he answered.

I took a while to watch the match, which had outstanding players such as Leon Messi, Ferdinand Suan and Cristiano Ronaldo. Soon enough, Barcelona scored and the bar erupted in cheers while the giant barman howled with disdain. Barcelona played an incredible game, controlling the ball for most of the match, but Madrid fought back and scored, whereupon the barman and the front row cheered and howled. If this was in the UK there would probably be a fight.

The next morning I packed at 8 a.m., took a last *café con leche* and croissant at the bar then strolled to the *estacion de autobus* through the park with my backpack stuffed full of cigarettes. I waited at the next door café, where I smoked my bootleg Montecristo Clubs and sipped coffee until the driver let me on board.

Several Spanish-looking ladies boarded the bus and bade *ola* to me as they took the front seats. Then at 11:05 a.m., we took off slowly, driving downhill past endless roundabouts with the steep mountains lining the valley. At the border, the bus slowly drove past the Policia guardpost then a European Union signpost for Spain.

After a few minutes drive, the bus parked in a *Guardia Civil* control point, and a huge Spanish civil guard officer in green with a flat hat marched across. The driver opened the door and the officer climbed up the steps to directly stare in my face.

'Do you have any money?' he asked. I gulped like Jerry in the Tom and Jerry cartoon.

'I have about one thousand euros,' I answered nervously.

'Are you *sure*?' he pressed. I decided to take out my wallet and counted about 1,400 euros and 80 pounds.

'Hmmm,' he muttered. He then alighted, and I tried not to look at his eyes as he ambled down the side of the bus to the luggage hold. The Spanish ladies were busily opening their cases. I began to fret – would I be commanded to alight? I tried to fix my stare ahead, not daring to look at him. After a nervous five minutes with the officer digging around in the Spaniard's bags, he walked off. Then the driver started up the engine as the Senoritas stowed their luggage again and boarded. With the hiss of the door closing, we were off. I watched the stern officer stride back to his guardpost room. I was through.

There wasn't much to see in Andorra but it was picturesque and enjoyable. There was absolutely no reason to return, unless of course, I needed a lorry-load of cigarettes and just happened to be in the neighbourhood.

Cigarettes – tick.

Country number 82 – tick.

6: Monty's Malta

As misfortune would have it, I needed to do some banking in Hong Kong but it had to be done over the counter. Darn it – I had to take a trip to Hong Kong to sort this out. That presented me with a variety of interesting options for stopovers on the way there. Maybe even on the way back? I pondered how many days I could get away with without my wife objecting.

I wanted to visit another one or two European countries to keep the pressure on Andy. So I spent a couple of days on Skyscanner figuring out the cheapest way to get from Manchester to Hong Kong via the most obscure ticket legs. Peculiarly, Malta and Romania were hotspots for dirt-cheap flights to various cities, so I bought a package holiday flight to Malta, onward leg to Istanbul then on to Hong Kong. It was less expensive than a standard airline such as the Middle-Eastern carriers or Cathay Pacific, so I had a sound excuse for my wife – who had given up with my pitiful excuses at this point.

Malta (No. 83)

The Ryanair flight 5209 was possibly the worst I had ever suffered. The legroom was not enough for Mini-Me from the Austin Powers movies – even the five-foot-tall middle-aged lady next to me had to contort her legs to fit in. In the row in front of me was an excitable three-year-old boy with blond hair and a fluorescent-green T-shirt who jumped up and down using the seat like a trampoline and shaking the backrest.

Right behind me was another three-year-old; this little flight-spoiler must have been a Sikh, for he wore an elasticated electric-blue beanie to cover his head. He continuously opened and slammed shut his tray table to my despair, and his mother, dressed in violet-coloured sheets, resolutely ignored him. I gave him a few looks of contempt through the gap between the seats – each time he would pose momentarily – then continue his torturous routine. I somehow wedged myself forward to take the pressure off my knees, put on my earphones and listened to Queen as loudly as I could to imagine I was not on the flight from hell.

The landing at Luqa Malta International Airport could not arrive quick enough. Upon clearing immigration, I took an airport taxi to the Silema district since it was too late for public transport. After calling his mates to get directions, the taxi driver dropped me outside the Jones Hostel in a deserted side street. After much ringing of the doorbell on the old limestone building, a young lady called Kuya let me in, and I paid my 32 euros (£25) for two nights in a four-bed dormitory.

I slept awfully – since the mattress was just a thin bed of springs which jarred in my back like a bag of bent spoons – and I cursed paying 16 euros a night for the discomfort. You may be wondering why on earth I stayed in a hostel again – and suffered another back-grinding bed another time. I can only suppose I hoped to get lucky with a comfy mattress someday to give me smug satisfaction at paying the lowest price possible.

I was relieved to get my wake-up alarm at 7:40

a.m., shower and get out of the hostel. A kind South African lady directed me to the bus stop for the capital, Valletta, and I turned right towards the promenade and passed ivory-coloured buildings with ornate balconies jutting out into the narrow street. It was spitting rain, and at the seafront, morning joggers and strollers passed back and forth as I propped myself on the sea wall waiting for my bus. After 9 a.m., bus number 13 picked me up, and I paid 1.50 euros (£1.17) and it trundled slowly along the seafront road.

Despite the awful start to my trip, I was excited to be here on the island of Malta. Strategically positioned in the Mediterranean and at the crossroads of Europe, North Africa and West Asia, Malta attracted the attention of in-vogue empires. The islands were ruled by the Phoenicians until the third century BC when the be-skirted soldiers of the Roman Empire swished in, then by the Byzantines in the sixth century AD. They were followed by the Aghlabids, then the Arabs took the helm in the 11th century until they were conquered by the Normans. The islands were donated to the crusade-friendly Order of St. John in 1530 until the pompous Napoleon came to town in 1798. Finally, Malta became a British possession until its independence in 1964.

Around Silema, the bus trundled past marinas jammed with hundreds of yachts – predominately modest – but which included a few that were too ostentatious for Khashoggi. After a further 25-minute journey through a tunnel, the bus reached the outskirts of Valletta where the marina was filled with vastly more spectacular yachts with their masts bobbing in the spring breeze. A great limestone city wall surrounded the capital.

The number 13 bus snorted and chugged its way

into the Valletta Bus Station, heralded by a sort of rotunda circled by green-and-white single-decker buses and three statues in the centre holding up a huge disc. The bus shuddered to an ungracious halt, the lights and engine abruptly powered off then everyone started to disembark. This must be it, I deduced.

I spied a café and decided that would do for my breakfast. Glass counters at the front offered an assortment of croissants and dinky little pasties. I ordered a greasy cheese pastie, chocolate croissant and a *café con leche*. The café owner was a balding grey-haired old man with a twizzled grey moustache and shuffled about in his grey cardigan.

I sat at a square plastic table facing the sea and the old Phoenicia Hotel, which was being restored. I was surrounded by construction workers and elderly gents supping espressos. So, there I was, ill-prepared in my haste to arrange my flights to Hong Kong, with sketchy ideas of what I was going to see. So what – I was elated at reaching country number 83.

After ten minutes waiting for my order, I had to get a move on. So I hastened the owner, who apologised and whizzed up a brew which he ambitiously called café latte. It was a half-pint beer glass filled with filter coffee, a fistful of sugar and UHT cream milk. It tasted like a *teh tahrik* in the Far East – sweet and addictive.

The weather was brightening up by the minute. The pall of low grey cloud was tinged light blue, the sun was poking through and the drizzle had stopped. It was going to be a great day, I figured. I thumbed through my Europe guidebook and planned my priorities over my cup of sugar with coffee in it.

I decided that my first priority was to see St. John's Cathedral, so I departed the cafe and headed towards the city centre. I crossed a modern steel bridge that appeared to have replaced a castle drawbridge centuries ago, and entered the walled city, which was paved with beautifully polished beige limestone. To the left was a Libyan Airlines office, and through the front window, I could see a lonely chap sat behind the counter. I was curious and entered.

'Hi. How much are the flights to Libya?' I asked.

'Sorry, we don't have flights to Libya. We haven't got permission from the Maltese government yet,' the chap replied.

I was tempted to ask him why on earth he was sitting in an office in a country which his airline did not fly to, but I kind of felt a bit sorry for him.

'Where do you fly, then?' I threw him a bone.

'We only fly to Egypt and Cyprus. The flights land at the American military base just outside of Tripoli.'

'How can I get a visa?' I pressed.

'You need to speak to the Libyan Consulate, I'm sorry,' he continued, 'it's a bit complicated. There are now three parties ruling in Tripoli. The Tripoli government, Benghazi and the new one installed by the United Nations.'

It all sounded rather complicated, and I had now lost my curiosity and appetite for baseless questions. The agent wanted to prolong the conversation, so I had to thank him and retreat. Maybe he only had one customer per day.

I continued through Pjazza Jean De Vallette, which was decked in polished coconut-pink limestone, and reached a pretty church on the right. A church official was lovingly sweeping the steps.

'Excuse me. What church is this?' I enquired.

'It is Italian,' he told me, 'Santa Caterina d'Italia.'

I thanked him and popped into the nine-sided Italian church for a short meditation. The interior was decorated in pale pinks and yellow pastel shades with a carved ceiling of biblical scenes. I then continued to the Co-Cathedral of St. John through narrow alleys lined with traditional shops with billboards and crates of produce stacked outside them.

Surprise, surprise – the cathedral was constructed from limestone. Unusually, the tower had three clock faces – one for the time, one for day of the week and one with the day of the month. The cathedral was built in the 1570s as the religious headquarters of the Knights of the Order of St. John, and I wondered if the day and date dials were glued on in later centuries.

Inside, I waited for what seemed an eternity behind some French tourists, who asked far too many questions for a bunch of normal people, then paid the 10 euros (£7.30) entrance fee and entered.

Inside, it was fantastically gilded in Baroque style and completely inlaid with gold carvings. The barrel ceiling had six sections painted by Mattia Preti to depict the life of John the Baptist and there were eight crypts which represented the eight languages of Europe which supported the crusades. The floor was exquisitely sectioned into inlaid marble tombs of fallen knights. Skulls seemed a popular theme along with Maltese crosses, lions, angels and Latin inscriptions.

The cathedral was originally an austere affair. In the renaissance period, the Grand Master's benefactors presented fine gifts and paid for extensive decoration of the crypts until it was dripping with marble statues, Belgium tapestries, silver lamps and marble altars. Grand Masters afforded themselves statues with their ashes stored in urns and flanked by statues of angels standing on skulls and turbans to represent the fall of the Ottomans. This cathedral was the king of bling.

After seeing the museum and the vessel which had

stored the forearm of John The Baptist until the mini-despot Napoleon stole it in 1798, I left to wander this interesting city. Old shops looked like they hadn't changed in a century.

'FINE FURNITURE'
'DRAPERS'
'HOUSE FURNISHER'

I stopped at the Cettina Café Luciano for lunch and ordered a Maltese mixed grill, which came with native sausage. It was an enormous meal with enough calories for a crusader. That night would have to be a light meal to offset that. I washed it down with a Cisk Maltese lager then pressed on.

The streets were thronged with pedestrians who strolled, shopped and dined in the attractive capital. It felt the size of the Isle of Man but was considerably smaller: barely over half the size. With a population over five times larger, Malta made it into the top ten list of most densely populated countries along with sardine city states such as Hong Kong, Singapore and Macau.

It was time to find the Lascaris War Rooms. I tramped back to the corner of the pedestrianised shopping street and St. Johns, and bingo – a sign pointed the way. Passing some more intriguing old stores, I followed the signs down a steep street that reminded me of San Francisco in California. The balconies jostled for space and were coloured various shades of green and blue contrasting the coconut-pink limestone facades.

Turning left past the Chinese Cultural Mission, the direction signs evaporated. Fortunately, I bumped into a couple walking a French bulldog who directed me down several flights of narrow stairs carved into the limestone, then I entered a long tunnel under the hill.

The tunnel was unusually dark with only a low-wattage CFC bulb along its length. Almost at the other end of the tunnel, I found the museum entrance and was greeted by a friendly couple of fellows, a Yorkshireman and a Maltese. I paid 10 euros (£7.30) entrance fee and watched the introductory documentary.

Malta had paid a pivotal role in the Second World War. It guarded the Eastern Meditteranean so was able to hamper German merchant vessels and warships provisioning Rommel in North Africa – so effectively that two-thirds of those vessels were sunk in the war. Hitler knew well that Malta had to fall and, from 1940 to 1942, the Luftwaffe and Italian Regia Aeronautica flew over 3,300 air raids to bomb the living daylights out of Malta. Almost two-thirds of the buildings on the island were destroyed: 5,524 homes, over 50 hospitals and educational institutes – in total over 30,000 buildings.

In preparation for the raids, the British military had dug like moles deep under Battery Park and established a joint command base for the army, navy and airforce to monitor the attacks and defend the territory. The Germans, in turn, tried to locate the fortifications and had sent reconnaissance aircraft to search for any signs. To avoid detection of the on-going defence works, the excavated material was smuggled out at night and dumped in building sites and anywhere else it could be secreted.

After the fascinating documentary, I entered the Sector Room where a map the size of two ping-pong tables showed Malta and Sicily. This was where the British defence forces tracked the incoming Axis bombers. Without a credible air force able to defend Malta, due to the Battle of Britain, the island was severely pounded and food supplies were almost exhausted. The population was placed on severe food rations and ate anything that moved. Maybe that was why I saw very few dogs about the island?

Churchill sent a fleet to resupply Malta, and two aircraft carriers including HMS Eagle with 32 Spitfires, a fuel tanker and 14 merchant vessels and destroyers were despatched from Gibraltar. The fleet was mercilessly attacked by the Germans and lost all but four of the merchant ships, but critically, the Spitfires left the sinking HMS Eagle and the tanker was decanted of its fuel before it sunk. This was enough to turnaround the desperate situation.

A bigger role was due for Malta, and the next room I entered was the control room for Operation Husky in July 1943. Eisenhower, Montgomery and Patton were secretly squirrelled into the complex and planned the rehearsal and invasion from this room. After the war, the facility was locked up and was forgotten about until 1999 when it was rediscovered.

The Husky operation room was two storeys high with an enormous map of the Eastern Mediterranean and a five-metre-high sliding ladder which ran alongside so it could be updated. The control room was rudimentary but effective: blackboards and chalk for updating status reports and a display board, much like an old airport electro-mechanical departure board, where status updates were slats dropped into slots in shutter-like frames.

Malta's people were fantastically brave in the face of the adverse pounding they suffered. For their bravery in the Second World War, Malta was awarded the George Cross by King George VI, and it was incorporated into their national flag at independence.

At the end of the tour, I walked back out the tunnel and climbed the limestone cliffs to Upper Barrakka Park which overlooked the Grand Harbour and Battery

Park below. An enormous flotilla of yachts lay across the harbour, with one Khashoggi-sized yacht sat in the closest berth to the peninsula.

It was getting cold, and I had to leave early to Luqa Airport for my flight to Istanbul. I took the number 13 bus back to Silema and bought a couple of tins of Cisk lager to sip while I did some online work with my laptop.

Malta was a surprising stopover. I had not realised the extent of its strategic importance to the Holy Wars or the Second World War, and the visits to St. John's Co-Cathedral and Lascaris War Rooms were eye-openers. Now the small state was chiefly a tourist spot for sun-starved Northern Europeans, and I hope to see it again. Some day.

A cute little tick – number 83. Done.

7: Ribbentrop Runts

After Malta, I took a Turkish Airlines flight to Istanbul and that was country number 84. It was a fascinating stopover but rather uneventful. And anyway, you went there for a holiday last year, right? I then continued to Hong Kong and did my banking errand. Now it was time slip in a couple more ticks on the way home to England.

I had discovered that Aeroflot was selling ridiculously cheap fares from Hong Kong to Eastern Europe. Armed with Skyscanner, I had trawled various cities until Chișinău in Moldova popped up at the insane price of 280 pounds for a one-way flight. The hairs stood up on the back of my neck – I had no idea what Moldova was famous for, or exactly where it was – but I would find out.

I had also discovered that there was a direct train from Chișinău to Bucharest, the capital of Romania. So I had bought an onward flight from Bucharest to Manchester and my return route home was locked in.

Aeroflot had changed drastically since the last time I had chanced my luck on this bargain-basement airline as a young man aged 22. I had flown from Kenya to Moscow on a Soviet-era Ilyushin 62 then on to London on a Tupolev 154, which in those days were a bit prone to crashing here and there. Traveller's tales were full of Aeroflot flights taking off with passengers standing due to lack of seats. Fortunately, it wasn't that bad.

But the Ilyushin was not a fuel-efficient aircraft, so

with a limited flying range, it had to stopover in Yemen for re-fueling. And in 1990, with the Soviet empire disintegrating, there were shortages of everything in Moscow. The Aeroflot crew had bought half a supermarket in Kenya and had filled a third of the overhead lockers with food, alcohol and cigarettes to do a spot of smuggling. I supposed it subsidised their meagre rouble salary. So I turned a blind eye, despite not having anywhere to stow my backpack on the flight, and had to sit in my seat with it under my feet like a penguin sitting on its egg.

Anyhow, I digress. As I had 100 times before, I took the A42 Airbus to Hong Kong's Chep Lap Kok airport. I then checked in and boarded Aeroflot flight SU 213 to Moscow's Sheremetyevo airport.

Moldova (No. 85)

So – where is Moldova?

I never really knew the answer to that one. I assumed it was a mythological communist country dreamed-up in the wicked mind of Sacha Baron Cohen. Could I remember a Moldovan football team playing in the UEFA championship? Or Moldova winning the Eurovision song contest? Or the travel agents selling package tours to Moldova? A stag party getting smashed in Moldova. Nope, none of the above.

How this country had remained off-the-radar I am not entirely sure. The Bosnia-Herzegovina conflict had hogged the British news in the early 1990s, so perhaps nobody had noticed the Transnistrians clashing with the Moldovans. One thing for certain, Moldova was off the tourist trail with only 121,000 foreigners visiting the country in 2016.

Formerly known as the SSR Moldova, or the Soviet Socialist Republic of Moldova, my first recollection of this state was when I was reviewing Andy's country-tracker spreadsheet. I had visited many regions of Europe in the year 2015 to early 2016 and was rapidly running out of places to visit. I surveyed the remaining dozen on my "NO" list. Moldova and Romania were right there. Were they near each other?

At that point, I didn't realise they were historically part of the same Romanian Empire of Principalities and were partitioned by Stalin and Hitler in the Second World War. Perhaps naive, but I didn't understand the geopolitical soup of Eastern Europe.

What did the Moldovans look like, I wondered? At gate 23 of Sheremetevo airport, as I waited to board flight SU 1844 to Chişinău, I had my first opportunity to figure out what they would be like. The waiting passengers looked rather an unusual lot – it felt like I was in Chalmun's Cantina from Star Wars. There were all sorts of faces from here and there, presumably oddball ex-Soviet republics.

I could figure out several Chinese and Central Asia-looking dudes and assumed the rest of the white-faced passengers would be either Russians or Moldovans. Certainly, I was the only western-looking face around. One Chinese-looking lady was approached by what I can only assume were officers of a Chinese bureau, for they interrogated the young lady, inspected her China identity card and asked for other papers. One other passenger looked remarkably like President Putin travelling incognito.

Once onboard, I was thankful to find that it was an Airbus A320, and the boarding crew and flight crew all greeted me in Russian. Did I look so much like a Russian? Fat and pasty-skinned? Or surly? Or maybe they were never expecting a Brit to be boarding a flight to Moldova.

I took my seat, or rather, was shoehorned into it. I was in the aisle row seated next to what I suspected was a Central Asia couple since the man was speaking in a Slavic or Turkic-type language. To my right was Santa Claus; portly and with his white beard flowing over his chest. A tall lady played on the front row with her cute baby girl and looked the odd-one-out. A giant of a man, who looked like a Russian army conscript, strode by with his giant knuckles clasping the seatbacks as he walked. He looked like Ivan Drago – the Russian boxing opponent of Rocky Balboa in the Rocky IV movie.

After three hours and a dinner of triple-layer sandwich of processed cheese and white gunge on German-type brown *brot*, the Aeroflot craft landed ever so gracefully on the runway of Chişinău Airport. The passengers simultaneously erupted into an impromptu clapping of hands. Maybe it was in appreciation of not crashing – Aeroflot had had over 720 air incidents and over 8,200 passengers had lost their lives. Today was our lucky day.

Both my suitcase and I got soaked since there was no passenger boarding bridge or covered baggage vehicle. Outside the crowded arrivals area, I was greeted by dozens of taxi hawks and hotel touts.

'Taxi?'

'Hotel? Taxi?'

I braved them and struggled to a money changer, where I exchanged a crisp 100 US dollar note for what seemed like an outrageously low 1,952 Moldovan lei. My wallet was also full of useless Russian roubles, so I dumped those as well to give me well over 2,000 lei (£80) to keep me going for two days.

I found the taxi stand in the terminal and was informed that the standard rate to the city centre was 100 lei (£4), so I followed the appointed driver, who was surrounded by a mob of hangers-on. One older gent tried to wrest my suitcase from the hands of the younger man assigned to me. I rebuked him and handed it back to the younger man, who smirked and led me to a yellow-and-black taxi.

It transpired that the suitcase-stealing older gent was the driver. As he climbed into the drivers seat to my utter confusion, several others thronged about discussing things that touts and hangers-on do. I just decided to go with the flow since my suitcase was battered, the locks damaged and it was full of dirty washing. If they wanted it, they could bloody well have it.

It was well after midnight, and the drive into the city was interesting. The taxi screamed along at a pace on the dark road, and every few minutes, the driver would grind to a walking pace as he reached a floodlit overhead gantry. As we passed underneath each gantry, a camera flash went off then he looked at me and said *politie*, which I understood immediately to mean police. Why would the police take photos of every car? Would some unfortunate have to flick through the photos, trying to match those who were going too fast? Were they looking for criminals behind the wheel?

The driver turned down a dark lane and stopped to scrutinise my hostel booking form. He seemed to have poor eyesight, for he struggled to hold it up to the car's interior lamp. Scratching his head, the driver then pulled out a cigarette lighter and proceeded to waft in front of the form. He then drove off again and stopped in front of a ramshackle compound of single-storey houses. He darted in and returned with a young man with stubble.

The man spoke to me, 'You have a booking with IQ hostel?'

'Yes, I have,' I was glad to see someone who was expecting me and spoke English.

Inside the hostel, the lounge was frequented by a few travellers: a Russian guy, a Bulgarian and a Moldovian lady. The hostel owner decided we should perform check-in formalities in the morning since it was already nearly 1 a.m. He issued me with a pile of bedding and pointed me to my upper bunk in a room that looked like a child's bedroom with stuffed toys peering down from high shelves. I quickly made my bed, plugged my smartphone into a wall socket to charge and changed into my shorts and T-shirt and fell asleep.

Sometime in the early hours, I awoke suddenly to a sensation of someone touching my leg.

'Wassat?' I called out then dozed off again. Sometime later, I awoke again. Someone was standing near me.

'Your snoring is so loud. I can't get any sleep,' the ghostly figure scolded me.

'Sorry mate,' I apologised.

Light was already streaming in the window, so I guessed it was 6 a.m. and decided to wait for my alarm to go off. I could hear the complainer tossing and turning in his bed and tutting and puffing from time to time. What kind of traveller was that? If Tutting-twit wanted a silent night's sleep then he should have stayed in a hotel.

I awoke at my alarm time of 7:20 a.m. and quietly clambered down the bunk bed ladder to avoid Tutting-twit whining again. I showered, dressed and hurried off to find the train station. I grabbed a city map on the way out and located the hostel on it but not the train station. Drat. I will ask in a café, I thought.

I found a small café on Ameneasca Street and ordered a café latte and a cottage-cheese croissant. I challenged the waiter's English by asking him directions, and he nervously pointed out the train station on the east of my map. I had been walking in the wrong direction.

I continued up the street and turned right on to the main Stefan cel Mare Boulevard, which was rigged with overhead trolleybus electric wires. Soviet-looking trolleybuses whined smoothly along the street stopping for passengers. They were bendy-bus types similar to the eighties-style ones I had seen on my visits to Moscow. A few looked quite new and flashy with curved windows – quite uncharacteristic of socialist public transport.

The traffic was mostly a mix of Western and Eastern European cars such as Dacia and Skoda. About a tenth were vintage communist-era cars, such as Lada 126s, and another tenth were flashy BMWs, Range Rovers and Minis. The footpaths were vintage communist-era with a patchwork of uneven asphalt, yet, some sections were being completely replaced by shiny-new block paving. The buildings told a similar story: old communist-era buildings were scattered here there, but the bulk were nondescript European blocks interspersed with flashy new blocks with mirrored windows – evidence of new investment.

I headed left at the road fork where the Liberation Monument stood – a tin-hatted soldier cradling a busty woman in dark granite. They looked like they were standing on the bow of the Titanic. Then I took a right fork to Yuri Gagarin Boulevard, which was dedicated to the lucky first man in space. As I observed the road sign, a street urchin with a cart of his belongings scurried towards me. He was shouting at me to get away from his turf.

'Piss off you little swine,' I shouted.

I decided to hasten my pace, though, for I had heard stories of real-life Bubble Gum Gangs in Romania. I didn't want to hang around and be surrounded by a gang of street kids with their little hands rummaging in every one of my pockets.

A few moments later, I noticed the train station on the other side of the street. It was built of beige stone and had Christian-Orthodox-style pink arches over the entrance and windows. I descended into the subway under the road, a labyrinth of small stores selling all manner of knick-knacks, and emerged fronting the square and the Pain Train monument. This was a train-carriage-sized granite block topped with human sculptures wearing painful expressions who represented the communist-era deportations of Romanians to various Gulag camps around the Soviet Union.

Inside the neatly renovated station, a gang of middle-aged ladies in uniform were furiously mopping the granite floor. I tiptoed over the wet floor area and found the international ticket booth, where I bought a first-class sleeper ticket to Bucharest for 771 lei (£30). Not particularly cheap, and I didn't know whether I would get a shiny new carriage or a Soviet-era dump of a train.

The block next to the train station was a busy flea market, and given the propensity for communist-era knick-knacks in Eastern Europe, I figured there could be something of interest I could pick up cheaply such as a T-34 tank commander's goggles or a cosmonaut's set of false teeth. There were dozens of Moldovans milling around next to their stuff laid out on sheets of cardboard or blankets. I had a nosy around and soon realised it was almost exclusively used clothes – probably peeled off dead people or nicked off washing lines.

I strode onwards towards the hostel, since I had to check out by 11 a.m. I passed the Monument to the Liberation of Moldova from German Fascists, which was a Russian soldier in a tin hat with a muscular Batman-style body and holding an enormous sword with a Soviet star on it. The liberated local next to him was a young Moldovan lady in a *Titanic* movie pose with her arms outstretched and hair sweeping in the wind. She was raised aloft, and they looked like a couple of ice-skating contestants.

I reached the hostel and the owner was nowhere to be seen, so I gathered my belongings and sat at the lounge table doing laptop work. I bought an onward flight from Bucharest International airport to London Stanstead for Friday evening. I would be arriving at 23:50. Ouch. How would I get home at that unGodly hour? The earliest train was at 6 a.m., which meant sleeping on the airport terminal benches for a few hours.

I waited for an hour to pay the owner then left to eat when he failed to materialise. I headed down Tighina Street, and after taking lunch in a Bavarian-style underground restaurant, crossed the road to the Museum of National Armaments.

I was surprised that I could enter the compound without being challenged. Newly-painted relics of 1950s to 1970s Soviet technology were on display. A 5я23 anti-aircraft guided missile, a MiG-21 fighter, a T-34 tank, BTR-60 armoured personnel carrier and various mortar batteries.

After fooling around on a few of them for amusement, I entered the building where I was greeting by a young lady dressed in a powder-blue uniform and wearing wrap-around glasses. I was surprised that she spoke decent English. After charging me 10 lei (£0.40) entrance fee and another 10 lei for a camera permit, she led me around the exhibit since I was the only customer that afternoon, or probably that day? Or even that month?

The museum was full of interesting artefacts about the world wars and explained the territorial changes to Moldova through the last two centuries.

It's fair to say that the history of Moldova and the greater Romanian people was complicated and had been under the control of the Ottoman Empire, Russian Empire and USSR. Chunks of territory including Bessarabia, Wallachia, Bukovina, Transylvania and Transnistria had been combined, hacked off and superglued to other states such as Ukraine over the centuries.

Between the wars, Greater Romania had been united with more or less a common language and purpose. During the Second World War, the Molotov-Ribbentrop Pact chopped Romania into two halves, and subsequently, the region east of the Dniester River become the Moldavian Soviet Socialist Republic under the control of the Stalin.

The Soviets had changed from the Roman alphabet to Cyrillic and brainwashed the population that they were different from the rest of the Romanian-speaking folk across the river. The Soviets ran their communications and wide-gauge railway tracks right up to the border at the Dniester River. They then deported anyone who disagreed with the decision or who were just plain intelligent and could threaten them. The dissenters were carted off in cattle trains to the Gulag camps in Russia, A total of 70,000 were despatched in conditions similar to the Jews who were sent to the extermination camps – and many didn't survive the harsh journey.

The Soviet empire came under strain in the late 1980s, and the Moldovans – as was fashionable in Soviet-bloc countries – took advantage of the situation. They organised protests, removed Russian as an official language and switched back to the Roman alphabet. The declaration was on 21 August 1989.

Since then, Moldova had struggled along with the lowest gross domestic product per capita in Europe. The entire country only had the GDP of the Isle of Man. The curator lady told me her salary was a meagre 1,000 lei (£40) – that was less than a Chinese factory worker. Less than half, in fact. Why were iPhones not being assembled in Eastern Europe, I wondered?

After my fascinating time at the War Museum, I returned to the hostel to check out and bid goodbye to the beardy-friendly hostel owner. Outside on the street, a white Dacia taxi was waiting for me, and I loaded my case in the boot.

'Train station please,' I informed the driver, and he returned me a blank look.

'Choo choo,' I tried my best train impression. Pointing at the train station on my Chișinău city map did the trick, and after much straining of his tiny Dacia's engine, I was dropped at the stately train station where the gang of cleaner ladies were still mopping the lengthy hall of granite. I found a café close to the platform and took an espresso and bread bun while waiting for the train.

A light-green shunting locomotive rolled into view, momentarily paused, then revealed a line of enormous passenger carriages painted light-blue with a mustard-yellow go-faster stripe down the side. After the locomotive uncoupled and trundled off, black-uniformed train guards opened the carriage doors, unfolded the steel steps then stood neatly to attention at each carriage. They were impressively choreographed and would not look out of place outside The Ritz.

I settled my bill, grabbed my wheelie suitcase and crossed the tracks to find carriage number three. While the guard checked my ticket, I scrutinised the train. It was a typical Soviet-era carriage with chest-high steel steps, enormous body and embellished with Cyrillic lettering which labelled everything of even vague importance. It was precisely the same as the Trans-Siberian train I had taken in 1990. After the intense ticket inspection, I was waved on, and I excitedly mounted the steep grated steps.

I entered the carriage corridor decorated with faux-beech melamine walls, grey-painted steel heaters, windows crudely fitted with a plain nets hung from café rods and shiny-gold curtains embossed with 'CFM Moldova' tied back in a vain attempt to give an air of class. I cluttered along the corridor, which was laid along its length with a Persian-style polyester rug topped with protective linen, and located my cabin.

My purported first-class cabin was just a regular one since it had four berths covered in burgundy vinyl. My cabin had the same polyester rug, gold curtains and nets. The bits of leftover curtain material were turned into a table cover to hide the heavily damaged table. I dumped my bags and left the stifling hot cabin to stroll in the corridor. A plump lady was trying to open as many of the windows as she could, which was futile since most were unopenable due to age.

At 4:30 p.m., there was a deep guttural sound as the locomotive reversed-up to the carriages and was coupled. I plugged in a power adapter to an electrical outlet in the aisle to find the power was now on. Soon enough, the carriage creak and strained as the locomotive gently tugged on the couplings, then an unintelligible station announcement heralded the departure and the train slowly creaked off. An overnight train journey on a Soviet train, no-one else to share my cabin with and a power outlet. I was in heaven.

The Moldovan countryside rolled by at a stately pace in the spring late-afternoon sun. Farms of grassy fields were punctuated by small scraggy trees, mature poplar and willow trees and low rolling hills, which provided a backdrop in the near distance. Stations rolled by with Romanic and Cyrillic names, brightly renovated and framed by willow trees. Communities of half-constructed houses and older bungalows glided by. I estimated we were rolling along at about 70 kilometres per hour, which sufficed to make progress without the ancient carriages jumping the rails.

I was tired after my semi-slumber the previous night due to the anti-snoring brigade, so I made up my bed of 'Calea Ferată din Moldova' printed linen and two mattress rolls for good luck and dozed off. I was rudely awoken at 7 p.m. by a large lady in navy-blue trousers and a chunky military-like sweater hollering at me in Romanian. Or was it Moldovian? Or Bessarabian? I figured out she was warning me about the border.

'I don't know,' I hollered back in a dazed state. I peered out the grubby windows and saw a sign 'Zone controle'. Was I already at the border? The timetable had indicated that the border would be reached at 2 a.m., so I arose and in the corridor met the plump lady peering out the window.

'Romania?' I enquired.

'No,' she tersely responded. I shrugged my

shoulders and lay down again. Next, another younger lady – similarly dressed and equally plump – appeared.

'Where you go?' she asked me.

'Erm. Bucharest,' I answered.

'Where you [come] from?' she continued.

'I flew from Moscow to Chişinău yesterday then spent my time in Chişinău city.'

'What [did] you do Chişinău?' she continued her interrogation.

'Erm. I visited the War Museum,' I hesitantly replied.

She grunted then demanded my passport. She leafed through my dozens of pages of immigration stamps.

'You travel a lot,' she remarked.

'Yes,' I confirmed.

'You still have money?'

'Erm. Yes,' I answered. She shrugged her shoulders, handed back my passport then wandered off. Next were two uniformed men who I presumed were customs.

'You smoke?' they asked.

'Yes,' I replied.

'Show me [your] bag.'

I pulled out my wheelie suitcase, opened it and pulled out my Istanbul duty-free shopping bag.

'I have 400 cigarettes,' I told them.

The stubbly customs official held my backpack open and swirled about inside with a torch. Then he grunted and returned the bag to me seemingly upset that I hadn't been hiding an enormous stash of cigarettes.

We were at the Moldovan border – that was for sure. I peered out the window to see dozens of train bogeys. So, this was where they were going to do their act.

Josef Stalin, being the paranoid delusional variety of despot, insisted on building his railway network with a wider railway gauge than the 4 foot 8 ½ inch "Standard Gauge" used across Western Europe. His huge railway network was built on the "Russian gauge" of 4 foot 11 27/32 inches because he thought that the European fascists would invade the Soviet Union by commuter trains from Berlin.

Stalin probably wasn't entirely deluded, nevertheless, this provided a problem for the cross-border train services. I had been through a wheel change before, when I travelled the Trans-Siberian Express. The switch was performed at the border between Outer Mongolia to China's Inner Mongolia in the early hours, and Andy and I had to disembark while the operation was clandestinely undertaken in a vast shunting warehouse.

Now was my chance to observe this transformation at close quarters. The carriage was shunted into a railway siding, and six giant hydraulic jacks surrounding the carriage at the corners and middles. The jacks were similar to those in tyre and exhaust garages – except on a huge scale with massive four-metre-high pneumatic units. Railway workers inserted giant forks of the green and yellow jacks under the edge of the carriage itself and scampered underneath the carriage. They removed the hydraulic hoses, did some jiggery-pokery with a coupling and attached a steel cable.

I watched the blue carriage in the next siding and observed the steel cables taughten then pull out a string of six wide-gauge bogies. Tethered behind them, another steel cable pulled in a string of six standard-gauge bogies positioned along the steel cable at the precisely right distance. Clever – that's how the buggers did it.

After locking and coupling the new set of wheels, my carriage was shunted off to be re-assembled into a single train again. The train was picked-up by a standard-gauge Romanian Railways locomotive – a Class 41 from the venerable days of communism.

The blonde-haired immigration lady returned with her four-star epaulettes. She was accompanied by a trim lady in a navy shell suit who wielded a passport stamper in one hand and a laptop mounted in a tray from a shoulder strap around her neck, like an ice-cream seller in the golden days of cinema. They looked at me, chatted then after a few minutes the ice-cream-seller lady *whumped* my passport.

I inspected the page after they departed. It was a Moldovan exit stamp with a little picture of a train in the top right corner. It looked cool next to my entry stamp with a little line drawing of an aircraft. I wondered – did they keep a stamp for every transport type at border crossing? One stamp with a little bus on it. One with a car? One with a cute motorbike?

I guessed that I was officially out of Moldova. They had chattered about my thick passport, changed my train wheels, *whumped* my passport and shunted me off to some sidings in the dark. Moldova was done. Would I be back? You never know. I might pass through again for some cheap food and a railway journey out to St. Petersburg.

Country number 85 done. Now I was putting some distance in front of Andy.

Romania (No. 86)

I had no particular desire to visit Romania. Sure, the thought of seeing the real Transylvania and Count Dracula's castle sounded interesting. But it was one of the poorer countries of the European Union, and I had read stories of street kids – like the Bubble Gum Gang in the *Hostel* movie – who swarmed tourists and picked their pockets. I had been pestered by street kids on my travels around Europe, especially in Italy and Paris, so these images and press stories were impressed in my mind – I was not looking forward to getting fleeced.

Still, it was another country – another tick. I *had* to see it. And there were no cheap flights out of Moldova. In fact, there were hardly *any* flights out of Moldova, so I had little choice but travel overland to Bucharest for a flight back to England. If I had survived El Salvador and Guatemala, then I could survive anywhere on this planet, I thought to myself.

So there I was, sitting on a dated Soviet-era train carriage at 9 p.m. in some railway sidings in Greater Romania no man's land. There was a storm overhead, lightning danced around the sky and rain poured down in bucketfuls. I stared gloomily at the barbed-wire fence outside. This was not a pleasing start and certainly not the sunny spring walks of Chişinău.

A polite bearded Romanian immigration officer entered my train cabin, asked for my passport and scanned it with a handheld terminal. He then looked me in the eye in a Clint Eastwood sort of way. A few moments later, a super-polite customs officer in army fatigues greeted me.

'Do you have anything illegal? Tobacco?' he asked.

I thought for a moment then decided that my two cartons of Marlboro were probably not illegal quantities.

'No,' I replied confidently.

'Are you a tourist?' he persisted, again quietly and politely.

'Yes. I am heading from Chişinău to Bucharest, then I will fly to England,' I replied.

'Thank you,' he answered then plodded off.

How nice he was. Maybe they were trying to impress the European Union by being uber-nice to fellow member citizens. Shortly, the customs officers filed off the train, the locomotive tooted and I was on my way again. The train picked up speed quickly on the Romanian side of the border, and I had visions of the bogeys becoming detached and the carriage flying off the track.

It was now 10 p.m., and I *had* to get some sleep, for the train was scheduled to arrive in Bucharest at 6:04 a.m. I stowed my rucksack in the steel chest under my couchette, rolled-up my jeans with my wallet and passport inside the pockets and hid it under my pillow for safety. I then changed into my shorts and T-shirt to sleep.

About midnight, I awoke with a start. Nobody was prodding me and complaining about my snoring, but I was shaken by something and just couldn't get back to sleep again. I tossed and turned, and worse still, I was dying to urinate. I had drunk half of my three-litre bottle of water and was desperate but didn't want to leave my valuables behind in the cabin. What was I going to do? I was in no mood to change into my jeans and cart my rucksack to the awful toilet.

An idea came to me. I could use the large water bottle. You know? I jumped up and gulped down as much water as I could before filling the half-full plastic bottle. I hoped that my neighbour in the next cabin was not listening to what I was doing. Despite emptying my bladder, I still couldn't get to sleep. By 2 a.m., I gave-up and fetched my smartphone to listen to Queen; perhaps that would help.

I dozed off again, but by 3 a.m., I had another toilet break due to drinking all that bloody water. The water bottle was now almost full, and I felt sure that if I waited until Bucharest I could fill that bottle to the brim.

I awoke in a sweat at 5 a.m. The train guard had turned on the cabin heating, and now it was too stuffy. Sod it, I took my washbag and train towel to the bathroom, where I delicately brushed and washed – praying that I did not drop anything on the nasty toilet floor. If I dropped anything then it would have to instantly get thrown into the nasty toilet and flushed right out onto the track via the poop pipe.

Finally, the train arrived at a station with long new platforms, and my next-door neighbour confirmed we were in Bucharest Gare de Nord with the fake Paris railway station name. It was still dark, and I yomped along the platform in the cool air attracted to a brightly lit McDonalds sign. My game plan was to eat breakfast in the station then wait until dawn came; I figured out I would be safer from the Bubble Gum Gangs in the daylight. Then I would head straight for the Palace of the Parliament.

I tucked into a delicious McDonald's breakfast of a sausage McMuffin and smirked to myself that I was now on country number 86. I was getting closer to 90 – that would be a fantastic milestone. I hoped that Andy wouldn't start to panic: I wanted to sneak up to 90 without raising too much attention.

Romania came under control of the Soviet Union in 1944 and was mismanaged by one of the world's maddest dictators, Nicolae Ceauşescu, from 1948 until 1989. Despite the poverty of his nation, he had deluded visions that Bucharest could be turned into the Paris of Eastern Europe. He bulldozered thousands of homes then built wide boulevards, a clone of the Arc de Triomphe and the colossal Palace of Parliament, which was so costly he near bankrupted the country.

Ceauşescu built up a fearsome secret police organisation, as any dictator worth his salt would do, to spy on the populace and even forcibly take away their children and lock them in orphanages as a penalty. At the same time, he outlawed contraception and abortion to boost the population. Perhaps it was to replace the incarcerated kids?

He completely bungled an industrial revolution in the 1970s, and Romania's foreign debt ballooned out of control. Ceauşescu was so obsessed with clearing the debt that he exported everything that the country produced – including medicines and foodstuffs – which his people desperately needed.

Among Ceauşescu's more personal acts of madness, he wore a different suit and new pair of shoes every day because he suspected the material may be laced with poison by assassins. It was rumoured that at bedtime his outfit would be sent for incineration.

Fatigued by Ceauşescu's incompetence and general shortages of food and medicine, the Romanian populace took to the streets culminating in the shooting of protestors in December 1989. Ceauşescu and his wife fled Bucharest by helicopter but were caught and, after a trial on Christmas Day, executed by a firing squad.

After a bit of pensive thought, I decided it was about time to dare the city and its kiddie gangs. With my possessions locked down, I exchanged my far-too-many Moldovan lei at a ridiculously low rate, just 10 cents on the dollar. At least they took the Moldovan currency off me, which was only fit for toilet paper outside its border. One foreign exchange bureau flat refused to accept Moldovan lei even though they were once the same country speaking the same language. What utter snobs.

I located the entrance to the underground Metro and walked down grey granite-tiled subways until I reached the metro line number one. I couldn't understand it. I had expected to be overrun with beggars and Bubble Gum Gangs, especially in stations, but I didn't see anything but clean thoroughfares. The metro train itself was also a great surprise – wider and cleaner than the London underground – and lightly loaded with passengers so I could easily get a free seat. I had specially put my rucksack on my front to guard against pickpockets, but I was sure I could have worn a rapper's gold necklace and a Nikon camera around my neck and nobody would have batted an eyelid.

I exited at the Pod Izvor Metro Station and found myself at the edge of a handsome park, Izvor Park, on the banks of the splendid Dâmbovița River. This area was formerly a warren of narrow streets and rickety houses which Ceaușescu had flattened. Heading south into the park, I passed through neatly maintained gardens tended by dull workers. Still no beggars. Still no Bubble Gum Gang. I crossed a wide road, the National Unity Boulevarde, and as I approached the People's Palace started to appreciate its immense size.

Perched on a low hill, the palace overlooked the city and Izvor Park. It was an immense oyster-coloured block with mature trees masking the lower floors. I counted about 30 windows along its length, and the main section was about ten storeys wide. The midsection had a belt of enormous arched windows – I presumed this floor was for function rooms or something – and above that, a terrace and balustrade wrapped around the building.

I followed signs for the entrance to the People's Palace which led me around the left. Once I was facing the palace, I could appreciate its humongous size from another angle. The front section alone, behind which stood the gargantuan main block, was four storeys high with two wings that angled forwards. This wing itself seemed to be about the size of Buckingham Palace. I passed through the gardens with manicured lawns, pointy trees and faux-Parisian period streetlamps to the main entrance, paid for a 9 a.m. tour and waited excitedly until I was called.

The palace was Ceauşescu's pièce de résistance, and he planned it to combine his centre of government and residence. At 365,000 square metres, this was the second-largest public on earth – second only to the Pentagon. It was the granddaddy of all palaces and large enough to accommodate Buckingham Palace, the Palace of Versailles, the Royal Palace of Stockholm, the Winter Palace in Saint Petersburg and Topkapi Palace – with enough room left over for an IKEA superstore. The Palace was the heaviest building on earth, estimated at over four million tonnes, and was so heavy that it was sinking at the rate of 6mm per year.

Ceauşescu started construction of his pet project in 1983, and 27 churches and a quarter of Bucharest were demolished to make space for his ego trip. It was only finished in 1997 – long after the revolution. The colossus housed over 1,000 rooms, 40 conference halls and 400 government offices. The immense scale continued underground with eight subterranean levels, access roads, catacombs and even a nuclear bunker.

The tour started. I followed the lady tour guide into an annexe outside the Great Hall, which I supposed Ceaușescu had imagined he would sip Grand Cru Champagne with the French President and other world leaders before swishing into the Great Hall. The annexe was the area of one-wide by two-squash-courts long with a vaulted lit ceiling and arched walls to house paintings. The floor was inlaid salmon-coloured marble with a huge teal-coloured woollen rug covering most of it. Busts of various famous Romanian nobility stood on plinths here and here.

I walked its length and entered the Great Hall, which was designed as a 600-seat theatre. It was a circular hall split into over two-dozen segments and three levels. The lower level had various entrance doors in each segment and the floor was filled with hundreds of red velvet seats. The mid-level had four rows of balcony seating and opera boxes, and the top-level had circular windows around it – perhaps these were for the secret service to spy on the attendees?

The centrepiece was an enormous round chandelier which weighed five tons. In total the building was graced with 2,800 chandeliers, which probably required a small army of lightbulb-changers to take care of. Unfortunately, the architects of the Great Hall forgot to build a side entrance to the stage for the actors, and the stage was too low to accommodate an orchestra at the front.

And there were just a few architects on this project – over 700 of them. And 20,000 labourers who worked 24 hours a day to build the palace. The stairs were rebuilt several times because the risers were too high for diminutive Ceaușescu's 5 foot 2 inches. The floors were entirely marbled – requiring one million cubic metres of stone to cover it.

Next, I was led through several lobbies of marble columns, vaulted ceilings and lit by dozens more chandeliers until we reached the Grand Staircase. The staircase was wide enough for James Bond to drive a cement mixer up, and the upper section had two flights of stairs to each side lit by a sixteen-metre-high window with curtains big enough to give a laundry-woman a stroke. Each curtain weighed 250 of kilograms; was there a washing machine in the world big enough to handle them, I thought.

When I reached the top of the staircase, I turned around to admire the stairwell. It was about six storeys high and large enough to house one of Sellafield's nuclear reactors. Prompted by the tour-lady, who kept tutting at me for dragging along at the back of the group, we then passed through five-metre-high carved wooden entrance doors into Alexander's Hall.

This looked like a place you would hold a speech: it had enough bone-coloured conference seats to fill an Airbus A380, a stage and double-storey bay windows along its length. It was ornately decorated in the style of Palais de Versailles with cream walls and gold accents.

I passed through a pair of bay windows on to the central balcony, where Michael Jackson infamously announced 'Hello Budapest'. I looked out across Ceaușescu's dream of Paris-in-the-Balkans.

A manicured oval lawn, adorned with more pointy conifers, and a dual-lane circular driveway as big as a motorway-exit roundabout fronted the palace. Beyond that, a line of flagpoles, and past that, the graceful Unirii Boulevard. In the distance, the boulevard was flanked by two banks of monolithic eight-storey government buildings – each one at least 200 metres-long each.

Unirii Boulevard ran as far as the eye could see and was modelled after the Champs-Élysées. It was built at any human or financial cost, as any crazed dictator like Ceaușescu would do, so that he could imagine he was of global importance while he sat munching cornflakes on his Michael Jackson balcony.

Construction of the palace had stopped during the revolution and its architect was exiled. After the architect returned to Romania, the building was completed and Ceaușescu never even got to live in his behemoth. At the time of my visit, 30 per cent of the building was occupied by the parliament and 50 per cent was unused.

After getting harassed again by Tutting-Tour-Lady, I passed into another of the palace's many halls, The Great Hall, which was rented out for exhibitions. It was lavishly decorated with dozens of chandeliers and a faux-skylight.

I had visited countless staircases, halls and corridors. It seemed that I must have seen as much as the size of Buckingham Palace after a couple of hours walk. I returned to the entrance, where I was shocked to be told by Tutting-Tour-Lady that we had only visited 5 per cent of the whole building. Utterly incredible. I wanted to sit down and think about that – but I was being shooed out by her.

I left the palace at 11 a.m. and walked back towards the city, my mind in awe of the enormity of the building. I headed north along Liberty Boulevard then back across the lovely Dâmbovița River, which resembled the River Seine too much for mere coincidence. The city was very metropolitan with French-style buildings.

I walked along the north bank of the river, down Splaiul Independenei and past Opera Park. At a crossroad, I turned right on to Ştirbei Vodă Street, where I discovered what I was searching for: the Casa Radio.

Officially known as the Dâmboviţa Center, the building was constructed in the 1980s as a museum of the Romanian Communist Party. It was never fully finished and was mothballed after the fall of Ceauşescu; another of his egomaniacal vanity projects. Each block was eight storeys high and the grand fronts were collonaded, but their ugly unfinished concrete sides were exposed.

I walked onwards past Count Dracula's local bank, Banca Transilvania, and towards the Gare du Nord. I took a final McDonalds meal, retrieved my suitcase from the luggage storage then took the Metro train to the airport for my flight back to Manchester.

I could never have imagined that Romania would be on my desirable travel list in a million years. The crazed handiwork of Paris-obsessed Ceauşescu, The People's Palace, went straight on to my top-ten list of sites alongside worthy adversaries such as Tiananmen Square in Beijing, St. Basil's Cathedral in Red Square, Moscow and The Great Jaguar Temple in Tikal, Guatemala.

Country number 86. Tick.

STALIN'S STATES

8: UFO-spotting in Slovakia

During the summer of 2016, I took my wife and daughter on a five-day driving holiday to Jersey – that was country number 87. Then I took a cheeky weekend trip: I flew to Guernsey then, early on Monday morning, back to Gatwick for work in London. I was astonished that I got away with that one without paying my wife a bribe. Tickety-tick – that was 88.

I never fail to be intrigued by things I stumble upon when travelling to a new country. I visited Castle Cornet in Guernsey and discovered it was the last holdout of the Royalist armies against Oliver Cromwell in the British Isles. Fascinating. Both Jersey and Guernsey were remnants of the Duke of Normandy possessions – and neither were part of the UK – but they *were* on Andy's country-tracker spreadsheet.

Following my visit to these two Crown Colonies, I took a long weekender to Portugal. This was a rather ordinary trip for me, although I did enjoy basking in the port area of Lisbon. That was country number 89.

Now I was poised to break into the 90 tally number – which was bound to alarm Andy – and I reckoned that it could provoke him into action. So I had to plan a cavale which would propel me way out of his reach – my current advantage of 12 countries against Andy's 77 was not enough buffer.

I analysed Andy's country-tracker spreadsheet, and given my limited holiday-leave entitlement of about ten days, concluded that it had to be somewhere in Europe where travel times were short. At that point, there were only ten European countries I hadn't yet visited, so that presented two options.

Option one was to visit Northern Europe, including Iceland and Spitsbergen, but that would be horribly expensive and involve a large number of flights: according to my calculation, at least eight sectors.

The second option was to visit Eastern Europe and hit the ex-Soviet Union republics. Of those, I had so far only visited the ex-Soviet Socialist Republic of Ukraine.

Over the occasional bottle of wine, my younger brother revealed that he was interested to join me on a crazy cavale. We agreed on doing this in May 2017 and had several selection criteria. Firstly, it had to be a dirt-cheap trip, so that ruled out the Northern Europe option. Secondly, and most importantly, it had to be an utterly unappealing trip to our two wives – so crumbly Eastern European countries would fit the bill.

Finally, our mind was set on visiting some Soviet Union-era architecture, so on those three counts, it was a no-brainer to decide that my seventh cavale would be to ex-Soviet Union Republics. We would also take in a couple of Warsaw Pact countries, and the adventure would start with the dirt-cheapest flight to Eastern Europe we could find.

Our objective was to find as many Communist-era relics as possible: Lenin statues, red stars, hammer and sickles, Lada and Volga cars, trains, pre-fabricated socialist housing blocks, KGB offices, spying infrastructure, heroic statues, Soviet military hardware and internment camps.

We were agog. Our wives were aghast.

Slovakia (No. 90)

Our journey started with a £40 flight from Birmingham, England to Bratislava, the capital of Slovakia. The RyanAir flight was full to the gunwales with Slovakians, and as far as I could determine, just two Brits: me and my younger brother.

The flight touched down at 21:57 local time, and we rushed through the European Union channel. I collected my backpack from the luggage carousel, and we exited into the warm, yet fresh, Slovakian night at 23:21 – just four minutes before the last bus departed Bratislava airport. Across the terminal road, the driver of the No. 61 bus was sleeping with his feet up on the dashboard. I tapped his window, and he indicated towards the bus stop 200 metres down the road where a handful of passengers awaited.

I read the signs around the bus stop; we needed to buy tickets from one of the light-green ticket machines. A gent leaned over to me as I perplexed myself reading the instructions.

'The price is ninety euro cents to the city,' he informed me.

'Erm. I only have euro banknotes on me,' I puzzled, 'do you have any change?' I proffered him a five-euro banknote.

'Sorry, I don't. But anyway, nobody will check for tickets at this time of the night. Don't worry,' he assured me.

Presently, the bus pulled-up and was completely dark inside. We boarded, ignoring the tangerine-orange ticket validation machines mounted on the handrails, and sprawled over a section of four seats in the bendy-bus. I observed that no other passengers validated their tickets.

'See, Jeffrey,' I told my brother, 'you wanted to pay for a taxi, you bloody tourist. Now we are going to get a free ride to the city.'

The bus took off with its interior lights flickering on intermittently. After a few stops, a crowd of two-dozen young men, jeering and looking the worse for wear, boarded to football-match-style chanting. None of them validated their tickets, and they occupied the rear section behind the bendy bit. A wiry gent aged about 60 and wearing a cloth cap made a beeline for us and sat on the opposite section of seats.

'Where are you from?' Wiry-Gent asked.

'England,' I replied.

'Ah, yes, England. We are celebrating our win at a handball game,' he nodded in the direction of the noisy mob who were now singing and dancing in the bus aisle.

The mob passed around a bottle of vodka and they swigged from the bottle with one hand and swung on the handrails with the other as the bus lurched around corners. After 20 minutes, the rowdy bus stopped in a leafy side street, and the driver spoke to us in Slovakian while packing up his belongings.

'This must be the train station,' I supposed to Jeffrey.

The sign 'Bratislava Hlavná Stanica' shone above the building, and we agreed it was the station. It was almost midnight, but Wiry-Gent had said it was safe to walk around the city at night, so after much fiddling with my Google map, we set off.

We took a right-left then yomped up Štefánikova Street then, after a mile, turned right to where the

Downtown Backpackers Hostel was still lively with drinkers in the bar. We dumped our bags in the pitch-black dormitory then sipped two 50cls of Czech Pilsner Urquelle before crashing on the wafer-thin mattresses of our bunk beds at 2 a.m.

After showering in the hostel bathroom, which I always found a challenging art in balance and avoiding touching anything that appeared unsanitary, we took a Bratislava breakfast of fried egg, bread and coffee. We then yomped back to the train station, where I bought couchettes on the 23:01 overnight train to Krakow, Poland for us. It would arrive in Poland at 7 a.m. the next morning, so we would save a night in a hostel.

The haughty, middle-aged ticket lady in window number one was not to be impressed by my about the shocking price of 68 euros (£57) for each train ticket. On my cavale to Eastern Europe with Andy, we had paid less than £10 for overnighters, and I grumbled that the European Unionisation of Eastern Europe had destroyed the cheap life of budget travellers, but unsurprisingly, I gained no sympathy with my rant.

It wasn't strictly true that I had not been to Slovakia before. Sort of. I had visited Czechoslovakia in 1990 with Andy on our European cavale. However, we had only visited the western region, which became the Czech Republic after the split of the former federation in 1992. Under our improvised rulebook, we couldn't count breakaway states unless we had physically visited the region before its separation.

We had debated weeks over this rulebook, which we had no name for. The problem arose because of Ukraine. We had taken the train from Budapest to Moscow before the disintegration of the Soviet Union, and the route passed through the former Soviet Socialist

Republic of Ukraine. Andy wanted to count Ukraine in his tally.

'But we travelled through Ukraine,' reasoned Andy.

'But we stayed on the train the whole time. We never even placed our feet on Ukranian soil,' I countered, 'you never even *touched* the country.'

'We did visit Russia,' Andy continued his contrived logic, 'and so we should be able to count former republics such as Ukraine and Belarus.'

'Come on,' I countered again, 'you never even put your hiking boot on Belarus soil either. That's a stretch.'

Along with other rules related to transit flights and border skirmishes, our rulebook was formulated. So there we go – let's call it the Ukrainian Protocol.

Anyhow, back to Czechoslovakia. You could suppose it was reluctantly Communist. Excepting East Germany, it was the most westerly of the Warsaw Pact states and shared borders with Germany and Austria. This reluctance erupted in the Prague Spring of 1968. A new government attempted reform by declaring a new constitution which afforded civil rights and liberties, and furthermore, a road-map to democracy was planned.

That was all too much for the Soviet Union leader, Leonid Brezhnev, who in August 1968 sent in an army from neighbouring Warsaw Pact countries – Hungary, Poland, Bulgaria and the Soviet Union – to brutally crush the government. The crackdown lasted until Czechoslovakia had a second attempt to topple Communism, the Velvet Revolution, in 1989.

Armed with bottles of mineral water and 90 euro cents bus tickets, we took the No. 93 bendy-bus through the old town, along Staromestská Street and across the River Danube where we alighted for Stari Most, also known as the UFO Bridge.

Built in 1972 during communist rule, the UFO Bridge was, well, like a metal UFO plonked on the top of a suspension bridge. To be more precise, perched 95 metres high on a pair of angled steel pylons at the southern end of the Stari Most bridge across the Danube. The funky bridge had just a single tower, and the five suspension cables were anchored at the southern end of the bridge, tensioned over the pylons below the UFO and secured to the central reservation around the mid-section.

We took a pedestrian underpass through a park and to the riverbank. It was a beautiful day with a cerulean-blue sky and only a few clouds on the horizon to the east. The river was coffee-brown and wide at this point as it flowed downhill from Vienna to the west. The southern riverbank where we stood was a park with shading trees and grassy areas where a few locals walked their dogs.

After I had admired the view for a while, Jeffrey interrupted me.

'Come on. Stop wasting time. Let's go up to the UFO,' he prodded me.

'You lead the way, tour leader,' I answered.

We entered a tiny ticket office at the base of the UFO tower. A couple of giggling young ladies sold us tickets for 7.40 euros each (£6.20), and we took the lift up.

'How does this lift work?' I asked Jeffrey, 'the pylons holding up the UFO are at an angle – shouldn't the lift car be tilted over?'

'Dunno,' he answered, 'maybe the lift car is dangling from steel cables?'

Jeffrey spent the rest of the lift journey scratching his head and inspecting the lift car.

At the top, we entered the UFO Bar Restaurant.

'Hey, this is like the Starship Enterprise bridge,' gasped Jeffrey. So it was.

Jeffrey stepped over to the bar, 'this is where Captain Kirk sat in the series. Come on – get the beers in.'

We took a seat in the window area.

'This is where Spock and Uhura sat,' he continued. I was never a big Star Trek fan – I wasn't fully sure. The window overlooked the Danube facing towards the old town. Huge 350-metre-long river cruise barges were docked on the north bank of the river, and behind lay the churches and buildings of Bratislava: a mix of centuries-old churches, communist-era government blocks and late-nineteenth-century tenements.

'Are you getting the beers in?' asked Jeffrey.

'Looks like it,' I answered.

I bought two 30cl glasses of Staropramen lager from Captain Kirk at the bar.

'Cheers,' we announced at the same time, clinking our glasses of refreshing beer.

We continued our Star Trek-themed discussion while admiring the Danube, then after our beers were finished, walked up two flights of stairs to the UFO roof-deck. Was Spock allowed on the roof, I wondered?

The views up top were superlative. To the west, the Danube gently meandered through the heavily wooded south bank from Vienna only 100 kilometres away. I turned to the south and faced Austria, which was only 6 kilometres away to the southeast. Hungary was only18 kilometres away to the southwest – this was the crossroads of Central Europe.

I observed the south of Bratislava was heavily wooded and interrupted with 1950s communist-era apartment blocks – they were pre-fabricated in haste to house the burgeoning post-war population. The highway continued from the UFO Bridge towards the new town area of Petržalka, which painted from a distance appeared to be gaily painted. It didn't seem like the depressed rotten blocks which resulted in its seedy reputation as the "Bronx of Bratislava".

'Let's go there,' pleaded Jeffrey, 'we need to see the dark tourism apartment blocks. I read that a dog was seen running around with a human hand in its mouth.'

'It sounds like a typical council estate. If it will make you happy,' I agreed, 'we can take the bus along the highway. It's a straight run I think.'

After soaking up the sun for a while on the UFO Bridge roof terrace and spotting buildings we planned to visit, we took the path back to the bus stop and waited for the number 93 or 94 bus to Petržalka.

Presently, while Jeffrey was inspecting the bus timetables at the bus shelter, a number 93 bus arrived.

'Come on! Stop staring at the timetables – the number 93 is here!' I hollered at Jeffrey.

I took the third entrance just behind the bendy part of the bus and turned around when I was on board to look for Jeffrey. I couldn't see him. I peered around the rear of the bus to see if he was hiding somewhere. Then I looked at the bus stop again and noticed Jeffrey was still engrossed in the timetable. At the same instant, the doors closed. I hammered on the glass, but the bendy-bus speedily pulled away. 'Shit,' I muttered to myself.

I alighted at the next stop along the elevated highway then called Jeffrey's mobile phone. Fortunately, he answered.

'Ding-a-ling!' I said, 'The number 93 bus was here.'
'But,' retorted Jeffrey, 'I was...'
'Bloody hell. Take the next number 93 and enter the third door. Text me when you are on the bus.'

Thankfully the plan worked, and we sat on the

bendy-bus admiring the Soviet-inspired housing blocks along the road. At the terminus, we alighted and walked about the area but saw nothing but plain block after bland block. One block was still under renovation with the old facade ground away to shiny-white concrete. Aside from a few kids on skateboards, a scavenger rummaging through the rubbish skips and an abandoned supermarket trolley, there was little of consequence. Petržalka did not live up to its rough reputation, and certainly, I did not encounter any feral dogs trotting around with severed body parts in their mouths.

We took a bendy-bus back north, passed under the UFO, over the Danube again and alighted at the old town.

'You lead the way, Jeffrey,' I asked him.

He studied the map, 'This way. Come on, slowcoach.'

We walked down some steps to a subway under the highway, which was splattered in graffiti, and along narrow stone touristy alleys. Jeffrey bought a red-white-and-blue baseball cap with 'Slovakia' on the peak, then we visited the impressive Gothic Cathedral of St. Martin where the Hungarian Kings were crowned in the sixteenth to nineteenth centuries. We then continued along Panska Ulica, passed the British Embassy and arrived at the blush-pink Primate's Palace.

'What on earth is the Primate's Palace?' I quizzed Jeffrey, 'is this the royal residence of the Planet of The Apes?'

Jeffrey just frowned at me, 'Hurry up! You're slowing us down.'

I traipsed up a red-carpeted sweeping staircase following him, paid the 3 euros entrance fee each then entered the Hall of Mirrors. I didn't find the hall impressive: it was just 10-metres cubed with unimpressive white-framed mirrors on the walls and two banks of red plastic chairs. It looked more like a furniture store than the Palais de Versailles.

'That was a waste of 6 euros,' I groaned, 'your tour is rubbish.'

'What about the dark tourism sights?' wondered Jeffrey, 'there's some decent ones to the east.'

We agreed that he would navigate, and I followed Jeffrey until we reached a park where the six-metre-high Fountain of Union stood forlornly in the middle of a huge drained and vandalised fountain pool. The Communist-era stainless-steel carbuncle was described as a linden flower – whatever one of those was – but look more like a split mushroom. The fountain tiles were hanging off and spray painted with black graffiti. The fountain was surrounded by colourful iron park benches which were sprayed with graffiti on every inch.

'Don't worry,' I informed Jeffrey, 'the European Union will give a few million euros to fix this up.'

How depressing some areas must have been, yet now, the people smiled, drank, ate and ambled around his handsome city with a spring in their step.

One final sight: Jeffrey was to navigate us to the Military Cemetery of the Soviet Soldiers, the resting place of over 6,800 troops who died liberating Slovakia from the Nazi's in the closing stages of the Second World War.

We crossed Freedom Square and staggered up the hill of Slavin, past the Chinese and Iraqi consulates and up some steep concrete flights of stairs. We were greeted by a well-tendered mausoleum topped with a 40-metre-high obelisk. Atop the obelisk was a Soviet soldier standing on a crushed swastika under his boot. Wreathe adorned the steps, and I randomly checked them to find they were from both Russia and Germany.

I sat down for a rest on one of the granite benches. I was rather disappointed that the place was not in grotty communist decay; crumbling and smothered in graffitied like the fountain. On the other hand, it was pleasing to see that the city of Bratislava, or the Russians – or someone – had taken the trouble to respect the memorial grounds.

Weary after a half-hour walk down the hill, we ordered a bowl of borscht soup and a plate of steak and chips each at the Antic Restaurant in the train station. It was a fairly reasonable 11 euros (£9) each including a 500ml of Staropramen beer. Then we ordered some more 50cls of Staropramen in the station sports bar to while away the time for our train to Poland. The clumsy fool of a waiter knocked my pint over – right over the table – and soaked my laptop. Fortunately, I was able to rapidly power it off then shake it dry.

At 17:40, we yomped to platform one, and on cue, the 18:01 sleeper to Krakow arrived, which was pulled by a Czech Railways Škoda 71E Edyta electric locomotive in blue livery.

'Yeah. This is like it,' Jeffrey said in excitement, 'it's like one of those trains on the Top Trump card games from years ago.'

'It's fantastic, isn't it?' I agreed.

We quickly located the blue-over-white carriage No. 357 with an orange go-faster stripe, and Jeffrey was excited to be the first one aboard. We took couchettes 12 and 14 in a three-berth cabin, and after spreading about our belongings, smelly socks and boots, the excitement died down and we fell asleep.

And so endeth country number 90 – my Eastern European cavale was well underway. And I was now in the 90s. And I was on a lift-off countdown to my target of 100 countries.

9: Commonwealth of Commies

Belarus (No. 91)

Krakow in Poland was the next stop on our cavale, but alas, it wasn't a new tick for me. We visited Auschwitz Concentration Camp then took the train to Lvov in Ukraine. Or was it Lviv? Ukraine was not a new tick for me either, but hey, it was my first visit to the city of Lvov. It was an enthralling visit to a post-communist economy of a Soviet Republic. We took a walk about the Lvov Train Station area and eagerly spotted Volga cars, Lada cars and rusty bucket-loads of urban decay. We oddly saw a street sweeper wearing a red Royal Mail postman's jacket and a station cleaner wearing a purple Sainsbury's shelf-stacker's shell suit jacket.

Our next stage of the journey was an overnight train to Minsk, the capital of Belarus, which I had pre-booked at great cost and trouble through a travel agency in London.

After a final pee for 3 Ukranian hvania (£0.10) in Lvov Train Station, we plodded to platform four where stern-looking carriage attendants were waiting at each blue carriage. They were Soviet-era carriages with corrugated sides, caravan-style windows and steep iron steps up to the shoulder-height floor. After a rather long conversation in Russian and English with an attendant, where neither party understood anything the other said,

I presented my ticket, and then we were pointed to wagon number two where we located our bunks 9 and 11.

The cabins were typical Eastern European designs: *kupe*-class four-berth affairs with seat-beds, pine-effect melamine-clad walls, faux-Persian rugs and lace curtains hanging from a café rod across the caravan windows to offer a bizarre sense of faux-opulence. After settling in, I ran to the locomotive to see what would be hauling us.

It was a classic Soviet-era monster: a VL80S unit, which was two carriages in length and built in the Novocherkassk Electric Locomotive Plant in the USSR in 1978. It was a knackered, rusty, dirty brute. And I adored it.

I ran back to our wagon with just three minutes to go, and the stout, blonde attendant had already climbed up the four-foot-high steps and waved her finger at me.

'*Nyet, nyet,*' the carriage attendant blocked my way.

'What? That's my carriage – number two!' I protested.

The skinny blonde attendant then popped her head around the corner and intervened. After a heated discussion in Russian, the stout attendant shuffled to one side to let me board. Phew.

'The locomotive is a 1970s monster from the Soviet Union,' I excitedly told Jeffrey.

'Cool,' he replied, 'I bet it was on the locomotive Top Trumps card set we used to play in the 70s.'

At exactly 18:38, the train slowly glided away. Jeffrey had finished preparing a dinner spread of white crusty loaf, salami, cheese spread and cheese slices using a pair of round-ended medical scissors and Swiss army knife. We heartily dined on our open sandwiches washed down by a bottle of Russian Baltika No.7

Export Lager.

We were in good company: the Belarussians were ranked by the World Health Organisation in 2014 to be the booziest country in the world with an average of 17.6 litres of pure alcohol consumed per year. That was more than the Norwegians and Icelanders combined, who I considered to be worthy piss-artists.

After eating my medically-dissected sandwiches, I headed to the bathroom to clean my hands, and Clarissa the attendant directed me to the stainless-steel sink inside. With gritted teeth, I looked around the utilitarian bathroom. The toilet was a decades-old pressed stainless steel affair with dimpled footrests embossed into the rim for those ex-Soviet citizens who preferred to squat.

I washed my hands and dried them with paper towels, but there was no bin. Clarissa was furtively watching over my shoulder like a fussy aunt and nodded where to throw it – in the toilet. I lobbed the towel in and pressed the toilet foot pedal, upon which the metal flap in the bowl popped open revealing the passing railway track below. The railway line to Minsk must have been scattered with turds and paper towels.

Back at the cabin, I watched the fields roll by in the late spring sun. The Herculean beast of a locomotive steamed along with a great trundling noise like an enormous steam roller.

'Are you looking forward to Belarus?' I asked Jeffrey.

'Yeah, cool. I hope it's like Ukraine. I love *commie* countries,' he eagerly answered as he watched out the window. By 10 pm I was falling asleep, so I made up my bed and fell into a deep sleep.

I awoke with a start in the night and checked the

time on my smartphone – it was only 1:30 a.m. I had one of those unnerving moments where you awake and have the feeling that someone has disturbed the room, so I focused my eyes in the dim light and noticed that the cabin door had been left open. Suddenly, an Ukrainian border guard, dressed uncannily like an Action Man toy figure complete with a chin scar and blonde crew-cut hair, filled the doorway. We were at the Goryn border crossing. Action-Man asked for our passports, and after rummaging through my pages, he *whumped* me out.

A 20-minute rumble later, the train screeched to a halt at the Belarus border. A parade of assorted officers visited our humble laminated cabin. First the immigration officer, who looked like a cross between a Spanish bullfighter and a North Korean general. He sported a pine-green military-looking hat boasting an impressive broad brim and a steeply-raked peak. He was puffed with importance.

Bullfighter asked for my passport in Russian, so I handed it over with a humble grin. He spent a solid ten minutes scrutinising my passport: the shimmer of the bio-page, checking every entry and exit stamp one by one and reading the emergency contact details with great intent.

'Minsk? Holiday? No fly [to] Minsk?' Bullfighter interrogated.

'Yes, Yes, No,' I replied.

Along came another officer, who was skinnier and less meticulous in presentation. Skinny bullfighter took Jeffrey's passport and asked precisely the same questions. We endured this double act as they continued to scrutinise our passports and ask more questions, until finally, they became satisfied and nodded agreeably to each other. Then they left one by one leaving a shorter officer to scan the passports and stamp us. He had a car-battery-sized computer terminal encased in black leather which hung from a strap across his chest. He appeared immensely proud of his enormous 1980s terminal.

The parade continued with several customs officers dressed in SWAT-style uniforms who invaded our cabin. One intimately searched under the bed storage spaces and mattresses while even a sniffer dog joined the prison-style shakedown. After what seemed like an eternity, the fuss died down and we were on our way; Belarus, here I come – country 91. Now I was in the nineties and ticking along nicely towards the century.

Before I had time to sleep again, the train stopped at the first station in Belarus, and a few-dozen passengers boarded. A man who looked about 40 years old and his teenage daughter opened our cabin door. Crap – I thought we were going to have the cabin to ourselves. I had to fetch down all my baggage from the upper bunks. I'd also swiped two mattresses and an extra pillow from the spare bunks, so I had to re-make my bed and handover my ill-gotten booty. I waited out in the corridor for them to settle down in the upper berths then got my head down again.

Arising at 7:30 a.m., I undertook my morning ablutions before the crowds awoke, changed my underwear and made the best of a challenging environment for keeping clean. Back at the cabin, I stripped down the bedding and rolled-up the mattress to make space for me and our fellow passengers.

'Fancy a coffee, Jeffrey?' I asked.

'Yeah. Do you have some Ukrainian hryvnia left?' he asked.

'No. I'm going to steal the coffee from Clarissa.' I quipped.

I bought two coffees using euros and watched the view from the train window until, precisely on time at 9:20 a.m., the train glided into the modern Minsk-Passajirskii Train Station.

I prepared my backpack and stepped into the corridor.

'Where have they all gone? That was quick,' I said to Jeffrey with surprise, 'there's nobody left.'

I changed some money at a *bureau de change* in the concourse then bought our train tickets to Vilnius for 18th March. I hadn't figured out the route to our accommodation, the East Time Hotel.

'You mean you didn't prepare a route to get to the hotel?' wailed Jeffrey, 'let's get a taxi.'

'No way,' I countered, 'we can figure this out. Look, there's a city map near the ticket counters. I know it's less than a half-hour walk from here.'

We spend a solid 20 minutes studying the city map, which was in Cyrillic, making it awkward to understand the street names. Furthermore, I had paid for the dirt-cheapest hotel, which inevitably meant that it was tucked away in the bowels of the industrial area.

'I think I've located it,' I prodded the map telling Jeffrey.

I took around ten photos of the map with my smartphone, then after a McDonald's breakfast, we headed east down a highway towards a power station. It was roasting hot, and I was having second thoughts about yomping across the city.

Eventually, I found a street sign which seemed to approximate Velosipedny Lane in Cyrillic. We fruitlessly searched the street, which was lined with warehouses and government offices. At the junction of a main road, Jeffrey spied a modern ten-storey building.

'Hey! This is a hotel – come on!' he shouted.

I wasn't convinced, but we were desperately hot and weary. Inside, Jeffrey approached the reception.

'Is this the East Time Hotel?' he asked. After raising his voice and repeatedly demanding to know which hotel we were at, a lady was called down from the upper floors. It seemed she spoke excellent English.

'Can I help you?' she asked. Jeffrey explained we wanted to check in.

'This is not a hotel,' she replied, 'this is an office.'

I would have found this amusing if I wasn't fatigued and sweaty from marching about the industrial zone.

'There is a hotel about a ten-minute walk on the left,' she pointed down the road.

We yomped along a dual carriageway and past industrial units selling cement mixers and compressors. Jeffrey spied a hotel in the distance, and sure enough, after cutting through some wasteland and the back of a car park, we arrived at the brand spanking new East Time Hotel.

We checked in, then the *receptionista* ordered us a taxi which took us to the city centre. We planned to find the tourist information centre, get a city map then go hunting for Soviet memorabilia. We headed down a side street when an older gent, smartly dressed in a dark-grey suit, apprehended us.

'How are you, my friends? What is your name?' he asked. I gave him the fictitious name of Donald.

'My name is Gerald,' he continued in a well-mannered voice, 'I used to work for the tourist authority providing guided tours. But they changed the staff at the agency and now they won't talk to me.'

I could tell this was a scam.

I whispered in Jeffreys ear, 'He's going to scam us for money as a guide. Let's go,' I warned him.

'But he's a nice guy,' whispered back Jeffrey, 'he could help us'.

'Were you born yesterday? I'm not going to pay him – he's a scammer. I'm going.'

I left Jeffrey to trail behind me with Gerald in tow, pestering him with stories. I stopped at a main road to check my directions, and Jeffrey and Gerald reached me at the kerb. Gerald thrust his hand in his blazer side pocket.

'Look,' he presented his outstretched hand to Jeffrey, 'it is my quarter from America. I have a coin collection, you know?' he claimed. Jeffrey faked a coo. I just knew what would come next.

'Do you have any coins for my collection,' pleaded Gerald, 'maybe some coins from England?'

'Told you,' I whispered in Jeffrey's ear and turned my back on Gerald's cupped hand.

I found the tourist information centre, and Gerald loitered outside – too afraid to enter. The young lady in the agency gave us a tourist map and suggested a visit to the Stalin Line. She told me how we could take a bus from the train station to get there, then we thanked her and escaped from the side exit to avoid being ensnared with Gerald again.

The centre of Minsk was based around an artificial lake surrounded by a brick-tiled promenade and manicured lawns. Grand government buildings were dotted around the lake – some older, some very modern. The day was beautiful with a light-blue sky and streaky wisps of cloud – it all seemed too lovely for a Soviet republic.

We visiting a cluster of central-government buildings and the brilliant-white St. Joseph's Roman Catholic Church to the east of the lake before crossing the Svislach River to a huddle of restaurants. We chose

ALONG THE WAY

Above: Sniper Alley, Sarajevo, Bosnia-Herzegovina.

Below: Sleeper train from Podgorica, Montenegro to Belgrade, Serbia.

Above: Monument to the Soviet Army, Sofia, Bulgaria.

Below: Pripyat, Ukraine.

Above: Changing wheels, border of Moldova and Romania.

Below: Palace of Parliament, Bucharest, Romania.

Above: Stalin Line, Minsk, Belarus.

Below: Qender Zjarri Bunker, Tirana, Albania.

Above: Skopje, Macedonia

Below: Gullfoss Waterfall, Iceland.

Above: Longyearbyen, Svalbard.

Below: Midvagur, Faroe Islands.

the Kavjarnja Bar Restaurant, where we took a table in the sun at the front terrace.

Ordering a local beer and dinner of black sausage and potato dinner each, we soaked up some sunshine before continuing. We proceeding along Starovilenskay Street, past Trinity district and around the perimeter of the lake. We visited the first of a long list of patriotic monuments, the Memorial to the Sons of the Motherland who Died Abroad, which stood on the tiny Island of Tears. It was dedicated to fallen soldiers of the Afghanistan war and was a small chapel inscribed with the names of the hundreds of Belarussian soldiers who had died in the conflict. The chapel was underwhelming and undeserving of its grandiose name.

Belarus was unmistakeably a Soviet-style country and reminded me of the Soviet Union when I visited Moscow in 1989. I had been confused about the exact name of this state for many years. It was known as Belorussia in my old Purnell's Atlas of the World, sometimes as White Russia, Byelarus or Byelorussia. That made me associate it with Russia in my mind.

And Belarus was still heavily intertwined with Russia even after independence in 1991. It was massively dependent on Russia for energy and half of its exports went to its giant neighbour. It continued the legacy of Communist Party control and the widespread use of symbolism such as the hammer and sickle, red stars and statues of Lenin. They adored the pointy-bearded leader of the proletariat.

The east lakeside was bordered by a huge complex of expensive-looking apartments – this was a clean and modern city able to compete with any Western European capital. Remaining part of the Russian Empire seemed to have served Belarus well, and their fortunes seemed better than Ukraine, which had tried to cast their lot with the West.

We walked through the handsome park, visited a DC-3 parked in a fenced-off area then headed towards the liberation monument. Officially known as the Minsk Hero City Memorial, the obelisk celebrated the liberation of the city from the Nazi's by the Russian army following a three-year siege. A long flight of grey stone stairs led up to the memorial, which was composed of ten triangular slabs fanned open, and at the centre, a 45-metre obelisk was topped by a gold star. We walked up past pots of patriotic red flags, and to the right of the obelisk stood a statue of a woman in a closed-neck dress holding up three musical horns.

That was enough patriotism for the moment, so we took a bendy bus down Pieramozcau Avenue back to the centre. We alighted at the major intersection and headed northeast up Niezalieznasci Avenue.

'I'm so knackered. Can we stop for a beer?' suggested Jeffrey.

I was hot and exhausted so rapidly agreed, 'Sure.'

We drank a 50cl of beer each in the terrace of the Il Patio café bar then continued up Niezalieznasci. We passed the Palace of the Republic on the left and reached the expanse of Kastrycnickaja Square, which was fronted by the Roman-temple-like Trade Union Cultural Centre.

After another 15 minutes walk, we passed Central Park, crossed the river again then reached the impressive Victory Monument standing in the centre of a roundabout in Pieramohi Place. It was a grey stone obelisk, which was twice as high as the surrounding five-storey buildings and topped by an ornate gold star. The base was emblazoned with a USSR hammer-and-sickle wreath, and below it, was a bas-relief of the usual patriotic soldiers holding a flag and hugging the peasants. Interestingly, the flag had a bust of Lenin on it – not easy to find following the break-up of the Soviet Union.

The motorists were whizzing around the roundabout at great speed so there was no way to make a dash to the monument. I looked around the place.

'Maybe there's an underpass, Jeffrey?' as I scanned about the area then noticed a flight of stairs behind a low wall, 'here!'

We descended the underpass and walked down a corridor into a squash-court-sized underground chamber. In the centre was a circular dome with an eternal flame burning merrily. Was it underground to avoid the harsh Minsk winter weather? To the rear was a fantastic Soviet-style poster: a red, yellow and orange mural of Belarus soldiers proudly waving a handgun and a huge red star with a hammer and sickle in the centre.

Outside on the roundabout, two soldiers stood guard and marched back and forth. I was hesitant to poke fun of them lest I spend a few months in a Belarus jail. That was enough sightseeing for the day, and we were famished, so we walked back to Central Park and passed a couple of hours in the terrace of a rather upmarket restaurant drinking beer and eating dinner before taking a taxi back to the East Time Hotel for the night.

Our plan for the next day was to visit the Stalin Line, which was a Soviet-era military hardware exhibition at the line fortifications commandeered by Josef Stalin during the Second World War.

We cleaned up and headed down for breakfast, which turned out to be the most ghastly food I had ever tasted. The hot breakfast items included cut slabs of omelette and boiled-pork sausages. The sausages were similar to those which had revolted me in Podgorica: the meat was a gooey *slutch*. They were like podgy human fingers with the bones removed, and I almost gagged on them.

'I wonder if there is any problem with radioactivity?' I supposed to Jeffrey.

'Why?' he asked.

'Most of the radioactive fallout from Chernobyl headed north to Belarus,' I informed him, 'it is probably still in the food chain. Those human fingers could be radioactive as well as disgusting.'

The nuclear disaster had made a real old mess of Belarus. An estimated 70 per cent of the radioactive fallout landed in Belarus and affected over 2 million citizens – nearly a quarter of the population. Not much was known of the clean-up operation due to the secretive nature of the Communist state, which remained intertwined with Russia.

I reluctantly ate a half-bowl of porridge, then we checked out and ordered a taxi to Minsk train station. Jeffrey made a beeline for the front seat then began interrogating the unfortunate driver.

'Do you know Manchester United?' Jeffrey asked.

'Yes,' came the reply in a heavy Russian accent.

'David Beckham?'

'*Da, da*. Beckham,' came the excited reply.

'The Queen. Do you know the Queen?' A blank look from the driver. Jeffrey looked at me.

'See, David Beckham is more popular than the Queen,' declared Jeffrey.

I thought of explaining that maybe the driver didn't know the English word for Queen – but then decided it was a waste of time.

We arrived at the train station by a circuitous route,

deposited our backpacks in the luggage storage then went in hunt of the bus to Molodechno, which would take us to the Stalin Line. We walked under the platforms then took the rear exit to the bus station. Thanks to the helpfulness of a road sweeper, we were eventually directed to a waiting yellow minibus marked 'Минск-Молодечно' in black Cyrillic lettering.

I paid my three roubles, then at 10 a.m. precisely, the minibus drove away, zoomed past the city centre office buildings then through Soviet-era prefabricated apartments in the suburbs. After fifteen minutes, we were driving along a modern countryside road through fields and patches of evergreen forest.

After some while, the minibus stopped and a young man carrying a length of finished wood and some carriers bags sat opposite me. He looked a bit like Steve McQueen: lithe and with short blonde hair and stubble. I nodded niceties in dreadful Russian, then after a while, I decided to enlist his help about where we needed to alight. I showed McQueenski the leaflet advertising the Stalin Line, and his face beamed.

'Me, me!' he pointed at his chest and made a sound like a rumbling engine. Perhaps he was a tank driver, I thought.

'T-34 tank?' I asked.

'*Da, da,*' he replied. Which seemed all rather coincidental. I Googled a photo of a T-34 tank using the minibus' Wi-Fi and showed him. His eyes lit up.

'*Da! Da! Da!*'

After 45 minutes journey, we reached the crest of a hill, and there were fantastic views of a flat valley of fields and evergreen woods. McQueen-Tank-Commander pointed to the military exhibition.

'*Linea Stalina*,' he excitedly announced.

We walked to the gate and paid our ten roubles

(£4) entrance fee each. The tariff also advertised the extra services, which included bullets, anti-tank rifle ammunition and a tank drive.

'Give me one anti-tank bullet and five regular bullets, please,' I asked.

'*Nyet. Nyet*,' the cashier waved her hand in a negative motion then pointed inside the gates with a stabbing motion, 'pay bullet.'

We made a beeline for the firing range, which was a covered market stall-type structure housing various weapons. Along the table on the left were a half-dozen Second World War automatic rifles, and on stands, a DshK heavy machine gun and a PTRS-4 anti-tank rifle. A throng of Chinese military officers were milling about and laughing heartily – some in army uniforms and others in air-force uniforms. They had just finished their shooting and were escorted by a Belarus officer.

A tall and elderly general-type wearing a pale-green uniform and a hat like General de Gaulle stood proudly observing the proceedings, and a short tubby lieutenant-type greeted us. Then Lieutenant-Type made a gun-firing noise and pointed his finger at the firing range target.

'Bullet?' he asked.

'*Da, da*,' I replied excitedly, 'anti-tank rifle.'

I paid 10 roubles (£4) to Lieutenant-Type who deposited it in the top slot of a cash box, then he pulled a 12cm slug from a metal locker and loaded it into the PTRS-4 magazine. He then flicked the safety lock up and handed me a pair of red ear defenders.

The rifle had wooden handles about a foot apart, which looked like the handle-ends of two spades. Between them was a small metal firing trigger. Lieutenant-Type motioned me to push the metal trigger upwards to release the cock and push the spade handles towards each other to fire the weapon.

'Fire!' Lieutenant-Type shouted. I squeezed the handles together and got the fright of my life.

'SHIT !' I shrieked. Even with the ear defenders on, it was deafening and eardrum perforating.

I also fired five rounds of an automatic rifle, which cost me 20 roubles (£8), and Jeffrey took a turn much to the hearty laughter of General de Gaulle.

I then walked up the single-lane road to a parking area, which housed the collection of armoured personnel carriers and tanks. They were predominantly Second World War-era and included a T80B Tank which had served in the First Chechen War and was very impressive at close quarters.

Around 300 metres walk to the rear of the exhibition was an impressive collection of intelligence vehicles and rockets. There was a P-15 "Tropa" radar truck from the 1950's with a pair of enormous parabolic dishes made of mesh stacked two high.

A BM-21 Grad rocket launcher looked menacing with dozens of rocket tubes atop a lorry, which was able to fire chemical-loaded rockets 20 kilometres into enemy territory. Another cool item on display was an S-75M Volkhov surface-to-air missile, which was over 10 metres in length and could fly at 82,000 feet.

The two finest exhibits were the last. A SCUD missile carrier with 10 enormous wheels, as proudly displayed during Victory Day parades in Moscow's Red Square, which could fire missiles a hefty 280 kilometres but with all the accuracy of a drunk in a game of darts. The other was some sort of intercontinental ballistic missile which stood vertically at an impressive 20 metres high with a grey-painted body and a red nose-cone.

I wondered whether they were sanctioned for

exhibition by the Russian military – they looked impressive and sensitive. There again, Belarus was in the Russian Commonwealth and the military was probably under common command.

The aircraft display included a MiG-25RB, which was the first mass-produced fighter jet to reach 3,000 kilometres per hour, and some ugly-looking, bulbous helicopters. I was highly disappointed I did not find any Sikorsky helicopters – particularly the enormous twin-rotor ones.

After overdosing on all the military exhibits, we walked to the Stalin Line trail. I entered an extremely cramped bunker. Five-foot-high doors separated the chambers, which were mostly around four square metres each, and I tried to imagine how life must be inside them. The intelligence room had three periscopes in a chamber the size of a small wardrobe, so there must have been three Soviet soldiers tangled together during a watch.

The Stalin Line was originally built in the post-revolution period to protect Russia from the West, and during the 1930s military build-up in Europe, the line had been extended. Long vertical arcs of defence lines, layered like a tortoiseshell, were constructed to protect key city areas from Leningrad to the north, Minsk and Moscow from invasion by the Nazis. After Hitler opened up the Eastern Front, the defence line proved barely challenging for the Wermacht and was overrun within weeks.

The Stalin Line had been abandoned by the Russians after the war and largely forgot, so it was largely intact. The trail led up to a hill past a double-row of anti-tank defences, and the views over the valley to the forests in the distance was magnificent.

After clowning around on a fixed artillery gun

perched on the hill, we headed to the log-cabin café to find lunch. I ordered a borscht soup, a frugal plate of chicken and boiled potatoes and a 50cl of anonymous draft lager. Jeffrey followed suit.

'We had better get going,' suggested Jeffrey, 'the road is in the middle of nowhere.

I agreed. I was worried about missing the night train to Lithuania. We walked along the dusty path along the road – with cars and lorries whizzing past at motorway speeds – until we came to a bus shelter. It was roasting hot, so I was glad of some shelter. We munched on double Mars bars and drank bottled water until, after a worrisome long period, we were rescued by a minibus heading to Minsk.

We loitered around Stantsiya Minsk-Passazhirskiy train station for a couple of hours, ate some lumpy food from the stalls and eventually realised that our train was waiting on a platform a good walk away from the main station. It was a shiny new Lithuanian Railways train: a silver-grey two-carriage unit made in Poland that looked more like an urban commuter train. I was quite shocked – I had been used to the Communist-era beasts we had taken so far on this cavale.

And so ended our cool visit to one of the last remaining communist strongholds of Europe, and we were on our way to another ex-Soviet Socialist Republic, Lithuania – which had taken a completely different direction.

10: Baltic Balls-Up

Jeffrey and I had exited Belarus and were now on our way to the Baltic states. They would be three easy-peasy ticks for me – they were small states and had half-decent transport. The Baltic states would propel me towards the magic 100 countries in just a few days. And Andy had no idea. I presumed.

Lithuania (No. 92)

The Lithuanian Railways-cum-Polish train was without question the most uncomfortable train ride I had ever endured. I cursed the Polish manufacturer with all my might as my legs were crushed against the partition wall in front of me. The seat was also thin – like a rubber shoe sole – and my bottom became numb. Fortunately, the journey passed relatively quickly in just two-and-a-half hours: Lithuania was a compact country at just triple the size of Wales. We arrived at the capital, Vilnius, at 11 p.m., and the diminutive train station was dim but not completely deserted.

'Taxi?' a tout called.

'No,' I replied tersely, 'no taxi.'

'Is Lithuania using the euro?' I asked Jeffrey. My guidebook was a few years old and indicated that the country was using litai.

'I think it's euros. Why does it matter?' he replied.

'You wanted to get a taxi to the hostel, didn't you? How are we going to pay for it?' I replied. Jeffrey grunted.

I studied a forex rate board hanging outside a closed bureau de change. There was no exchange rate for euros, so I assumed they must be using euros. We tramped outside into the pleasant night air, and a beaten Volkswagen estate taxi was parked right in front of the station exit. A slightly-built middle-aged driver with mousey hair and metal-rimmed glasses approached us.

'Taxi?' he asked in pretty good English.

'Sure. Do you know the Downtown Forest Hostel and Camping?' I enquired.

'Yes, I know that place. Ten euros,' he confirmed.

Jeffrey and I debated a while over the £8.40 cost, but this was the only taxi. And walking around the city at midnight wasn't a great option, so we dumped our backpacks in the estate hatch and were on our way. I surveyed the narrow and dimly lit streets as the driver proceeded to tell us his life story.

'I lived in England before, you know? I have a daughter living in London,' he started with.

'Nice,' I answered, 'why did you return to Lithuania?'

'I have no idea. This government is completely useless. There are no jobs and everything is so expensive,' the driver carped.

'Did the prices increase when Lithuania converted to the euro?' I asked.

'Yes. Everything is so expensive now. Our salaries are lower than ever, and the cost of everything has gone up,' he droned on, 'This government is so useless.

Joining the European Union seemed to have had varied success for the Lithuanians. It was destructive for the country's population, which was three times smaller than the city of London. Thousands had emigrated, and the country was shrinking by about the population of Swindon every five years.

'Hey, I will take you past the city centre – you can see it's beautiful,' Droning-Driver continued.

He drove past the city hall and took a left at the main square where the buildings were bathed in floodlights and diners were eating at tables in the street. We circled the town then headed up Paupio Street, which was a quiet suburb lined with parked cars. Droning-Driver turned right in front of a pair of iron gates and across a gravel driveway in front of the hostel building.

'Do you want a private tour?' suggested Droning-Driver, 'If you like, I can take you on a tour of the city. Or how about a gentleman's club?'

'We'll think about it,' I replied, 'maybe you give me your card.'

After I took his card and paid him ten euros, the driver left, and we scrunched along the drive to the rear of the hostel. It appeared to be a grand old house with several floors, and inside was a front desk and bar. A few tables were dotted about where some travellers nursed bottles of beer and played with their laptops.

We checked in, dumped our backpacks in the small bedroom and bought a couple of Svytury's Ekstra bottle beers to celebrate a new country.

'Country number 92 for me,' I told Jeffrey as we clinked our beer glasses. Warning bells should have been ringing for Andy.

The next morning, I rose early and showered; I had slept well in my single bed. Our mission for the day was to buy onward bus tickets to Riga, Latvia and tour the city of Vilnius. After Jeffrey was ready, we checked out and took a city map to plot our walkabout. Jeffrey was the tour guide for the day and recommended we take breakfast in Užupis – an artsy district which had cheekily declared itself an independent republic.

We yomped along the narrow cobbled streets, past decayed residences and several churches. Many of the houses in the suburbs were pretty jaded from the days of Communist rule but not collapsing. We entered a small business compound bordering the clear, babbling Vilnia River, which meandered through the city. The riverbanks had several graphic statues including a graphic female torso and a six-foot-high marble penis. Around the corner, we reached the Užupis constitution, which was etched into stainless panels bolted to a wall. I read some of the constitution clauses.

'12. A dog has the right to be a dog.'

'13. A cat is not obliged to love its owner but must help in time of need.'

The Lithuanians were a quirky lot. The International Institute for Advanced Studies compared the weirdness of 250 different nations and created the 'Bizarre Index'. The irksome French were rated 15.5. The Lithuanians were off the scale – rated at 135.2 – which was the highest reading globally. Unusual quirks included giving odd-numbered bunches of flower as gifts and reserving even-numbered ones for funerals.

The Lithuanian language was also an olde-worlde oddball – more related to ancient languages such as Sanskrit and Ancient Greek. Their diet was equally quirky with dishes including sour-cream potato with cannabis seeds, potato pudding with pig's ears and black sausage made from wheat and barley boiled in blood and stuffed into pig intestines.

After a pig's-ear-less breakfast of omelettes in an outdoor café with the slowest service in Eastern

Europe, we continued walking in the hot morning sun until we reached the Ecolines sales office in front of the bus station. I entered the tiny air-conditioned office, which was deliciously chilled, and bought a couple of one-way tickets to Riga for 2:45 p.m. We deposited our backpacks in the luggage storage so we could visit the city.

'Where to now, tour leader?' I asked Jeffrey. He was getting right into the role of chief navigator.

'Let's see the Frank Zappa statue. He was banned in the days of the USSR,' he confidently proposed.

'So what? Just about every western singer and band was banned in the days of the Soviets,' I responded.

I couldn't convince him otherwise, but anyway, it was on the way to the parliament building, so we marched off in the heat. And marched we did – for what seemed to be about an hour – until we reached the compact Reformatų Park.

'So, where is your statue, huh?' I taunted Jeffrey. He stared at his city map intently and pretended he knew where he as going – but it was nowhere in sight.

'What kind of a crappy tour is this?' I teased him. After another long march for 30 minutes, stopping for a cool beer along the way, we reached the parliament building. It looked like a 1970's town library with vaulted sides and central gates. It was here in 1991 that the Soviet military tried to suppress an uprising by the Lithuanians, and a barricade of concrete blocks had been erected.

'So, where's the barricades?' I quizzed Jeffrey.

'Here,' he answered after a pause.

In front of the parliament stood a grey granite bollard, which was square-shaped with a pyramid top. A plaque identified it's role in the independence movement. After two hours of gruelling marching in the heat, all we had to show for it was a town library and a two-foot-high bollard.

'This is rubbish tour. Where now?' I asked Jeffrey.

'Cathedral Square. Let's take a taxi,' he commanded. Okay, I played along.

We quickly hailed one, which was driven by a butch woman who slumped in the seat at an unusual angle. She nursed the gear stick in a bit of a sexual manner, which was alarming. Jeffrey asked her how much to get to the main square.

'Twelve euros with meter. Ten euros no meter,' Butch-Lady-Driver replied in a gruff voice.

Right. So if she didn't turn on the meter then it would be cheaper: cash in hand.

'Bloody rip off,' grumbled Jeffrey. Butch-Lady-Driver accepted our offer of ten euros, turned off the meter and roared off down the bus lane chancing a police ticket. After a couple of hairy turns, our hairy Butch-Lady-Driver abruptly came to a halt in the bus lane facing the cathedral. I thanked her, and we crossed to the large square fronting the cathedral, which had a sort of tower to the right. The tower was the Belfry of Vilnius Cathedral.

'Why does the belfry have no cathedral attached to it, Mister Tourguide?' I asked Jeffrey.

'Well, I dunno,' he replied with a blank look.

It was at this very square in 1991 where the people of the Baltic states held a peaceful protest against the Soviet occupation. They created a chain of an estimated two million people from Tallinn in the north, across the three Soviet Socialist Republics, to Vilnius in the south. The southern endpoint was at the Stebuklas Tile – a stone tile which reputedly performed miracles. I wandered about searching for the tile, but miraculously, could not find it.

After several sweeps, I located the chessboard-sized granite tile. It was a bit of a blow to find a rather simple tile, which was easily overlooked. And it was a new tile.

'This tile is new,' I whined, 'it can't have been performing miracles for very long.'

Jeffrey shrugged his shoulders.

'This tour is just crap,' I groaned at him, 'the biggest attractions are a parliament building, which is like a town library, a bollard and a floor tile. We've spent hours traipsing around the city, and the most interesting thing I had seen so far was a taxi driver who looked like a drag queen.'

Jeffrey shrugged his shoulders again and ambled off towards the cathedral. I followed him and entered the cathedral itself, which was beautifully decorated like a white-chocolate cake. It looked more like a Roman Temple. I said a quiet prayer then left.

'Are you hungry?' Jeffrey asked me.

'No. But we need to eat before our bus ride. Let's go,' I agreed

We walked to the right of the cathedral and Jeffrey spied a *touristy*-looking cobbled street lined with bars, cafés and parasol-shaded tables. After 200 metres, we hit the cafés, and after giving the first few a swerve due to high prices or unoriginal menus, I happened upon one which advertised Lithuanian dishes. I ordered pigs blood sausages and sautéed cabbage with a 50cl glass of Svyturys wheat beer. The meal was served on a black oval hotplate and was most delicious.

The Lithuanians were all busy knocking back 50cl glasses of beer. They were the third-highest alcohol drinkers on earth. Maybe all the alcohol and pigs blood sausages were not too healthy since they had the third-highest crude death rate in the world – even behind

Afghanistan.

'Lithuania is too cleaned up,' I groaned to Jeffrey, 'we haven't seen any Soviet monuments or Communist-era architecture. Even the train was a rubbish new one. I hope Latvia is better.'

'Don't worry. It gets better,' he replied while chewing his meal.

Then it was time to run. Literally. We legged it back to the main road and jumped in a waiting taxi, which took us to the long-distance bus station with only ten minutes to go before our 2:45 p.m. departure. I ran to the bus driver to confirm our seats, while Jeffrey ran to the luggage storage to collect our bags.

The Ecolines bus was modern and comfortable. I watched the scenery roll past: a mix of scrubby farmland, scattered homesteads in dingy pastel shades and trees which were becoming more evergreen as we headed more north.

That was indeed an easy-peasy tick: country number 92 done.

Latvia (No. 93)

Riga had a reputation as a party town – infamous for stag nights and hen parties. Cheap beer and spirits were a cast-iron guarantee to attract Brits for a party. However, the Latvians had adopted the Euro – and the question was – had it had dented the price advantage that had attracted the tourists?

I had high hopes for Lativa since Lithuania had been a bit lame. In many respects, these Baltic states were twin brothers: they had 99% the same land area, were both ex-Soviet Union Socialist Republics, achieved independence on the same day in 1991 and had experienced drastic double-digit shrinking of their populations every decade since.

Our Ecolines bus from Vilnius arrived in Riga, the capital of Latvia. It headed down a dual carriageway along the east bank of the Daugava River then turned right into a bustling bus station with about 20 bays. It was 7:45 p.m., but with the late-spring sun and clear sky, Riga was begging for a traipse around the city.

'Are we going to walk to the hostel, or what?' I asked Jeffrey as I grabbed our backpacks from the driver who handed them to me.

'No, we are going to get the tram. I know where we are going,' he confidently replied.

'Okay, you lead the way,' I conceded.

We entered the bus terminal and bought a bus ticket out to Tallin, Estonia for the next day at the LuxExpress lines office. Jeffrey also picked up a city map from the tourist information counter.

The hostel didn't seem so far away – only one or two stops on the tram. Jeffrey was handy with the city maps – figuring out the trams, buses and walks around the cities – and I was contented to let him do all the thinking while I admired the views.

The number five tram stop was on the other side of a causeway, so we had to take an 'n'-shaped walk along the riverbank, across a bridge and back to the front of Riga Central Market. The market was composed of four buildings with arched roofs similar to British train stations. They were former German zeppelin terminals that had been converted into an indoor market.

'I love markets,' claimed Jeffrey.

'Boring,' I retorted, 'that's touristy stuff – looking at fish on slabs. Where's this tram?'

As we neared the tram stop, I looked for a way to buy tickets. From the start of our cavale in Slovakia, the tram passengers had hopped on and off without ever paying for a ticket – and Jeffrey loved the idea of not paying for tram tickets any more.

'Where do we buy tram tickets from?' I said, looking about.

'Don't need 'em,' Jeffrey replied.

'We're gonna get caught someday, you know,' I warned him. He grunted.

At a nearby newspaper kiosk, the vendor told me to buy a ticket on the tram.

The tram trundled up – an older 1970s-looking double-ender contraption with white and blue livery. It wasn't too full, so we boarded at the driver end, and I paid 4 euros (£3.30) to the lady driver through a small cut-out in her cab security window.

'How many stops?' I asked Jeffrey. He peered at the map.

'One. Near the Victory Monument.'

I surveyed the city as the tram ground its wheels with a screech as it snaked on to the main street, Zigfrīda Annas Meierovica Boulevarde. This was a visibly wealthier city than Vilnius, and the investment was apparent. The streets were neat – not dishevelled and lined with grimy Eastern European buildings. We trundled along the border of Bastejkalna Park then alighted when we noticed the Victory Monument in the centre.

'The Liberty Mansard Hostel is above the McDonalds,' chirped Jeffrey.

We crossed the road and found the brand spanking new hostel on the fourth floor of a typically European neo-classical building. The hostel was decorated in a very modern orange-laminate panelling and accented with grey metal fittings. Our room was above the reception on the fifth floor – so tiny that it was barely bigger than the steel bunk bed we would be sharing.

'Let's go and get a beer,' suggested Jeffrey.

'Sure, and we can figure out which sights we can see this evening,' I agreed.

We continued up Zigfrīda Whatsit Boulevard then took a left fork, which veered off into the old town. We bagged an outdoor table at a café and ordered a couple of 50cl draft Cēsu lagers. After studying our tourist map and some lively debate, we decided to head straight for the Latvian Academy of Sciences Building, which was also known as Stalin's Birthday Cake due to its prominent Stalinist architecture.

We took the number five tram back to the market then walked along the side streets to the rear, until I gasped at the sight of the sandstone-coloured 21-storey building in front of a grassy park area. It was like a shorter Russian version of the Empire State Building.

'Now, this is what I am talking about,' I exclaimed.

The Academy was architecturally similar to the Moscow State University, and I could spy hammer-and-sickle bas reliefs on the facade,

'Hey, how are you?' came a warbly voice behind me.

I turned around, and there were two fellows sat on a park bench. One of them, the smaller fellow, was nursing a plastic bottle half full of some clear spirit. The Lithuanians were the third-heaviest boozers in the world – just ahead of the Russians. That figured. I approached the bench seat and chatted to the smaller Latvian. Jeffrey had just received a phone call from his wife, so I decided I may as well chat with the layabouts.

'Where are you from?' Shorty-Layabout asked me.

'England. And you?' I asked back.

'Oh, good. I'm from Latvia, but I was two years in London. What are you doing my friend?'

'I'm looking at your wonderful building,' I replied and sat down next to him.

'What is happening with Brexit?' Shorty-Layabout asked me with mildly slurred speech from drinking his bottle of hooch.

'It's a fantastic opportunity,' I replied, giving him a mild shock, 'because the European Union is just like the Soviet Union. They control our lives, and many Brits want independence.'

Shorty-Layabout took another swig from his bottle and thought deeply as he tried to reconcile my surprise answer.

'How about Latvians?' I challenged him, 'did you enjoy being ruled from Moscow? With the Soviets controlling every aspect of your lives?'

He stared at me and frowned, then Shorty-Layabout and his larger friend nodded in unison.

'We hate Moscow. They sent lots and lots of Russians to our country – now half of our country is Russian,' Shorty-Layabout declared, turning towards to his drinking buddy, 'my friend is Russian-speaking. I am Latvian-speaking.'

In fact, about a quarter of the population were ethnic Russians, but anyway, I sympathised with his concerns about the population becoming diluted.

I decided to dig deeper, 'How long ago did you adopt the euro?'

'Hmm. Maybe two years ago,' Shorty-Layabout answered.

'Did prices rise?' I asked.

Another pause – another swig from his bottle.

'Yes,' he sighed, 'it's so hard to get a job, and things are much more expensive now.'

'So, you should get back your Latvian currency, then..." I told him.

That caused him to think extra hard, and he turned to discuss the matter with his friend. So I took the opportunity to stand and make a hasty exit.

'Hey. Can you buy some drinks for me?' demanded Shorty-Layabout.

I handed him a two-euro coin, and my new-found friends were as happy as Lenin.

Jeffrey had finished his phone call to his wife.

'Let's go and take a look inside the building. We might be able to see the Stalinist lobby,' I suggested.

The tall wooden front doors were propped open, and inside was a kiosk with a poster advertising tickets to visit the observation platform on the 16th floor.

'Come on, let's do that,' Jeffrey urged.

We paid five euros (£4.20) each, and armed with tickets, we headed to the single lift. The building was quiet, but there again, it was already 8 p.m. and relatively late for tourists. The lift was empty, and we trundled up to the 15th-floor lift terminal and walked up to the 16th floor.

Outside, the observation platform ran around all four sides of the tower, and there were incredible views over Riga in the late sunny evening. The sun was glowing a fiery yellow and gently lowering in the sky to the west over the River Daugava, which bathed the old city and the zeppelin market in light. Spires of Russian-style churches towered above the city buildings, and my eyes led across the cantilever bridge across the river to the few government building dotted in the greener west bank of the city.

A group of girls dressed in nurses uniforms were laughing and giggling on the corner overlooking the river. They were taking group photos of each other like a model shoot. I suspected they were on a hen night, and they were talking in an Eastern European language.

I caught one word.

'Slovakia!' they giggled in hushed tones. My brother was wearing his red-white-and-blue tourist baseball cap with 'Slovakia' emblazoned on the peak.

'Hey, Jeffrey, they think you are from Slovakia,' I laughed.

We headed back down, passed the zeppelin market again and took the tram number five back to the old city. We alighted at the centre and walked past House of the Blackheads to the square of Old Riga. It had been converted into an outdoor beer hall with wooden bars and outdoor decking where live bands played.

'Let's get a beer, I'm knackered,' I suggested, and I found an empty table. The wooden fence around the decking advertised Black Balsam, and a waitress appeared and highly recommended it.

'It must be a local stout,' I supposed to Jeffrey.

'I'm gonna order two for us,' he eagerly decided.

He ordered two glasses, and the waitress returned with two tall shot glasses full of jet-black liquid.

'What the hell is that, Jeffrey? This was your bloody idea!' I protested. The waitress beat a hasty exit.

I took a small sip – it was completely disgusting and tasted like bitter cough medicine. It was brewed from 24 different plants, buds, flowers, berries and oils, and it was a fantastic cold remedy. But that didn't do anything to compensate for the taste. I swiftly knocked back the medicine and then ordered a 50cl of beer each and a sharing platter of ribs, wings and sausages.

I enjoyed a celebratory Monte Cristo cigar to celebrate my 93rd country with Jeffrey, then at midnight, we strolled back to our hostel. We passed Irish Bars packed with stag night revellers spilling on to the streets, dubious bars with pole dancers and a motorbike gang.

'Hey, pole dancers,' Jeffrey pointed at a particularly raucous bar in excitement, 'let's have some more beers.'

I thought for a moment – if we went inside it was going to be impossible to drag him out again.

'We have an early bus,' I sighed, 'we can't be stuck in there all night.'

I woke early at 6 a.m., showered, then Jeffrey and I had a breakfast of coffee and toast in the hostel kitchenette. We deposited our backpacks at the bus station's luggage storage then took the number ten tram to the west bank of the river to find the Soviet war memorial. The Latvian National Guard had destroyed most of the Soviet-era landmarks after independence, but this huge memorial had allegedly survived.

As we arrived, I noted a tidy – but empty – park containing a huge soaring column, which I had spied from the observation platform of the Stalin Birthday Cake. It stood on a concrete plinth with '1941*1945' etched in concrete cubes each the size of a washing machine, and the column was shaped like a giant Mexican *churro* stick.

To its left was a typical Soviet patriotic statue of an athletic woman standing on one leg with her cloak sweeping in the wind and hand out-stretched to the sky. To the right of the main exhibit, on another platform tiled with red granite, were three enormous statues of Soviet soldiers grandly pointing their arms and machine guns to the sky. The statues were chunky in limbs and almost eight-metres high each – they must have been too mighty for the Latvian National Guard to destroy.

It was time to head back to the city, and we took the number ten tram back across the bridge to Victory Park. Latvian soldiers were guarding the Freedom Monument, which was dedicated to the fallen of the

Latvian War of Independence. As luck would have it, we arrived at the moment they were changing the guard. A van arrived, and out goosestepped three soldiers who strutted to the left of the obelisk. They stopped 20 metres in front of the monument then doubled back to relieve the old guard who were frying in the 24 Celsius heat.

Our next destination was the KGB headquarters. Following several blocks walk, we arrived at The Corner House, which was named after the corner entrance where citizens could enquire at the KGB front desk about their missing relatives, or perhaps, rat on their annoying neighbours.

I entered the corner door of the granite-clad, nondescript building and entered the small lobby. A KGB sign in bold-blue Cyrillic letters, КГБ, was stencilled on the reception sliding window ahead of me. To the right corner was a white bakelite phone where civilians could call a KGB agent. They would have usually been enquiring about a missing relative – suspicious that they had been picked up by the KGB. The Latvian branch of the KGB were notorious for using delivery vans to roam the streets and snatch their victims by surprise. Their favourite transport was a bread delivery van.

Next to the phone was a wooden box with a slot for posting correspondence to the KGB. I was admiring the box when a lady appeared and asked if we wanted the tour. We paid 5 euros (£4.20) each then entered the main exhibit hall. I read the displays while waiting for the tour leader, and presently she arrived.

The building had been used by the KGB since the end of the Russian revolution, and except for the period of Nazi occupation, until 1991 when the Soviet empire collapsed and the Russians withdrew. After independence, the building was occupied by the Latvian police then finally abandoned.

'Follow me please, everyone,' called the tour leader. There was a group of about two dozen of us by now, and we filed into a wide hallway where a steel cell door was at one end.

'This is where,' KGB-Tour-Lady informed, 'people, whether guilty or not, were brought to the detention area. Many of them were innocent and had been wrongly accused by friends or neighbours. Accusations included listening to Western radio stations or telling political stories.'

'He's been listening to Radio One,' I pointed at Jeffrey, 'lock him up.'

KGB-Tour-Lady glared at me then continued. She told the story of one woman who had been sentenced to ten years of hard labour in a Siberian gulag based on an anonymous report. After independence, Latvians were given the right to access their public records, and she discovered that her flatmate had accused her of crimes against the Soviet regime to gain exclusive use of their shared flat. Who needs flatmates like that?

We were led down to the interrogation room, which was 10 foot by 12 foot room and decorated with light diamond-printed wallpaper. In the centre stood a wooden desk used to interview suspects and a rubber truncheon to intimidate and clobber them. At one end of the room was a one-way observation mirror, and I ventured into the small room where KGB agents formerly observed interviews. A chill went down my spine to think that, not so long ago, innocent people were beaten, tortured and accused of crimes against the Soviet Union in this very place.

I walked down the main cell corridor, which was lined with small holding cells to both sides. The cell block was utterly decrepit with peeling paint – it reminded me of Alcatraz – except it was more claustrophobic. I entered one of the cells, which had a plain concrete floor and a steel-framed bed. I could not imagine the desperation of the Latvians who were incarcerated here: they could be detained for years without reason – even shipped out to a gulag in Siberia.

It was time to go, for we had to take the bus to the final destination in my seventh cavale, and we only had 40 minutes before it departed. I calculated that we were a mile away from the bus terminal and would need to jump in a taxi.

I thanked the KGB-Tour-Lady, and she unlocked a steel door and led us away across the prisoner's exercise yard to the exit. It felt like I was being released from Alcatraz – it was a chilling experience, and the hairs on the back of my neck were standing up.

We trotted back towards the Freedom Monument looking for a taxi, but none were to be found. Luckily, I chanced upon the Radisson Blu Hotel facing the park and found a ride back to the bus station. After fetching our bags and buying some pizza slices and croissants to eat on the bus journey, we boarded the LuxExpress coach to Tallinn.

Country number 93 done. What a tickfest this was turning out to be. Woohoo.

Estonia (No. 94)

Jeffrey and I had tired ourselves out: we were utterly knackered with walking around Riga all day. The cool climate of the black LuxExpress bus was welcome, and after the bus had driven for about two hours, we had somewhere crossed the unmarked border into Estonia.

The houses were steadily becoming less of the jaded and gloomy Eastern European concrete boxes, and by now, were mostly Scandinavian-looking wooden chalet-type residences. The countryside had become more heavily wooded, and the birch and deciduous forests had given way to pine trees

By dusk, our bus had reached the city of Tallin – woohoo, that was country number 94. I felt that it resembled Rovaniemi in Finland: the buildings were spartan and functional with boxy windows and blinds. But of course, it was an ex-Communist Baltic state with bundles in common with its two long-suffering southerly neighbours. The whole country had a population barely bigger than the city of Birmingham and yet had shrunk by a quarter of a million since its independence from the Soviet Union.

The bus parked in a dimly lit station, and I fetched my backpack from the bowels of the vehicle. I recollected there was a law in Estonia to wear safety reflectors when walking in the dark. I considered telling Jeffrey about the 400-euro fine.

We yomped down the neat streets towards the city centre. We took a right at a branch of Hesburger and entered the courtyard of the Red Emperor Hostel, which was colocated with a bar. It was funkily designed with graffitied walls and odd piles of junk stacked along the walls. Through the bar upstairs and following the signs, I found the hostel reception, and we took our two dormitory bunks in the "Samantha Room" which housed three iron bunk beds.

'Sorry, you're on the top bunks,' regretted the lithe, young *receptionista* festooned with facial piercings.

It was 7 p.m. but still bright outside, so we decided to head out to explore the city in the hope of finding our first Soviet-era landmarks in Estonia. We navigated the cobbled streets towards the seafront and passed locals ambling in the late spring evening. The promenade had collapsed into the sea – the victim of a huge storm-surge which had wrecked it. We continued west until finding our first Soviet symbol, Patarei Prison.

Originally built by the Russians in the 1800s as a fortress and barracks, it was converted into a notorious secret police prison in the 1940s to lockup resistance fighters and dissidents. After independence from the USSR in 1991, the Soviet agencies abandoned the facility, which had subsequently degenerated. The tan-coloured brick building was two storeys high with a red tin roof and barred windows. Rusting red lookout towers watched over the perimeter – in the days of the Soviet Socialist Republic to watch out for escapees – now abandoned to the elements.

We decided to reach the prison via the promenade so walked along the crumbling seawall. Unfortunately, the perimeter entrance was barred with high mesh fences due to the danger of falling debris. We walked to the front and peeped through the fences, but the prison was as difficult to get in as it was to get out.

We headed back to the main promenade, where hundreds of Estonians were enjoying the weekend strolling around the wrecked seafront. They drank beers in temporary wooden bars and pretended all was fine among the collapsed concrete promenade. We strolled back to the city, through the city gate of St. Catherine's Passage, and eventually found an inviting street bar. I puffed a few Partagas mini cigars, and we drank Saku Original lager and toasted the end of our journey.

'Cheers. We made it. Seven countries, five ex-Soviet Republics and 2,000 kilometres.' I announced.

'Yehay,' said Jeffrey as we clinked our beer

glasses.

'And it's my country number 94,' I continued with another clink of glasses.

By midnight, we supped up and ambled back to the hostel. The Red Emperor had now taken on its night duty as a grunge rock bar, and I was interrogated by a shaven-headed doorman at the main door. The entrances and corridors had been confusingly reconfigured into a completely different layout, which confused me enormously. We somehow ended up in the bar, which was staffed by three ladies and seriously outnumbered by drinkers beckoning to be served.

'Shall we have a nightcap?' I asked Jeffrey.

'Yeah, let's go for it,' he nodded.

I ordered two 50cls of Saku Original from the bar, and we entered the main lounge area, which was industrial-themed and fitted out with old airplane seats. Crowds of young folk were noisily chatting or playing beer pong on a wallpaper paste table in the centre, and we discussed the next day's itinerary before retiring for the night.

We slept well in the dormitory, despite it smelling like a teenager's bedroom, and rose early at 7 a.m. to search for breakfast. After a croissant and mediocre coffee in the main bus station – served by a miserable-looking, bespectacled student type – we boarded the packed number 34a bus. I squeezed myself into the corner of the back seat next to an old gent with a wry expression. The single-decker rumbled out of the city centre and along the picturesque highway running east around Tallinn Bay.

'Where are you from?' Wry-Gent asked me.

'England. And you?' I cheekily asked.

'Me? I am Estonian,' he replied.

I suddenly realised that he was a kind fellow and that my answer was discourteous. Wry-Gent was dressed smartly in a beige-coloured macintosh and a flat cap. I studied him, trying to guess how old he was, and estimated that he must be in his eighties. That would make him a boy during the Second World War. He must have been able to read my mind.

'I'm ninety-five years old,' he proudly told me and held his arms aloft in a machine gun gesture making a *tat-tat-tat* sound like one.

'Ah, yes – you fought in the war?' I proposed to him. He nodded.

'Where did you travel from?' asked Wry-Gent.

'From Riga. It was exciting. We visited the KGB headquarters,' I answered.

Wry-Gent looked a bit puzzled: I had over-reached his English comprehension. I pulled out my smartphone and swished to the photo of Jeffrey and I in the Corner House standing next to the KGB sign. Wry-Gent made a rasping sound then pointed at himself.

'Me,' he firmly announced.

Was he saying he had been interrogated by the KGB? Or was he a KGB agent? I wasn't to find out, for our bus stop had arrived. I waved goodbye to Wry-Gent and his wife, and we were deposited in the hot sun at the edge of the highway, Pirita Tee. We crossed the road towards the yacht club, which was a few hundred metres away.

The yacht club started life as the location of water events for the 1980 Moscow Olympics. Being far from the sea, Moscow obviously couldn't stage them, and this purpose-built village was constructed. We walked along the marina, past the club main entrance and lines of yachts and boats, some of which were being tended to by their owners in dry dock. The floating walkway to the jetty was fenced off.

'I know what to do,' said Jeffrey confidently, 'we have to speak to a skipper to get in.'

Jeffrey spoke to a fellow and got permission to enter. At the end of the jetty was an original monument from the Moscow Olympics: a five-metre-high tower-shape of red steel tubes standing on a concrete plinth emblazoned with Olympic rings. At the top of the tubes was a Soviet red star. The Singing Revolution had overlooked this ex-Soviet symbol in their plan to erase any sign of what they considered an illegal occupation.

We walked back to a café near the yacht club entrance, and I nursed an apple juice while plotting our hunt for more Soviet-era trophies. We wouldn't be visiting the markets or churches: we were on a mission to find dark-tourism sights of the Soviet Union.

Refreshed from the heat, we walked past the Moscow Olympics Village, where the apartments had housed the athletes, then back to the main road heading to the city. The huge village car park was overgrown with weeds and deserted except for a couple of odd-looking locals who were parked in the corners cleaning their cars.

We walked for 20 minutes along the promenade alongside Pirata Tee. The sun was blazing and the cerulean-blue sea was inviting. We reached a spot where a tennis-court-sized concrete plinth stood on the beach – this was supposed to be a Soviet heroic monument.

'It looks like the revolutionaries have knocked down the statue,' I sighed.

We took the tram number one back to the port area of the city, took lunch in a sports bar then headed to Linnahall. We passed pre-fabricated eight-storey apartment blocks, which had seen better days, and were excited to see a few Russian cars including an immaculate Lada 1200s estate. We finally reached Linnahall and were in awe of its scale and dilapidation.

This enormous Soviet-era building was constructed as an events hall for the 1980 Moscow Olympics. It was so heavily built that Western intelligence believed it was designed as a defence structure against invasion from Finland. It had a floor space big enough to fit three hypermarkets with a 5,300-seat concert hall and a 3000-seat ice event hall.

Great concrete staircases cascaded down from the main roof area. We climbed up and were greeted by a decrepit and heavily-vandalised expanse the size of a football field. The dirty-grey concrete structure was littered with broken glass, loose concrete chips and spray-painted by the local youths who spent summer evenings up here admiring the sunset and downing bottles of liquor.

I walked along the centre strip, past concret garden boxes with light-blue promenade lamps, and absorbed the structure. It was built like an enormous nuclear bunker and felt like a Spectre secret base in a James Bond film.

I studied a set of stairs, which lead down like an underground station entrance. The cut-away section of the roof was a metre of solid concrete – a tad excessive for a sailing event hall. My mind wandered to the music video of Alan Williams' hit song, Faded, which was partially shot here in post-apocalypse style.

At the other end of the roof strip, we climbed the final two storeys to the highest point of the events-hall-cum-nuclear-bunker, and I looked down towards the rear of the building. It extended into the sea and appeared that patrol boats or submarines would be able to cruise under the rear section into the bowels of the bunker – Francisco Scaramanga would love this as his secret base.

The views of the bay and city of Tallin were fantastic from the rooftop – no wonder the local youths enjoyed getting wasted up there. We descended the staircase to the rear through the broken glass and took a taxi.

'Where are we going now?' I asked Jeffrey.

'To the Sokus Hotel Viru,' he replied.

'Why are we going to a hotel?' I wondered.

'Don't ask. Trust me,' he replied as he made a shush with a finger on his lips.

The Viru was built in 1972 and owned by the USSR tourist agency, Intourist. It was infamous as the hotel where visiting foreigners were directed to stay. Coincidentally, the 23rd floor was a sophisticated spying suite that monitored guests. The KGB tapped phone calls of foreigners, which included visiting diplomats, and sixty of the guest rooms were wired up to the spying suite. During the independence revolution, the KGB packed their bags and fled. The secret spying suite was so well concealed that it wasn't discovered until three years later.

We entered the modern lobby and visited the coffee lounge to the left. We took a solid wooden table facing the lobby and sat in the comfortable green-fabric armchairs. I ordered two Viennese chocolate cakes and coffees from the cashier at the counter, who looked like a USSR female shot-putting champion.

During the days of the Soviet Union, a half-dozen of these café tables were bugged by the KGB to snoop on foreigner's conversations.

'Do you think this is one of the tables that was bugged?' I asked Jeffrey.

He looked about the café, 'Probably. It's a solid

table.'

Following our afternoon tea at the spy hotel, we walked back to the hostel, collected our backpacks and found a taxi to take us to the airport. The elderly driver was spritely and slung our backpacks into the Opel saloon, and we were on our way. I asked him about life in Estonia under the European Union, and he thought long and intensely.

'Everything [is] expensive after we change to euro,' he glumly replied.

'Do you prefer the European Union or the Soviet Union?' I cheekily asked him. There was a long pregnant pause.

After careful thought, he shrugged his shoulders, 'it is the same.'

'Margaret Thatcher,' the Commie-Driver decided.

'Sorry, what?' Jeffrey asked.

'Margaret Thatcher. I like Thatcher. Strong.' Ah, he liked strong leaders.

'How about Putin?' I proposed. Commie-Driver's face beamed – even almost elatedly.

'Yes, Putin. Yes, strong,' Commie-Driver stared at me in his rearview mirror with excitement, 'Putin strong. Good leader,' he waved his fist.

'Are you from Estonia?' I asked Commie-Driver.

'No. Ukraine. Here in Estonia [for] 45 years.'

'Do you like Belarus?' I probed further. It was a pro-Soviet state, so I assumed that this would confirm his political leaning.

'Yes, Belarus people good. Russia, Ukraine, Belarus. We...' Commie-Driver tapped his index fingers together, '...like we are brothers. We together.'

We were now at the low-rise airport terminal, which looked like a modern bus station. I thanked and tipped our USSR-loving driver then quickly located the check-in counters 10 to 11 for Polish Airlines. As we reached the front of the queue, I had the presence to remember that I may have inadvertently left one of the bullet casings from the Stalin Line in one of my pockets.

So I unpacked my backpack and rummaged through all my pockets – thankfully it was all clear. After we both checked in, we found our way to a bar near to our departure gate, where a stern-looking bar lady served me a draft Staropramen and Jeffrey an Estonian Amber Ale. I had just sat down when I heard my name over the Tannoy.

'Would Mr Rice Colin please contact the transfer desk.'

Bloody hell, I thought, there must have been something wrong with my check-in baggage.

'Stay here, Jeffrey, I'll see what this is about.'

At the transfer desk, a tall ginger-haired lady in a navy pantsuit was waiting with a walkie-talkie.

'You called me on the Tannoy. Is everything okay?' I asked

'Your bag has a problem. Come with me,' Pant-Suit-Lady firmly informed me.

I'm in deep poo, I thought to myself, I must have missed one bullet casing during my search.

'You have a battery in your luggage...' she informed me as we walked towards the duty-free shop. Phew – that's not too bad, I thought.

'...and a bullet,' Pant-Suit-Lady continued.

Okay, I could be in deep trouble here, I thought in a bit of a panic. Possession of a bullet casing in an airport is not good news – in Manila and Hong Kong airports you would be promptly arrested. Pant-Suit-Lady beeped her proximity card on a door marked 'Airport Staff Only' and we passed down some iron stairs into the luggage processing hall below. Luggage conveyor belts and x-ray scanners were busy at work. Pant-Suit-Lady led me along walkways marked by yellow lines to a roll-cage in a corner.

'This is your bag,' she pointed at a bright blue backpack.

I rolled my eyes: it was *Jeffrey's* backpack, not even mine. The bugger. Pant-suit-lady took the backpack out of the roll-cage and placed it on to a wheeled trolley.

'Find your item,' she told me.

I quickly found the battery, which was a smartphone charger, in the side pocket. I stuffed into my jeans pocket. I rummaged in my brother's backpack among his foul-smelling dirty washing until I found the bullet in his jacket side-pocket. Pant-Suit-Lady quickly grabbed it off me and deposited it in a clear plastic zip-lock bag.

'Sorry about that,' I apologised to her.

'You're not allowed bullets on the aircraft,' she admonished me.

'I know. It's a mistake,' I replied sheepishly, hoping for leniency.

Pant-Suit-Lady furrowed her eyebrows at me then turned on her heels and led me back to the duty-free area.

I found Jeffrey sipping his amber ale and clouted him on his head with his smartphone charger.

INTERLUDE

While waiting in Tallinn airport nursing a 50cl of Staropramen lager, I checked my email and found an email response from Andy.

'Right. This is serious. Two years ago I was miles ahead of you in Europe, and now you are four ahead. I haven't had a new tick since 2013,' he grumbled.

I got the idea. I was now at 94 countries and in spitting distance of the magic 100, while Andy was now the one languishing behind – stuck on 77. I grinned a devilish grin to myself and took another sip of chilled lager.

'So,' he continued, 'I've compiled a list of countries I can visit.'

He rolled off a list of his remaining countries in Europe, flight stopovers in the Middle East and a lengthy list of Caribbean territories.

'I could go island-hopping to Anguilla, Aruba, Bahamas...'

A rather long list of 27 expensive, yet highly *hoppable*, destinations. I could sense his sudden desperation – that I had sneaked so far ahead of his tally. I smirked to myself smugly and took another sip of my lager. A while later, another email came in from Andy – he had been busy on Skyscanner.

'Right. I've booked a return flight to Antigua. Maybe I can hop to five other islands. The fightback starts.'

I replied to him with an impish grin.

'Well, at least you will get the opportunity to use some of those hundreds of travel guides you have bought :-)'

I began projecting numbers in my head with mild concern. Suppose Andy added ten new countries to his tally in 2017; that would take his tally to 87 – still seven behind me. But the gap would be closing, and with an all-out effort in 2018, perhaps he could reach the magic 100. I *had* to keep up the pressure – I was only six countries away from the century.

I sat in the terminal staring at the ceiling in deep thought. How could I keep ploughing ahead? I had already ticked off almost every place within three hours flight of England. I needed to identify a string of neighbouring countries I could visit on a cavale. I could steal his suggestion of Armenia, Georgia and Azerbaijan – but that would only be three. Damn it!

I thought and thought on the flight home to Manchester. There was no choice: if I could not add six more countries to my tally in 2018, then Andy would get to the century first. I decided to tick off a couple of weekend trips first, then I would design a cavale of three to four countries in May 2018 to finish off my mission. That was it: I could probably reach Albania and Macedonia on a short trip – or even Iceland. But which countries for my final cavale?

The heat was on.

Back in England, Andy and I met for dinner with our partners. Over some tapas dishes and a glass of rioja, he delivered the news I didn't want to hear.

'I have talked to my boss about taking a one-year sabbatical.'

'And what did he say?' I asked pensively.

'He's fine with it – I can return after my time off. I could even do this every year.'

Yikes. I'm dead meat if Andy does a tickfest every year.

'When are you thinking of doing this?' I nonchalantly enquired.

'Maybe next year. How many countries did you visit in one year?' Andy asked me.

'I managed 37. Although I didn't travel continuously – I still had to arrange my relocation back to the UK, take care of my daughter and so on.'

Andy had no real responsibilities: he had no kids and his closest relatives lived 200 miles away. Given a year, he could probably visit 60 countries, I supposed to myself.

I thought about it or a few nights and scoured Skyscanner to identify interesting and low-cost options. Eventually, I discovered a cost effective way to get in and out of Albania and Macedonia, so I locked them in. That would leave only three European countries for me to visit; I was now within the grasp of completing an entire continent.

Then a lightbulb moment enveloped me – I could *not* let Andy complete Europe first. Forget the Caucusus – it had to be a cavale to Northern Europe in May. And that would leave me with 99 countries and only one more to go to the century.

At my fiftieth birthday party, I negotiated with my wife to allow me to visit Albania and Macedonia as my birthday treat. The next day I bought my flights and booked a hostel. Locked and loaded. The heat was on.

BATTY BALKANS

11: Bonky Bunkers of Albania

I was rather pleased with myself for negotiating trips to Albania and Macedonia without any financial or material bribe to my wife,

Albania had already defeated me once – on my sixth cavale – when I had attempted to travel from Budva, Montenegro to Shkodra in Northern Albania. The exasperating problem with Albania was the poorly developed road system based on narrow winding roads connecting the towns. This was compounded by mountain ranges running north to south and resulting in east-west travel being horrendously routed around them.

As for the trains, they were utterly obsolete and a national joke. There were no national bus lines – the bulk of routes were served by minibuses, which are known as *furgons*. Oh, and the buses only departed in the mornings, so getting stuck in towns for the night was a given. And, did I tell you that there were no bus stations in Albania?

At the time of my visit, there were no domestic airlines, which frustrated attempts to get in the country and ways to hop around. Albania had had seven airlines in the previous two decades – and all had spectacularly flopped. It included the aptly named Albatross Airway, which survived two years before it was grounded due to unpaid bills, and Ada Air, which had operated a Soviet-made Yak 40.

With the odds stacked against the traveller, this was going to be a challenge.

Albania (No. 95)

My luck turned: I discovered that the Greek island of Corfu was just a stones-throw from Albania, and also, regular ferries ran across to the Southern Albania town of Sarandë. That was going to be my route in; forget Montenegro, Macedonia or Kosovo. I took a low-cost Thomas Cook charter flight from Manchester to Corfu at the un-Godly hour of 05:55.

After sight-seeing the castle and Corfu Old Town, I yomped to the New Ferry Terminal. Opposite the terminal entrance, I bought a foot-passenger ferry ticket for 19 euros (£14) from a pretty smiling saleslady. It was a runway-length walk in the searing heat from the port entrance to the immigration building, where I joined a line of passengers queuing next to a sign.

'To ALBANIA'

After a passport check and bag X-ray, I sat outside on some steps for my ride. After a good wait, an ugly red-and-white ferry chugged into view and berthed at the pier. A loading ramp folded down, and two tiny cars with Albanian plates were emitted – which appeared to be its entire roll-on roll-off capacity.

It was a Finikas Lines ferry, the *Marina*, which was registered in Albania. We were ushered aboard and welcomed by a crew member hollering to leave our luggage in the car bay area. This monstrosity was so top-heavy, at three-storeys high and with only a cars-width loading ramp, that I guessed they needed as much ballast as possible to stop it toppling over.

After a few moments it gurgled away, and I sat on one of the white wooden benches on the sky deck admiring the sun and distant mountains of Albania. It looked remarkably like the geography of Hong Kong to me with steep mountains plunging precipitously into the cobalt-blue Aegean sea. After 30 minutes, the vessel rounded a headland where perhaps 100 white houses clung randomly to the cliffs.

As the *Marina* approached the port of Sarandë, I started to have second thoughts. I started to fret that I was cutting my schedule too fine – what if I lost a day due to bus trouble and missed my flight from Tirana? This trip could be a transportation nightmare.

Albania was becoming an enigma to me – even before I had landed. After the Second World War, the country had isolated itself from the West under its communist chief of state, Enver Hoxha. He admired Josef Stalin and had adopted many of his tactics to intimidate and control the population – even decades after Stalin's death.

Among the myriad of things Hoxha took offence at was religion, and he proclaimed Albania as the first atheist state in 1967. Western music and movies, beards and even long haircuts were banned. During Hoxha's tyrannical reign, there was even a barber stationed in Tirana Airport to shave any arriving offenders – which even included visiting international football teams. Of the few things that Hoxha liked, he adored Norman Wisdom movies, and subsequently, the comedy star achieved a God-like status in the reclusive state.

The ferry reached the handsome port of Sarandë, where medium-rise apartments and hotels crowded the hills surrounding the bay. Colourful lights twinkled from the buildings – this looked alright, I thought. I disembarked, withdrew some Albanian lek from a cash machine and tried to avoid the congregating taxi touts.

'Taxi?'

'Where you want to go?'

'Hey, my friend.'

I wasn't being harassed, but there were dozens of them – and on every corner. I took a left turn out of the port then a right past some travel agents. Then another chap with a shaved head approached me.

'Colin? Are you Colin?' he asked.

How the hell did he know my name? Maybe he had seen my passport in immigration and this was a scam?

'What is your name?' he asked again,

'Jim,' I retorted in order to buy time.

'Are you Colin from England?' he persisted, 'I am [from the] hostel.'

It then dawned on me – he was from the hostel I had reserved.

'You book hostel? Come, check in,' he persisted.

I followed him across the road, up some stairs and he led me into the heavily graffitied hostel, Saranda Backpackers. I paid 10.50 euros (£7.70) for the night. The hostel owner, Teddy, gave me some great travel tips. He highly recommended that I visit the mountain town of Berat, which was five hours ride by *furgon*.

'Don' you worry,' Teddy reassured me, 'the *furgon* leaves at 8 a.m. I am gonna go with you to find the right bus.'

'Hey I appreciate your help,' I thanked him.

I decided to head to the beach for dinner. I had already eaten a little, but it was still early and I didn't want to hang around the hostel. I crossed the street and descended a long flight of granite steps to the promenade, which was lined with café and bars.

Sarandë was endowed with a beautiful bay and a wide sandy beach lined with palm trees and dotted with beach furniture; if it was across the bay in Greece it would be overrun by British tourists. I found an inviting restaurant, the Allday Grill, where I stuffed myself with kebabs and draught Elbar beer.

By 9 p.m. I was whacked, so I plodded back to the hostel, where the balcony outside the dormitory was occupied by a gang of lads chatting loudly and smoking cigarettes. I was too tired to wash so changed into my sleeping shorts and T-shirt then crashed. The noise of Sarandë main street with cars roaring past, the balcony boys chatting, smoking and the humidity, amounted to a challenge. But I was so knackered that I rapidly fell asleep.

In the morning, I found Teddy rummaging about in the kitchen preparing breakfast. He gave me a cheerful good morning without even turning around, and I greeted back at his sturdy bald head. He cut up several large loaves of bread, fried some eggs on a battered stove and served it up with Austrian blackberry jam and sliced salami. I couldn't refuse his efforts, despite the yucky cooker, and wolfed down my breakfast.

'Come,' beckoned Teddy while putting on an unusual flat cap made of whicker, 'I will take you to get the Berat *furgon*.'

I loaded up my backpack and followed Teddy through the backstreets of Sarandë. Along the route he said hello to everyone and shook their hands – it was like a politician's walkabout.

At the town centre main crossroads, opposite the supermarket, was parked a white *furgon* which was already pretty full. Teddy shook hands with the driver, an older gent with quaffed hair and a green polo shirt over his bulging stomach.

I thanked superstar Teddy and boarded the bus. All the seats were taken except the back row where a guy sat, sporting sunglasses, a neck pillow and sportswear. I couldn't make out his nationality because he just grunted an unintelligible word as I sat down at the opposite end of the bench seat. He looked like the Albanian version of Zach Galifianakis from the *Hangover* movie.

By 8 a.m., the driver collected the 1,200 lek (£8) fare from each of us, started his engine and chugged off. Which was fortunate since I was sweating like a pig in the stifling air of the *furgon*. I was so tired that I slept most of the first couple of hours, only waking occasionally to admire the hills and tended plains of Gjirokast County. By 10:30 a.m., we stopped at the Restaurant Gjoni rest stop in Qesarat, the utter middle of nowhere, and we all bailed out for a break. The driver darted inside and heartily scoffed a breakfast.

I bought an espresso then sat outside at a patio table in the sun. Hangover-Guy was on the next table, and I smiled and took a photo of the scenery.

'Want me to take your photo?' asked Hangover-Guy. I near fell off my Albanian chair, for I hadn't figured out he was a Westerner – I had guessed he was a rich, eccentric Albanian.

'No. It's fine,' I replied, 'where are you from?'

'Los Angeles,' he replied, 'and you?'

I told him that I was English, which seemed to please him, and we spent the rest of the journey talking. He seemed to have some military background since he talked authoritatively on China's Pacific fleet and North Korea's ICBM program. He was well-travelled, having lived in Thailand and spending the last nine months touring Eastern Europe, ostensibly due to being kicked out of the Schengen Zone.

'Hey, I admire you guys for doing that Brexit thing,' piped-up Hangover-Guy, 'did you vote for Brexit?'

'A thousand per cent,' I replied, 'The European Union is like the Roman Empire and Jean-Claude Junker thinks he is Napoleon IV. The power has gone to their heads.'

'Cool,' he replied, 'you Brits will be better off out,' he agreed.

After a few more hours, we arrived at a dusty bus terminal area, and the remaining passengers alighted.

'*Terminali*?' I asked the driver in pseudo-Italian, which I had figured out was the most readily understood European language in Albania.

'*Si. Terminali. Finito*,' he confirmed.

Hangover-Guy had booked a guesthouse for four nights in Berat, but I had made no preparations whatsoever.

'Do you mind if I follow you to the hotel and see if there are any rooms left? I haven't booked anything yet,' I suggested.

'Sure,' he replied, 'I'm going to walk there.'

'Erm. I think it's one or two kilometres out of town and 90 Fahrenheit in the sun. Are you sure?' I questioned Hangover-Guy.

He was travelling with two large wheelie suitcases, and it seemed improbable they would survive the badly maintained paths. He cradled a tablet computer on his palm.

'Why don't you see how far it is to walk? I would take a taxi, you know,' I told him.

'I can't use Google maps. Too insecure,' Hangover-Guy informed me. I guess that meant he really was somehow mixed-up with the military – or perhaps he was on the run?

'No problem, I will use my mobile,' I answered.

I checked my smartphone and discovered that the hotel was 1.2 kilometres away.

'No way – you can't be dragging those suitcases along in this weather. Let's take a taxi,' I said.

We took a taxi and stopped in the main touristy street of Berat.

'It's okay. We will walk from here,' said Hangover-Guy to the taxi driver.

A tout trotted across to pester us, and I politely told him we were sorted. We were facing a mountainside steeply terraced with stone houses climbing 100 metres above the street. The buildings were festooned with windows: this was the "town of a thousand windows".

Following my Google Maps, we trailed up the stone paths between the shop fronts and up the mountainside until we found a walled house with an arched gate. An old lady instantly opened the gate and peered out.

'Here,' she beckoned.

How did she know we were here? Did she have CCTV cameras in this fourteenth-century walled village? The hotel was, in fact, a guest house with only two rooms – and both were booked. So the kind lady telephoned a friend to see if they had a room. After a moment, an older gent popped his head around the gate – it was the tout from the main street.

'Ah! It is you!' he pointed, 'I thought you had a room? Okay, okay. Follow me.'

I bade goodbye to Hangover-Guy, who wanted to have a siesta, and we agreed I would bang his door after my day's sightseeing.

Tout and I descended to the main road, then 20 metres along, climbed another rough-stone alley into a gated courtyard. Tout's name was Stefan, and he showed me the back room priced 13 euros and the front room priced 25 euros (£18). It was a simply decorated room with a wooden floor, faded rugs and an iron-framed bed with ugly blankets. The only redeeming feature was three sash windows with gathered net curtains which overlooked the river.

'I will pay 20 euros – last price,' I told Stefan-the-Tout sternly.

'Okay, okay. I am not [the] manager. If I find another man for room, you share? Then you pay only 10 euros.'

I agreed. Stefan-the-Tout left to scour for "other man", and I set off to sightsee.

I returned to the main road, Rruga Antipatrea, which was well maintained with a brick-paved promenade along the Osum River with black steel railings and period street lamps. The river itself was a muddy tan-colour and half the width between the riverbanks; I presumed it was dry season.

I crossed the Austrian-built suspension footbridge over the river, which swung quite precariously as pedestrians crossed it. Halfway across, I looked back to the mountain and admired the Ottoman-period whitewashed houses with clay tile roofs, which were tightly packed together up the mountain. Together, several hundred plain Lego-style windows faced from the mountainside – the UNESCO World Heritage List area's 'City of a Thousand Windows'. I was in no mood to challenge UNESCO and count them one-by-one.

Across the dried river-bed, I climbed the stone alley Rruga Nikolla Buhuri, past the orthodox church and into the old town of Gorica. The stone paths were in awful shape, but the elevation of the old town afforded panoramic views of the 800-windows-cum-

10,000 windows. After soaking up the view, I decided to tackle the mountain climb to the castle. Or was it a hill? It looked incredibly steep, and at its peak, an Albania flag fluttering proudly over Berat.

I crossed the river again and walked up the narrow stone "roads" between the densely packed houses, past Hangover-Guy's guest house then zigzagged up the hill with great frustration since it was a maze of dead alleys. I realised the only way out was to the main road up the hill, Rruga Mihal Komnena.

I wouldn't like to be an Albanian postman for all the Turkish coffee in the Balkans, since the road was a good 30 degrees incline and ran for a full kilometre straight upwards. Worse still, the houses did not have street numbers on them – so the fuss on the internet was mostly true – Albania had no proper street addresses. Although there were clear street names. And they did have a bus station in Berat, so that myth was busted.

The road was constructed of beige limestone cobbles, which was highly polished through constant wear, which made it rather slippery underfoot. I trudged along, stopping occasionally to admire the view and catch a breather. Two young fellows strode past me and turned off up a stony path, so I decided to follow them.

The path was knackered and had degraded into stones and dirt for most of its length – completely worn away to the soil in some sections. I slowly chugged my way up, taking care not to lose footing on the loose rock, until I reached the castle wall. I ascended a staircase within the wall and rejoined Rruga Mihal Komnena again – and thank my quadriceps – it was almost level. I turned left towards the flagpole and walked the last 200 metres to the viewing peak.

And what a breathtaking view it was. The windowed houses of Gorica clung to the verdant green hill opposite, and the vertically grooved mountain to the north were similar to Hawaii's cliffs. The semi-dry Osum River meandered from the cliffs in the distance, past Gorica and along the plains where cherry orchards and olive groves flourished. The town spread out to the south, and beyond that, the spectacular Mount Tomorr towered 7,900 feet over the plain like a smaller version of the Andes I had seen in Santiago, Chile.

The handrails at the viewing balcony were mostly damaged and hardly suitable to prevent tourists from tumbling down the cliffs on to the hotel touts below. A young Albanian man was having his photo taken by his ageing father. He approached me.

'Please. You take [my] photo. My father, he...' he nodded his head, 'he don't know how,' he lamented.

'No problem,' I said.

After helping the fellow with his photo, I climbed back down the broken trail as slowly as possible to avoid tripping down the hill and getting admitted into an Albanian hospital. I reached the foot of Mihal Komnena Roadmade with no broken limbs and located an inviting-looking bar-restaurant. I took a table on the terrace and ordered an espresso and bottle of mineral water to hydrate. Feeling peckish, I also ordered *djath I bardhe*, which was a meal of baked sheep cheese in a dish of pepper and tomato sauce. Paying my bill of 250 lek (£1.70), I departed to see if Hangover-Guy was ready after his Albanian siesta.

Up in the old town, I banged on the gate to his guesthouse, but there was no noise from within. Never mind, maybe my evening would have ended up as a real *Hangover* movie, I thought. So, I took a *pica gorja*, a Greek-style pork pita, and two bottles of Korca beer at the Heaven's Kitchen Cafe before retiring for the night ready for my bumpy ride to Tirana.

My guest house was well and truly locked up with a giant padlock on the front gate. I let myself in then bolted it from the inside. On the doormat of the guest house was a small piece of writing paper.

'Hello, Colin. After 22:00 if no other guests you may *clouse* all the doors and big door by inside. Have you a good night. Stefan'

I locked myself inside and bolted the front door. I was the only person there, and it was a creepily quiet and dark alley. I reassured myself that I didn't feel unsafe, yet travellers could potentially be a target for burglars. So I inspected the various windows, which were all open for ventilation, to make sure they were barred. They all were except for the bathroom window, which was only covered with chicken wire. I locked the bedroom door with the hefty seventeenth-century key then took the single bed to sleep.

I awoke in the night dying for a pee. It was 4 a.m., and I didn't want the hassle of unlocking all the doors to go to the bathroom, and besides, it was a dark and creepy outside. I looked about and found my almost empty plastic bottle of mineral water. I drank the remainder then urinated in the bottle. Note to self: remember to throw that before Stefan-the-Tout arrived at 7 a.m.

My alarm went off at 6 a.m., and I unbolted the room and went for a shower with the piss bottle in hand. I locked the bathroom door, which was more of a wooden gate, then stared about. Damn it – the toilet roll was missing. I searched around and noticed that it had been knocked off the toilet cistern by the blowing curtain and fallen inside the toilet bowl. Bloody Nora – I couldn't leave it like that. So I looked about for something to fish it out.

There was a long-toothed comb on the edge of the

sink. Hmm, that would do. So I fished the toilet roll out with the comb, dropped it in the bin then left the comb on the side. Before I forgot, I poured out the plastic bottle into the toilet, rinsed it a little then wondered where I could dispose of it. The bathroom bin was too tiny, so I searched the kitchen – no bin. Hmm. I felt like Frank Spencer from the television series *Some Mothers Do 'ave 'em*, trying to cover up all my wrongdoings. I noticed there were several empty plastic bottles lined along the window sill. I pulled back the net curtain then stood it next to the other empties.

The shower was not a shower as we know it; it was a shower hose head mounted on the wall next to the toilet and pointed at the floor. Well, at least the toilet would get a free clean as I showered. Inevitably, the bathroom became a lake, and I had to throw a hand towel in the flood to dam a corner where I could dry myself.

After much cursing about the unconventional Albanian bathroom facilities, by 7 a.m. I was ready and Stefan-the-Tout arrived with a happy smile. He called an acquaintance for a taxi then led me down to the roadside, where we sat and chatted while he puffed on a cigarette.

'You should make a business here,' Stefan-the-Tout opined, 'one English man – he made a hostel here. *Goood* money. See that house with no windows, there?' Stefan pointed to a windowless building perched on a steep ledge on the hillside of Gorica, 'that will make a good hostel. It is *shitet* – for sale. I know the owner. His mother died, and he has no wife. He is selling for 60,000 lek.'

Buying a windowless building halfway up a mountain with no access road – in the middle of Albania – somehow didn't appeal to me. Even if it was only £400.

'I will think about it, Stefan – it does seem *shitet*,' I told him. He smiled back.

'You know, I was interviewed by a BBC Russia journalist from Estonia. They ask me everything about Berat: economy, people, customs...' continued Stefan-the-Tout.

I nodded in feigned interest until a portly driver pulled up in a banana-yellow Mercedes taxi. We agree 300 lek (£2) for the ride to the bus station, and I shook Stefan's hand and bade him farewell.

Safe in the taxi, I wondered about who would rent the room next. Would they find the plastic-pee bottle and fill it with water to wash their hands? Then maybe comb their hair with the poop-comb? I mischievously chuckled to myself, and the taxi driver glanced in the rearview mirror with a puzzled look.

At the *terminali*, there were about two dozen buses awaiting departure.

'Bus Tirana,' I instructed my driver.

He dropped me next to a 1980s Mercedes-Benz coach bus. I paid 400 lek (£2.70) to the driver and hopped onboard. At 8 a.m. the bus departed, and I felt relieved that I would soon be safely in Tirana to catch my outbound flight.

The road was well maintained – thankfully tar-sealed – and ran along a billiard-table-flat valley floor with low hills running a few kilometres in the distance. The vegetation was a little desiccated and appeared Mediterranean: perhaps a Southern Spain or Greece. The fields were divided into smallholdings about a tennis court width and as long as a football field. I assumed that they had been subdivided into Marxist-friendly strips during Hoxha's days.

The crops were chiefly corn, grapevines, cherry

trees, olive trees, watermelons and grass, which I assumed was for feeding livestock. The dried, harvested cornstalks still stood in some fields, while in others, they were gathered into wigwams. Some turkeys strutted about at the roadside, while at the side of a petrol station, some scrawny sheep were grazing on the scraps of grass here and there.

After a couple of hours, I figured we were surely in Tirana city. The bus turned off the main dual carriageway, lurching side-to-side as it pulled into a bus terminal of sorts. The terminal was crowded with buses and *furgons*, which displayed red signs in the windows for every corner of Albania. I climbed off and fetched my backpack to be immediately bombarded with taxi touts.

'Are you even a real taxi driver?' I asked one.

'Sure, follow me,' he answered.

'Erm...how much, first,' I asked. He held up eight fingers.

'800 lek. You must be joking – I will pay 400 lek,' I responded, which was about £1.70.

The driver played hard to get. I shrugged my shoulders and walked off towards the highway with the taxi driver trailing after me like a feral sheep. I stood at the kerbside and looked about for transport, while he irritatingly stood at the rear of his banana-yellow taxi with the boot open and patting the bodywork.

I counter-offered 500 lek (£3.30) but he kept waving his eight stubby fingers at me. If he was not going to negotiate then I would rather walk. I noticed an approaching bendy-bus, which was chock-a-block with passengers and the doors were open. I approached the driver.

'Skanderberg? *Centrali*?' I asked. He waggled his head and beckoned me with his middle finger. So I barged on with my backpacks, and the conductor fellow charged me 40 lek (£0.27).

Since I hadn't found any internet to download the Google map data, the GPS co-ordinates in my hostel booking just showed a blue spot on a threadbare map. Still, I could trace my journey, and after some 15 minutes, the bus turned off at the Zogu I roundabout where I bailed out to walk the rest of the way.

I stopped at the Bar Picasso to have an espresso and a chocolate-filled brioche while charging my smartphone and downloading the Tirana Google map from the free Wi-Fi. I also checked my email and found one had come in from Andy. I had emailed him the previous day that I had hit my country number 95, and it must have set him into panic mode, for he had just booked six weeks unpaid leave. Unpaid leave! That must have cost him a pretty packet in lost salary. I emailed him back.

'You can get quite a few ticks with six weeks leave...' I suggested. His reply came almost immediately.

'I have some project work to do on my new house. I won't use all that time for travel.'

I was quite suspicious. Was he planning a sudden flurry of travel? He had already booked a Caribbean holiday for December; that would be a respectable tickfest. Albeit, half of the islands he planned to visit had been wiped off the map by Hurricane Irma. I suspected that he had been irked by his loss of perhaps four ticks in the Caribbean and my additional tick: he would be five further behind than his plan.

How many ticks could he achieve in six weeks? I estimated he could achieve a new country every three days. That was 42 days divided by 3 – that was perhaps 14 ticks. On top of his existing 77, he would be at 91. I calmed down a bit and packed up for my yomp to the hostel.

Back to my yomp, I followed Google Maps until I reached a communist-era block of flats. The Hostel Albania was on the top floor, and after walking up the staircase in the sweltering heat with my two backpacks, I was sweating profusely and eager to get some air-conditioning. After signing in and paying 10.50 euros (£7.70) to the child-sized *receptionista*, I was granted use of a single bed near to the window due to concerns of me falling on a hapless fellow traveller and killing them. I took a city map and some advice from the *receptionista* then set off down Kavaje Street heading for the former secret police spying headquarter, the House of Leaves.

I walked along the narrow residential streets and happened upon a tobacconist on Naim Frasheri. I discovered they had a respectable selection of cigars and bought a Guantanamera Crystale for 400 lek (£2.70). That would do for a celebration of country number 95 tonight, I thought.

After a half-hour walk, I reached Skanderberg Square, which was fronted by the National History Museum building to the north. It was a simple two-storey concrete building with a huge mosaic mural of an angry mob of Albanians through the ages with bows and arrows, swords, muskets and rifles. The lady in the centre held aloft a rifle with an athletic forearm the girth of an arm-wrestler's and wearing a white flowing dress. She looked like the offspring of The Sound of Music and The Terminator.

To the southern side was one of those pesky "hero-on-a-horse" statues, which the Balkans were so fond of. This was allegedly George Castriot, better known as Skanderberg, who led a rebellion against the Ottoman

Empire. He looked like a super-hero with a crusader cape, angry face, pointy beard and a shallot on his head. I inspected my city map and realised that I had overshot the runway and doubled back to the House of Leaves.

The *Sigurimi*, the Socialist state's secret police, operated its technical operations centre in the building known as the House of Leaves. They performed mass state spying and eavesdropping on foreigners and enemies of the state from the end of the Second World War until 1991. It was estimated in a survey that 13% of the population had family members who were imprisoned as a result of the *Sigurimi* operations.

The Albanians were trained and technically assisted by the Soviet Union in perfecting their art of spying until 1961 when Hoxha fell out with the Warsaw fact. He then got all chummy with the Peoples Republic of China, who supplied spying equipment until they also fell out with each other in the 1970s. With no more commie friends to sponge off, Albania began to manufacture its own bugging devices. These home-made bugs, the size of an LCD, were implanted in everything from handbags to umbrellas, ornaments, foreign Embassies and hotels, where they recorded all the conversations on Chinese switchboards wired to West German tape-recording devices.

In one of the old monitoring rooms, I decided to be naughty and take a selfie at a Chinese-made switchboard. Murphy's Law stepped in, and a curator lady entered that instant and caught me red-handed holding a 1960s Bakelite phone handset.

'What happened to the sound?' I asked in faithful Basil Fawlty style, 'I thought I could hear spying devices in this room. What is going on?'

The curator lady was not a Fawlty Towers fan nor wanted to humour an old fool, for she insisted to call a technician to solve the problem. She twiddled with the West German sound recording devices, then at once, the sound came on and voices from guests in the other exhibit rooms were streamed to the operations console.

I placed back the handset, 'See – there you are,' I continued my charade.

I didn't fancy spending the rest of my trip being questioned by the Albanian authorities, so I decided to quit fooling about.

I pondered how much spying was done in these former Socialist and Communist states, from East Germany to Russia. And was almost certainly on-going in this modern age in states such as China and North Korea. It was fabulous to imagine that MI6 agents would still be required in the world of espionage.

After my brush with the guardians of the Albanian Secret Service, I headed back to Skanderberg Square but was prevented from passing through by three policemen and a military officer.

'What is going on? Why all the police?' I cheekily enquired to one police officer.

After explaining that I was English, which seemed to satisfy him, he told me that there was a NATO summit being held in the People's Culture Place. I found it amusing that construction of the Palace began using Soviet funds gifted during the leadership of Nikita Khrushchev – then completed in 1966 using communist Chinese money under Mao Zedong – and now had been commandeered by NATO, the army of the evil capitalists.

I skirted around the cordoned-off square and headed east down Abdi Toptani Road. Tucked behind the Ministry of Transport, I came across one of Albania's concrete bunkers, known as "Qender Zjarri", which had been converted into an art museum. The country was dotted with over 170,000 of these artillery-proof bunkers which, in the days of Enver Hoxha's schizophrenic obsession with invasion by NATO, were built to provide pillboxes for resistance fighters. The four-metre dome design meant that artillery and bullet-fire simply ricocheted off it.

My younger brother had some inexplicable fascination for George W. Bush Avenue, so I continued along Abdi Toptani Road and took a right into the oddly named avenue. I took a selfie at the street sign to shut my sibling up. Then I headed south, across a bridge over the River L'ana, to search for the Pyramid of Tirana. I turned right on to Bajram Curri Boulevarde, which sounded like a dish from a curry house, and walked along the riverbank. The river was only a few metres across – it was more like a stream.

The Pyramid of Tirana was a derelict concrete building designed by Enver Hoxha's daughter, Pranvera, as a museum dedicated to her late father. Predictably, it became out of fashion after the fall of communism. On its slide to obsolescence, it became a conference centre, then a command centre in the Kosovo War – until finally being abandoned to the vandals.

The pyramid, which looked like a cone affixed with triangular slabs, had smashed windows and was liberally smeared with graffiti. A backpacker girl had climbed the apex and was doing an impersonation of Christ the Redeemer in Rio. For a millisecond, I contemplated following her up the sloping sides of the pyramid, but then I noticed that the gap between the slabs was a skylight from base to apex. If I slipped, then I could crash through the glass and be spending the rest of my days in an Albanian intensive care unit.

A block further along, I reached Blloku, which was

the former residence and entertainment area of Tirana during communist times. Until 1991, this area was strictly off-limits to anyone except Communist Party officials and favoured diplomats. The streets were narrow but well-maintained, and the tall buildings had ground-floor shops of jewellery, handbags and luxury goods, along with dozens of bars and coffee shops.

I turned left, walked along a long row of shops then took a right to Ismail Qemali Street in search of the former residence of Enver Hoxha. It was a bit confusing to know which building was which: there were three candidates on that block. I took a table outside the middle one, the Vila 31 bar-restaurant, where I ordered a Kuqalashe Pilsner beer to figure things out. It set me back 250 lek (£1.66), which I thought rather reasonable for a five-star restaurant.

Some tour guides were taking groups to the farthermost building, which was a Chinese-themed alfresco restaurant; some groups visited the Lincoln's Centre of Albania, which shared the building with Vila 31; and some briefly studied the decrepit, dusty building behind me.

The Vila 31 had patio tables running along the pavement, which encroached a few metres in front of the decrepit building. I Googled 'former residence of Enver Hoxha' and was delighted to find that my encroaching patio table with a red parasol was right outside the correct one – the dictator's pad. It was a modern two-storey residence with a flat roof, huge windows and balconies. It looked uncannily like a Central American consulate.

I lit up my Guantanamera cigar to celebrate my successful trip and reaching country 95. I pondered that until 1991, I would not be permitted to even enter this zone. Now here I was – drinking beer and smoking

Cuban cigars – right outside Enver Hoxha's front gate. Mischievously, I waited until nobody was watching then flicked some cigar ash into Hoxha's front garden. There!

I requested a menu from a skirmishing waiter, which seemed to task his English language capabilities, so he called over a young fellow with an anchor-type beard from the next table.

'I'd like a menu please,' I requested.

'Oh, I am sorry,' Beardy-Fellow apologised in perfect English, 'the restaurant only opened a week ago and the menus are not ready yet.'

He proceeded to roll-off a menu of five types of ciabatta sandwiches and an elaborate Albanian platter of meat and cheese.'

'I will try the Albanian platter, please,' I asked.

'A great choice. It includes Albanian sausage and local sheep milk cheese,' Beardy-Fellow commented.

After translating my order to the waiter, Beardy-Fellow sat down again and we struck up a conversation, beginning with where are you from, and so on.

'I studied in Oxford then in Birmingham University,' he explained, 'I was in England for six years.'

From his conversation, I realised that he was the owner-cum-manager of the restaurant. I decided to press him for more information on Hoxha's former residence.

'Do you know exactly house was Enver Hoxha's residence? I've watched tourist groups visiting all of them,' I questioned him.

'Funny you should ask,' he replied gleefully, 'just a couple of weeks ago, during the fit-out of the restaurant, there were a group of old men chatting outside and one of them collapsed. I tried to help him, fetching a blanket, offering water and calling an ambulance.'

'Was he alright?' I asked, wondering what this had to do with Hoxha.

'I spoke to the old man for a while – I thought he was in his 70s – but it turns out he was 92 years of age. Then he told me that he was the chief of security for Enver Hoxha during the communist era. He was visiting the house again where he was stationed.'

I suddenly became very interested in the story, and Beardy-Fellow continued.

'We Albanians had no idea what went on inside these houses – it was highly secretive. So I asked the old man where Hoxha slept at night. He told me it was in a bedroom upstairs with a huge bay window. He knew that for sure because he was always being called into Hoxha's bedroom while on duty.'

'So, which house did he live in?' I asked.

'The house that I have converted into this restaurant is the original one. Later, Hoxha had the one on the right built and moved his whole family in there. However, he still loved his bedroom and continued sleeping there every night.'

Ah, so I supposed there was no simple answer: both houses were occupied by Hoxha and his family.

'Where exactly was Hoxha's bedroom?' I asked.

'It's upstairs at the back of the restaurant. You can take a look if you want. I need to leave right now, so I will tell the waiter to show you after your meal.'

'Cool, that would be fabulous,' I replied, 'I appreciate you doing that for me.'

So, I was sitting outside the railings of Hoxha's new house, where his family had lived, and he spent the day. Based on Beardy-Fellow's account, I was flicking my cigar ash in Hoxha's actual front garden.

The Albanian platter arrived on a wooden cheese board and was one of the best dishes I had ever tasted. Delicious chicken wings, herb sheep cheese and the Albanian sausage was tasty, albeit rather like a British one. I wondered whether Beardy-Fellow had smuggled some British bangers back from Birmingham.

After polishing off my third bottle of Tirana beer, I paid the English-challenged waiter 600 lek for the platter (£4) then went inside and asked if I could see Hoxha's bedroom. A tall, skinny waiter approached me and his English was less awful.

'Hello. You want to look?'

'Yes please,' I eagerly replied.

I followed him up some classy stairs to the restaurant's upper floor where an amazing bar terrace overlooked Blloku. Then he led me to the rear of the restaurant and to a room on the left. It was full of junk including bar stools, curtain rails and boxes of odds and ends. I stepped over them and surveyed the former bedroom. It had a huge bay window the width of the room, which faced a rear garden – just as Beardy-Fellow had told me. Mature trees grew right outside the window, and I could appreciate why Hoxha preferred to sleep right here.

I thanked the tall waiter then left the five-star restaurant to head back to my one-star hostel. Tirana was booming: it seemed to have more coffee shops than Paris and was thronged by classy restaurants with incredible outdoor terraces spilling into the streets. Luxury goods shops were everywhere – there was a boom feel to the city.

The route back was confusing, and I became lost in dead-end alleys and backstreets. Eventually, I succeeded in finding the apartment block tucked away behind a row of shops. I booked a taxi with a wiry ZZtop-looking guy manning the hostel front desk then crashed on my kiddie-sized bed.

I slept awfully and suspected I was being bitten by something in the night. At 6 a.m. I showered and changed into fresh clothes, then after breakfast, I took the taxi to the airport for my 11:40 a.m. Alitalia flight 585 to Rome's Fiumicino airport. And there endeth my Albanian experience.

Albania was a pleasant surprise. I was full of preconceptions based upon the bad press during its Communist era and years of Balkan civil unrest. I had anticipated a dreary communist aftermath of ugly apartment blocks and miserable-looking people. I instead found a beautiful country with tons of potential, friendly and honest people who welcomed me with open arms and some fun dark tourism.

Perhaps, someday, I would return.

Tick number 95 done. I had edged closer to 100, and Andy was – by all accounts – becoming increasingly nervous.

12: Routemaster Rip-offs

Macedonia (No. 96)

I had finished my Albanian trip, and only one Eastern European country remained on my to-do list: Macedonia. I had been researching a cost-effective way to reach it without any luck. What was wrong with this country? Did it really exist? I felt like the European explorers attempting to reach the ancient fabled city of Timbuktu. I was determined to reach Macedonia one way or the other.

I realised that I wasn't alone: I researched Macedonia and found typical questions asked on Google search included 'What was Macedonia before Yugoslavia?', 'Is Macedonia Greek or not?', 'Is Macedonia a real country?' and 'Is Macedonia poor?'

The biggest news was its ongoing battle with Greece over the rights to use the name Macedonia. Greece disputed that it was entitled to the rights, and so Macedonia was relegated to the unwieldy 'The Former Yugoslav Republic of Macedonia'. The confusion and ensuing international debate came from ancient Macedonia being much larger than the modern-day one. The modern state of Macedonia only covered two-fifths of the original region – the rest of it encompassed regions of Greece and Bulgaria.

After my trip to Albania, I spent the remaining months of 2017 scouring the internet for a way to get to the obscure and clumsily named state. There was a paucity of flights, particularly direct ones. I bought a Wizzair flight from UK to Ohrid, and after a few weeks, it was curiously cancelled. National airlines were charging a fortune for the privilege to reach Skopje and required multi-sector flights, which endured travelling the best part of a day. Not an option.

I pondered which bus or train services were within a few hours travel of Macedonia. Thessaloniki was on a main railway line to Skopje, but the Greeks were so upset about the ding-dong over the former Yugoslavian republic using the name Macedonia that cross-border train services had been suspended years earlier.

Flights to Pristina, the capital of Kosovo, were intriguing – only a 90 minutes onwards bus journey to Skopje – but flight schedules were limited. Albanian land transport was abysmal – I had figured that one out – so I binned that option. I spent three months analysing flights to Greece and Kosovo in the hope of a miracle.

Then I had a brainwave. I randomly looked at other Balkan states and found there were international buses from Sofia, Bulgaria to Skopje. Flights from UK to Sofia were cheap, so I booked a flight on Ryanair to Sofia and a return flight from Skopje to London Luton. If the bus from Sofia to Skopje didn't travel on certain days of the week, or there was inclement weather, or the bus was full, or – I would run out of time and be in trouble.

The day came, and I took the Ryanair 6338 flight from Liverpool to Sofia and arrived at 00:20 in the morning. I stayed at a hostel just a few minutes walk from Serdika Central bus station, and the next morning, I anxiously showered and yomped briskly to the bus station. Inside the terminal, there was no ticket office for Matpu bus line. Nothing on the electronic departure board.

'Hello. Do you need help,' a middle-aged fellow with flat cap, thick glasses and an official-looking identity badge asked while tapping me on the arm.

'Erm. Yes. I am looking for the Matpu bus to Skopje,' I asked.

'Follow me,' he hustled, then he darted hither and thither in a feigned panic, 'the Skopje bus [is] leaving now. 7:30 a.m. Quick.'

I looked at my smartphone and realised it was already 7:40 a.m. But he was off in a rush again, and I trailed after him to the main departure board. Helpful-Hustler twizzled his stubble while he studied the display. That wasn't particularly helpful: I could read the board myself and clearly there was no Skopje bus.

'Quick!. Follow!' he said as he dashed out through the revolving door exit.

I squeezed myself through the narrow door and found Helpful-Hustler pointing to another terminal

'Skopje. See. There is [the] bus stop,' he proudly informed me.

Why he didn't just tell me earlier? I gruffed and walked back into the terminal to get some breakfast, and Helpful-hustler stepped in the way. He held out his hand.

'Help me with money,' he grovelled.

Much to his disgust, I gave him one Bulgarian lev (£0.40) and dashed back inside the revolving door with the hopeless helper in tow. I somehow lost him, took a Turkish coffee and croissant at a café then visited the terminal convenience store to buy provisions for my journey. I bought a bottle of mineral water then noticed they sold flaky goat-cheese bread. The bespectacled cashier frowned at me.

'One of this bread please,' I pointed to the crinkly

roll as she huffed and pouted at me.

I indicated with my hands that I wanted a six-inch stick cut from the large roll. She took the whole roll, plopped it in a brown paper bag and weighed it. My gosh – it weighed 0.6 kilograms and cost 9.22 lev (£4.20). I decided not to argue and reluctantly paid. As she placed the bag of bread in my hands, I realise it was enough to feed a whole bus.

I headed out and located the Matpu ticket office, where I bought my bus ticket to Skopje from another surly lady for 30 lev (£11.40). I took another Turkish coffee in a small bar facing the terminal, anxiously waiting, then at 9 a.m. returned and was rudely ushered out. I waited outside next to a rubbish bin overflowing with coffee cups and smouldering cigarette butts. A portly old gent in a grey flat cap and black mac shuffled across with a huge bag and his even portlier wife.

'Skopje?' I asked.

'*Da, da*,' they answered in unison. I was elated; I felt like Mungo Park who had discovered a bus stop to Timbuktu.

Another fellow approached.

'Skopje?' I asked again.

'Yes,' he replied in perfect English, 'where are you from?'

'England,' I answered, 'and yourself?'

'I am from Bulgaria,' he answered dolefully, 'I am hoping for a confederation.'

I was perplexed. What kind of confederation was he talking about? Of Southern American States? A new Yugoslavia?

'I believe in a union – we need to stick together. Unlike you British. You are leaving the European Union,' he groaned.

'Well, do you think that Bulgaria is better after

joining the European Union?' I challenged him.

He seemed rather despondent and glanced towards the overloaded rubbish bin, 'If you ask my parents – the older generation – they say no. If you ask the younger generation than me – the answer is yes. A quarter of the population has left Bulgaria – there is no-one left,' he lamented.

It was time to board the bus, and I stowed my backpack and clambered up. I took a second-row seat and after a few minutes was confronted with a girl waving her ticket at me. Apparently, I had taken her seat number 6. I realised that I should be in seat 29 but the old gent with the portly wife was sprawled over it. I resisted a fight and found a seat at the rear.

Europe had just been through a severe polar vortex cold snap, and although there was a foot of snow on the ground, the mountain scenery was sunny and beautiful along the road west to Macedonia. Aside from a pee stop, the scenery rolled by for over two hours until the bus shuddered to a halt at the border.

A Bulgarian border guard in olive-green fatigues boarded the bus and collected the passengers' passports one by one. He stared me in the eyes and compared me with my passport photo. I was slightly nervous; it all seemed too good to be true that I was within a stones' throw of Macedonia.

After a good while, the Bulgarian border guard returned and handed back a wodge of passports to one of the passengers, and as the bus drove off, they were dished out. Fifty metres further on, we shuddered to a halt again at the Macedonian border. A border guard wearing a blue macintosh rapidly collected all the passports back. One Mongolian-looking young man handed the border guard an identity card, which incurred his wrath.

'No. Kazakh. No,' he waved dismissively at the poor fellow as he clomped along the bus in jackboots. On the way back past the man from Kazakhstan, he sternly wagged his finger at him again.

'Come,' he beckoned to him.

Fortunately, the Kazakh fellow was let back aboard, and after another 20 minutes, we got our passports back and rumbled off. I let out of a sigh of relief: finally, I was in Macedonia – and I was now on 96 countries. Which was edging closer to the magic hundred. Hallelujah.

It was also my 48th European country number, and I only had three more to go before I reached the milestone of visiting every country and territory in the whole continent. My next cavale to Europe was already planned for May, and I hadn't leaked the news to Andy. I smirked to myself as I imagined telling him that I was visiting European country number 51, the Faroe Islands. That would be a massive milestone. I grinned to myself in a sinister movie-bad-guy fashion.

The mountain scenery continued in Macedonia with winter trees, rustic mountain houses with piles of cut logs stacked outside and scary passes with precipitous drops over the edge. Soon, the bus was 37 kilometres from Skopje and hit a decent-sized town. I was getting stir crazy after four hours on the bus and looking forward to stretching my legs.

After a final stretch of toll motorway, the bus turned past the impressive Hotel Continental into a bus terminus. Everyone darted for the exit, so I assumed this was the end of the road. I took my leftover brick of goat-cheese bread and retrieved my backpack. I asked seat-stealer the direction to Fort Macedonia, Skopje's faux Arc de Triomphe. He pointed me through Skopje train station where I was instantly mobbed by taxi drivers.

'Taxi? You want [a] taxi?' they hollered. I waved my hand to indicate not, and I passed through the bus terminal and popped out the other side on to Nikola Karev Street. After asking a couple of ladies at a bus stop, they pointed me to walk straight up the street then turn left at the next block. I yomped off and took a left along Kuzman Josifovski Pitu Boulevard as they had instructed.

My first impressions of Skopje were assorted. I noticed that the ladies were mostly dressed to impress, with well-coiffured hair, tons of make-up and smart dress clothes. The streets were slightly unkempt and definitely felt like Eastern Europe – possibly vintage Ukraine – but with less potholes. I noticed very few Russian motors running about, unlike the Baltic states and Ukraine, except for a few Yugos which were abandoned in front gardens and the like. The shopping centres reminded me of Bosnia, with functional designs of mirrored glass and exposed round columns in brushed aluminium style.

As I yomped along the boulevard, I noticed a great, fat red double-decker bus. Was it an illusion? I had only seen major fleets of double-deckers in UK and Hong Kong; what a surprise. I noticed one of the beasts halted at a bus stop outside the Vero Center Mall, so I picked up my pace to take a closer look.

It looked similar to a 1970s AEC Routemaster with a half-width driver's cab and sloping rear upper deck. As I approached the curious vehicle, I noticed that it was Chinese – a Yutong City Master. I think it had broken down since another bus pulled up behind it and everyone began leaping off to transfer to it. I also noticed that the red LED destination sign on the disabled bus seems to have been scrambled.

To the wonderment of the passengers, I took a photo and admired the Chinese retro-clone before I continued on my way. After asking several more smartly dressed ladies along the way, I reached the city centre, crossed a major intersection and passed along 13 November Street on the south bank of the Vardar River. I passed four bridges until I reached Macedonia Square and found the horse statue, which was noted in my travel guide.

The statue was officially named Warrior on a Horse but was reputedly Alexander the Great. This great conqueror was another victim of the ding-dong with Greece. Macedonia claimed him as their heroic son due to his birth under the ancient boundaries. This riled Greece because his town of birth was near Thessaloniki in Greece. The statue, whoever he belonged to, was impressive at almost 100-foot high.

I then took a left turn down 11 October Street and reached the Macedonia Gate, a blatant clone of the Arc de Triomphe. It was a reasonably decent duplicate in cream and sand colours but was 40 per cent of the height of the original and with all the Napoleon stuff stripped off. I wondered why the Macedonians had taken such a shine to grandiose monuments. Could it be to attract tourists? Or perhaps to outshine their ex-Yugoslavian cohorts?

I had booked a bed in the Skopje Hostel, and they had sent me instructions by WhatsApp to wait under the Arc and send them a message. I sent a text and waited next to a taxi. There was a shopping centre next to the Arc, and while I waited, it emitted a steady stream of high-end German cars and smartly dressed shoppers on foot. They wanted to be noticed in swanky clothes and driving flashy cars, so I guessed the government also wanted to clothe the capital in grand-looking monuments.

I waited and waited. I was so bored that I took a selfie with an uninteresting fellow-on-a-chair statue. After half an hour, I began to worry that it was a fictitious hostel. So I decided to turn on my data roaming and call using WhatsApp, after which a young lady appeared.

'I am so sorry. [I] am late,' she wheezed out of breath, 'have you been waiting long?'

'Yes, a long time,' I replied.

It wasn't really, but my backpack was heavy, and I was wasting precious time as the weather was sunny and clouds loomed on the horizon. She led me across Dimitrie Chupovski Avenue to an iron gate in a building similar to apartment blocks in Budapest. Inside, she took me to the third floor using the ancient Yugoslavian-era lift then beckoned me into the hostel.

'Please. You remove your shoes. Here,' she handed me some carpet slippers.

It was an immaculate hostel with two main dormitories and a decent bathroom, which was worthy of a hotel. After check-in formalities, I selected a lower bunk and she left me to sort out my things.

The priority was to buy my wife's cigarettes before it was too late, so I scoured the local shops and managed to buy enough Marlboro Gold to keep her coughing until Christmas. Then I headed back to the city centre.

I walked to Macedonia Square to further admire the enormous bloke-on-a-horse statue – it was immense. The Macedonians were completely into statues, which were dotted all over the city centre. Some were littered along the river banks, and the main footbridges across the Vardar River were lined with dozens of them. Some buildings even had their balconies and facades festooned with the stone figures. Was there a Macedonian statue factory that was obligated to sell a wagonload a week to the government?

The statues didn't appear to be anyone of any consequence either. London has bucket loads of statues, but we have dozens of famous kings, queen's, prime ministers, inventors and artists to choose from. Macedonia only had Mother Teresa who was globally recognisable – the rest seemed to be scraping the barrel. They were probably parking wardens and pub landlords.

I crossed the weathered-marble square to the steps leading down to the Vardar River, which was muddy brown and gushed violently. I walked gingerly down the steps and noticed that there were no other people down there. A Roma-looking couple of young men were watching me from the Stonebridge above. Were they eyeing me up? I shall keep a beady eye on you, I decided.

At the river, branches, rubbish and even trees were violently sweeping past. Was the river normally this turbulent? Or was it run off from the polar vortex melting rapidly in the mild weather?

I noticed a woman standing in the river wearing a red swimsuit. She was about to dive into the water, but then an instant later, I realised she was a statue. Crikey, they had run out of land for the statues and had started dumping them in the river.

I walked back up the riverbank steps then did a U-turn back on to the marble-decked bridge, Stone Bridge. It was from the sixth century AD and supposedly renovated in the 1990s, but the marble was heavily corroded and pock-marked. The proud Macedonians were strolling across in droves taking selfies of the views. I paused at the peak to admire the landscape, which was now a bit murky – I assumed due to the coal smoke that hung in the air.

On the horizon, to the west, was a hefty range of snowcapped mountains from where the river appeared to gush from. I guessed they were the ski resorts on the border with Kosovo.

Much renovation work was in progress around the riverbanks, where old, graffiti-damaged communist-era limestone cobbles were being replaced by shiny new sand-coloured marble. I turned to face the east, where the most enormous neoclassical Constitutional Court dominated the north riverbank – fronted by yet another anonymous bloke-on-a-horsey statue.

Very odd additions to the river were three massive faux-galleons. They were crudely modelled after English or Spanish galleons, but probably double the size, with pretend ripped sails and angular shaped. They were bolted to the riverbed as floating restaurants and I could spy diners on the decks admiring the plethora of statues in every direction.

I crossed Stonebridge and passed a cluster of new-looking fountain statues. On the left were the statues of Saint Cyril and Methodius, the former being the unsuspecting preacher who created the Cyrillic alphabet so loved by the Soviet Union and adorned on intercontinental ballistic missiles and Soyuz spacecraft.

Yards further, and there was a fountain statue dotted with mothers with humongous breasts clutching their babes-in-arms and toddlers. Then yet another, of three men on a circular fountain with their pet lions on the tier below.

Continuing past the Stonebridge Hotel towards the Ottoman Bazaar, corroded marble steps led up the hill into a pedestrianised market of narrow streets. Roma beggars prostrated themselves on cardboard boxes on the ground and some coddled infants. The beggars seemed to have great expectations: instead of the usual plastic coffee cups you may see in London, they were carrying large cardboard trays. What were they expecting? Bundles of banknotes? I tossed a few coins to a Roma woman then climbed the slippery steps.

The bazaar was a real tourist trap with handbag stores, tailors and all manner of trinket sellers. The shops selling fashion items and gold jewellery were rolling down their shutters, and the beggars were rising from their cardboard mats and dusting off their clothes.

I meandered through the bazaar along Salih Asim and came upon a small square on the right where several restaurants had their tables spilling out into the street. I admired the menu of the closest, the aptly named Ottoman-era Turist Café, and peeked in the window to watch several cooks frying minced-beef sausages and stewing beans. A diminutive waiter appeared and ushered me to a table in the square.

I ordered five sausages, a dish of beans, an unleavened loaf of bread and a 50cl of draught Skopsko lager. I lit up a Marlboro Light cigarette, swigged the delicious lager and kicked back to admire the roaming beggars waving their cardboard trays at random passers-by.

When my order arrived, it was most delicious. I made myself some kebab-style pockets of loaf stuffed with the meaty sausages, lettuce, onion and a spoonful of the baked beans. It looked rather like it was going to rain, so I paid the reasonable 295 dinar (£3.80) bill and retraced my steps navigating past the pesky statues and beggars.

It was now dusk, and the plethora of vanity-project buildings and innumerable statues were illuminated by spotlights. This city was under a great deal of renovation and certainly had a peculiar charm about it – potentially a future tourist trap.

I needed to sleep very early because my flight back to London was at 6 a.m. I figured out I needed to sleep at 8 p.m. and wake at 3 a.m. so decided to have a few more lagers to help me sleep. I located a cluster of outdoor bars at the riverbank and selected the Telkom Bar, which had a tennis-court-sized outdoor area shrouded in plastic walls and a canopy. Gas heaters and table electric heaters looked promising to keep off the evening chill. I took a seat on a comfy sofa and ordered a bottle of Zlaten Dab beer. It was drier than the Skopsko and more like bottled Belgian beers from mass supermarkets.

I puffed on a further mouthful of cigarettes and had fun watching the beggar children. They were incredibly persistent and slipped into the closed area of the bar while the waiters were not watching. The beggars flitted abut the bar waggling their cardboard tray at the diners and drinkers. After a few moments, one of the waiters would notice and escort them out – only for the crafty urchins to feign exit and scoot back inside again. It seemed the waiters were a bit sorrowful for the beggars and did not give them a hard time.

It was now 7 p.m. and time to head back to the hostel. Navigating through the main square, past the giant horsey statue of non-Macedonian Alexander the Great, through the fake Arc de Triomphe and dodging the fake Routemaster double-deckers on Dimitrie Chupovski, I arrived back to the hostel entrance. It was now completely dark, and a tramp with his bags of belongings huddled in the doorway. I went in and checked the main door was properly locked behind me.

I didn't sleep well due to my recent odd sleep

patterns and awoke at 3:18 a.m. That was close enough to my alarm, which was set to 3:30 a.m., so I showered, packed and left the hostel where my taxi awaited near the Europharm pharmacy at 4 a.m. It was raining heavily, and I felt like I was leaving an old friend behind - this appealing city had ample oddball sights to warrant a visit.

Despite some scary hydroplaning on the motorway, I arrived safely at Skopje airport at 4:30 a.m. for my Wizz Air 7701 flight to Luton. Despite some questions about my horde of cigarettes, I made it to boarding safely and sat next to a Macedonian fellow who was returning to the UK.

Macedonia was an oddity. I was elated that I had made it after much failed planning. I discovered a proud and interesting nation worth a visit for a couple of days to see its fake London double-deckers, crudely-copied galleons and grand statues of people you have never heard of before. Oh – and it was the home of Mother Theresa.

I felt that my time in Macedonia was more than enough. I would have gone crazy if I had to pass another hundred statues.

Country number 96 and Eastern Europe ticked.

VIKING CLEAN-UP

13: It Ain't The Arctic Circle

I was running out of excuses to travel but needed to finish off Europe as fast as humanly possible before Andy rumbled me. I needed to get a northern cavale locked in – but how could I get my wife to agree? Would bribery would work again, I wondered?

I had agreed to buy her a new Ford Ecosport car in the Philippines as compensation for my trip to Central America. Could the same ploy work again? She had a new car in England, a Ford Focus, but had fallen in love with Mini Coopers. 'No way' was my stock answer. Could I bargain a cavale to Northern Europe in exchange for a new Mini?

Eventually, she relented. The lure of a brand spanking new Mini Cooper was too much to resist. She signed an agreement on the back of a napkin in a Chinese restaurant in July 2017, then I sent an email off to the Mini dealer and spent the weekend searching for affordable flight options around Scandinavia. I unearthed suitable dates in May 2018 and documented my itinerary. My plan was coming together.

By April 2018, I reminded her about my pending trip.

'Honey, it's two weeks until my Iceland trip,' I pointed out.

A barrage of expletives later, then a frantic search

for my scanned copy of the July 2017 treaty, I was back on track.

Iceland (No. 97)

The day arrived, and it was a gloriously bright day in Manchester with clear, sunny skies and 21 Celsius. I took the train to Manchester Oxford Road and changed to the airport train. Everyone was wearing T-shirts, and some even wore shorts on their bank holiday day out. And there was me – in hiking boots, four layers of clothing and a ski jacket. I took some unusual looks and grinned back.

At Manchester airport, I checked in to the Icelandair flight 441 to Reykjavik and joined the queue for baggage search. It was stifling in the hall, and a man in a linen shirt and board shorts scoffed at me as I took off my double-layer ski jacket in a sweat.

I wondered if I was over-doing it a bit. But as I descended the airstairs at Keflavik Airport after my 2 hours 45 minutes flight, there was a flurry of hailstones and a chilling wind, and I recalled the smarty-pants tourist on his way to Costa del Sol.

Airport staff pressed the arrivals to join the automated passport check queue.

'European Union?' an airport official lady asked me.

'Erm. Just about,' I replied.

'This way,' she pointed, 'the European Union queue.'

I joined the European Union queue, which had a bank of automated passport machines, and the European Union flag was proudly emblazoned above the turnstiles. The queues were all three deep, and I joined the closest one. I waited and waited, and the queue was going nowhere. So I peeked around and noticed that the passengers at the front were frantically rubbing their passports on the scanner, tutting and shrugging their shoulders. Another wonderful European Union project, I thought.

I left the queue and walked around to the 'Other Citizens' queue where nobody was waiting. I walked straight up to a plump border guard lady who smiled, checked my passport in two seconds then waved me through with a smile. I looked back to see the European Union queue still tutting and whining.

I located the tourist information counter in the arrivals hall, and after a short wait, a smiling blonde-haired boy asked how he could assist.

'Hi. Is there a bus to Reykjavik?' I enquired.

'Sure. The FlyBus or Reykjavik bus shuttles are over there. It will cost almost 3,000 króna to get to the city.'

I gulped – that was £21.50. That was way too much.

'Is there a *normal* bus.' I asked, 'I am sure you don't come to work on a 3,000 króna bus.'

'Sorry,' replied Tourist-Troll, 'our policy is not to tell you that.'

'Hmmm. Where is the local bus stop,' I pressed.

'Through the rear of the terminal,' he pointed in the direction, 'but it doesn't leave for another one hour and fifty minutes.'

Maybe Tourist-Troll was fibbing to discourage me from trying the local bus. Anyway, I certainly wasn't going to wait that long and I felt the tide was against me. I reluctantly bought my shuttle bus ticket and ventured out into the wind and hail to locate the orange-coloured bus.

My first impressions of the landscape, as the bus hit route 41 highway, was bleak. The scenery reminded me of the Big Island in Hawaii, which had been cloaked in lava fields and was still trying to recover from the desolation. The land around Reykjavik Airport was flat with no tree cover; what little forest the island had had was cut down by the early settlers. The horizon was fringed with snow-topped hills at a great distance.

The land was strewn with rocks and boulders – barren except for stretches of pale straw-coloured clumps of grass, which reminded me of Scotland. Some areas of rock were flint-grey and devoid of fauna whereas others were dabbed with moss. The rocky areas were hilly and reminded me of the Hoggar Mountains in the Sahara Desert. Only one per cent of Iceland's land was arable – and it seemed an overestimation to me.

Punta Arenas at the southern tip of Chile; Dunedin in the far south of New Zealand; Incheon in South Korea. As Iceland's landscape changed in various hues of desolation, it reminded me of all those bleak and remote places I had been on my travels. Why would anyone live here, I thought?

The frigid North Atlantic Sea was visible across the tundra, and the bus passed several townships until after 40 minutes it reached the outskirts of Reykjavik. I alighted at bus stop number 10, which was evident from a neon-pink sign. I thanked the bearded driver, collected my backpack from the hold and yomped up Snorrabraut Street to look for my hostel.

After 200 metres, I was already freezing despite my four layers of winter clothing. The wind was chilling my face, and flurries of hail were a constant irritant. I was surprised to see lots of graffiti, which I thought was rather uncharacteristic of Scandinavians.

The two-storey houses to my left were grey and drab, much like communist public housing in Eastern Europe, and to my right were newer but equally drab three-storey buildings.

At the corner of Snorrabraut Street and Flókagata, I reached the Reykjavik Village Hostel and checked in. I was in dormitory room number one in the basement, and as I barged in with my bags, I shocked a blonde-haired girl who was inside. There were three bunk beds, and I was assigned bed number two on the top – they were going to regret putting me there. I dumped my bags and walked back upstairs to the reception.

I grabbed a city map and walked back down the length of Snorrabraut to the seafront. It was a wide bay with a long promenade and a road running alongside it. The seawall was a row of polished pink-grey granite boulders the size of fridges, and the steel-blue seawater in the bay was framed by snow-dusted mountains on the other side of the bay. The occasional brave German tourists passed by, but by and large, it was a beautiful backdrop but too cold to enjoy unless you were an emperor penguin.

I began to think about what an unusual place Iceland was. It was not even fully part of Europe based on geological evidence: it was like a car straddling two parking spaces – half on the American continental plate and half on the Eurasian continental plate. Iceland was as close to Canada as it was to Southern Europe, and despite its wintry name, was not even inside the Arctic Circle.

With a population of only 337,780, Iceland had a population smaller than the city of Bradford. It's was so distanced from Europe that it had a unique civilisation formed from the harsh life and remoteness from invaders and other influencing civilisation. It was the last place in Europe to be populated, and the settlement was established in 874 AD by a Viking chieftain from Norway. In the ensuing decades, more Norsemen populated the island, and it is believed that they brought along Celtic slaves and women from Ireland and Scotland. Even today, the Icelandic language was almost unchanged from ancient Norse and the population was 93% pure DNA from the original settlers.

After some reflection at the chilly promenade, I trekked back up the hill and turned right into Laugavegur. It was the main touristy street, and I paused for 30 minutes at a Subway sandwich bar, which I reckoned would be way cheaper than any of the local cafés. I bought a special subway of the day and a diet cola, and after my stomach fill and a warm-up, I trekked off again down Laugavegur.

The narrow street was lined with souvenir and clothes shops. I ventured in a few and was shocked to discover that the simplest souvenirs were 1,490 króna (£10.70) each and a T-shirt was 1,990 króna (£14.30). I decided that I would buy as little as possible in Iceland or I would need to re-mortgage my house. I found a Bonus supermarket, which was bustling with locals, and bought a two-litre bottle of water for 109 króna (£0.78), which I thought was exceptionally good value.

Cold and uninspired by the city, I turned up Frakkastígur towards the cathedral. There were mainly residences here, which were more pleasant on the eye. They were mostly fabricated from corrugated pressed-steel sheeting and painted in pretty combinations of colours such as flamingo-pink and grey, sage and white, cobalt-blue or silver.

It was uncomfortably windy at the top of the hill. The cathedral was an unusual modern design, like a grey-cement space shuttle made of Lego pointing to the grey sky. A green copper statue of Leifr Eiríksson towered in front of the cement cathedral, and on the rear, a sign proudly proclaimed that the "Son of Iceland" had discovered the Americas. If so, why hadn't he bothered to inform anyone else in Europe, especially the Spaniards and Portuguese?

Heading back down the hill to Laugavegur, I passed the old Parliament Building, the modern City Hall and finally arrived at a frigid promenade at the compact Lake Tjörnin. Known by the locals as the City Pond, since it was a stretch to call it a lake, its waterfront was thronged with mallard ducks and grey-backed gulls. I then decided that the city was not handsome enough for me to exhaust myself or die of hypothermia, so I should find somewhere warm and cosy to drink a pint of beer.

I headed back up Laekjargata Street and stumbled upon an Irish bar tucked away in a backstreet. I bought a cold pint of Boli Icelandic lager and took a much-needed rest before I wandered back to the hostel and crashed in the basement dormitory.

I slept awfully that night on the upper bunk. The whole frame creaked and shrieked every time I tossed and turned. The mattress seemed fine when I first lay down, but the wadding seemed to disappear under the springs, and I found myself lying on a crunchy bed of coiled springs in the early hours. I tried to lie on the edges of the mattress where there was more wadding but couldn't get comfy. I tried lying on my front with my arms underneath me, but soon enough, my arms began to ache from the metal pressing into them. About 5 a.m. I gave up and went to get a shower.

The basement bathroom seemed clean but was

devoid of anywhere to place toiletries, so I had to secrete them around various nooks and crannies. The shower had lovely hot water, which was unusual for a hostel, but there was an eggy-sulphuric smell when I took my shower. Perhaps the drain U-bend had dried out, I thought.

Today was a big day, for I had booked a Golden Circle Classic Day Trip Tour – which was a bit of a mouthful. The tour would take most of the day and encompassed the main *touristy* sites within a few hours drive of Reykjavik. I drank from my bottle of Bonus mineral water and munched two brioche, which were from a bag of dozen I had bought in Sainsbury's, for my breakfast. Then I walked up Snorrabraut in the drizzle and cold to bus stop 11 outside the Austerbaer Museum.

By 8 a.m., a feeder minibus took me to the Gray Line main bus terminal, where I immediately transferred to the tour coach. I took a seat in the second row behind a guy who looked Afro-American, and at 8:30 a.m. it promptly departed.

The coach drove out of Reykjavik city, along highway 1 then right on to highway 36, which was a battered, pot-holed straight road which passed through marshy land and was virtually undeveloped. We passed Lake Thingvallavatn on our right, the largest lake in Iceland, then eventually reached Thingvallavatn National Park area, which was just 48 kilometres to the east of the capital.

The gap between the American and Eurasian continental plates opened by two centimetres each year, and over tens of thousands of years, it had grown into a rift valley three kilometres wide. As the tectonic plates pulled apart, new magma had risen in hotspots from the earth's mantle to fill the void – much like a scar forms across an open wound. It was estimated that in the last half millennium, Iceland was responsible for a third of all the emitted lava on earth.

We arrived at the Thingvellir National Park office, which overlooked the valley. I climbed the wooden ramp to the observation point and there were amazing views over the valley and Lake Thingvallavatn, which was replenished with the run-off from the surrounding glaciers. The sky was steel-grey from the rain clouds, and the scenery was bizarrely monochromatic with the straw-coloured scrub grass providing the only real colour. The dramatic scenery and dull hues reminded me of the spectacular landscapes of Antarctica and South Georgia.

Great fissures snaked around the park area, which were created by the enormous forces generated as the rift valley slowly split apart. I decided to take a closer look and was peering inside when I realised my hands were red and numb with the cold. The temperature was 4 Celsius and the freezing rain was pelting down. I wondered why the original settlers had chosen to live here in this barren land with utterly awful weather. I couldn't imagine how the Icelanders had tolerated life before cars, central heating and cable television.

After a short while, the bus departed again, and the road continued as a narrow B-road through the marshy and rain-driven landscape. Was the whole country like this, I wondered?

We shortly stopped at the Thingvellir Commonwealth assembly area. It was a 300-metre walk from the bus park on a raised section of rocks overlooking the rift valley to the south. To the north side of the meeting place was a natural rocky wall about three metres high and about 100 metres long – the precise location chosen because of the acoustics that amplified the speaker's voice. This was where the

Icelandic parliament, Althingi, was convened over 1,000 years ago. All very Lord Of The Ringsyish.

I was the last one to board the bus, and the driver was revving his engine to hurry me along. The tour guide was laughing,

'The driver's name is Horses. He will leave without you, huh?'

I knew he wouldn't. But I didn't want to take a chance.

After an expensive coffee stop, where I was served by a miserable-faced Icelandic lady, I chatted to a couple from Nottingham and the guy from the seat in front of me, whose name was Brandon. He was from Trinidad and a resident in New York, and he thought I was from the USA, which made me chuckle. Then we were on the road again.

Even though it was May, the flowers were not yet blooming because Iceland was sub-Arctic tundra. But as we drove further inland, there were wild blueberries, more marshland and less rocks. We crossed a ridge to the east, which was the edge of the North American tectonic plate – we were now driving on the Eurasian plate. It felt like a monumental moment – like passing from one continent to another. Which it was – in a away.

The bus turned left on to highway 365, which was as straight as a die. To the distance on the north side, black basalt mountains were topped with glaciers, snow and ice. The land was a 400 metre-high plain with moss-green-lichen-covered rocks protruding through the snow cover. The land to the foot of the mountains was marshy due to the glacier runoff; boggy and dotted with small pools of water. The dark grey clouds continued to billow overhead in various shades, and showers lashed the bus on and off with great regularity.

After 25 minutes drive, we passed Laugarvatn, which was on the north shore of Lake Laugarvatn – an interesting body of water that didn't freeze in winter due to the geothermal activity underneath.

Thermal power generation was a big thing with the Icelanders who got over half of their total energy requirements courtesy of the volcanic activity under the island. In geothermal plants in the rest of the world, engineers needed to drill 2.5 kilometres down through the earth to tap into useful energy sources. However in Iceland, they could drill just 100 or 200 metres down to get enough kilowatts of energy to heat and provide electricity for a few houses.

By 11:45 a.m., we entered the geyser area 28 kilometres east of Laugarvatn. We drove past the Geysir Visitor Centre towards the Gullfoss Waterfall. The falls were on the Hvítá River (White River), whose source was the Lángjökull Glacier (Long Glacier) about 40 kilometres to the north. This enormous glacier was about 30 kilometres long and over 900 square kilometres in area. It all sounded rather impressive.

I met up with Brandon, and we walked past the café and down a long flight of stairs to a narrow canyon where the Gullfoss Waterfall cascaded down with a huge plume of spray. I was quite surprised by the scale of the waterfall; I had imagined it to be more modest. It was perhaps 30 to 50 metres across and the noise was almost deafening. I descended a gravel path to a natural observation platform of black rock.

The south-flowing river made a sharp turn west above the falls and flowed turbulently over a wide stone staircase right in front of me. Then it plunged over the next drop of about 10 metres – then another – then the final drop of 30 metres into a canyon. The sight was breathtaking.

The canyon was a couple of kilometres in length, and the plume of spray from the final plunge billowed above the canyon. I stayed and watched the bigger plunge for a while but was getting absolutely soaked from the spray.

Next, we went to the geyser itself, or *geysir* in Icelandic, which was a few minutes drive away. The bus stopped at the visitor centre, and Brandon and I crossed the main road to the trail up the hillside.

To the left were streams of hot sulphuric water trickling down from the geyser pools, and they fed several small pools, which steamed away merrily. The ground was a variety of colours due to the minerals brought up to the ground: red from red clay, white from gypsum and green from something or other, which was green under the earth. The water was 100 to 120 Celsius and formed steam as it escaped the fissures in the ground.

The stream area was roped off, and small 'Keep off the grass'-type signs were posted at the rope with a symbol of a hand being burnt in 100 Celsius water.

'Do you think it's hot?' asked Brandon pointing to one stream, 'I can't see any steam from this one. I reckon it's not very hot.'

'Er. I wouldn't chance it,' I shuddered, 'I don't want a layer of skin to peel off my hand,' I replied.

Brandon was braver – or more reckless – than me, for he suddenly stepped on the red mud and placed his hand into the stream. I waited for him to scream, but fortunately, he didn't. He turned towards me and beamed while waving his wet but scald-free hand.

'Come on. Let's go and see the geyser before you find some really hot water to burn yourself,' I told him.

Up the track was the Little Geyser, which seemed to be dormant, then another 100 metres up the track was an area the size of a basketball court and was roped off to stop tourists from getting scalded in the mother itself – The Great Geyser. We stood at the north side and waited – and waited. After about eight minutes, there was an almighty whoosh and the spray shot 20 metres in the air.

'Whoooaah,' we shouted in unison together. The plume initially erupted as a telephone-box-sized phallic shape, then within a second or two, expanded to a cylindrical jet the size of small windmill tower. Then the shape collapsed as the whoosh stopped, and the cloud of mist transformed into a small cloud which dispersed randomly in the cold wind gusts.

'Shall we watch another?' I asked.

'How about we watch it from up there?' suggested Brandon pointing up the hill.

We walked further up the trail where several mineral pools the size of a jacuzzi were steaming with navy-blue and emerald-green minerals deep in the clear water. Then we faced towards The Great Geyser down the hill and waited. And waited. And waited some more. When it blew, the noise was more like a fizzling whoosh from that distance, and the steam dispersed into a large cloud.

'Ours was way better than that one, wasn't it?' said Brandon.

'Yeah. That one was trash,' I replied.

After perusing the visitor centre, we visited the village of Skálholt before the bus headed back to Reykjavik. I was soggy and tired but had thoroughly enjoyed the sights. I checked my Facebook account to find my brother was rabbiting on about eating puffins.

'Your task of the day. Find and eat puffin heart (local delicacy I believe).'

I thought a while then tapped Brandon on the

shoulder in front of me.

'Do you fancy eating puffin?' I asked him.

'Sure. Why not. Do they eat them?' he replied.

'Maybe,' I replied, 'my brother seems to think so. Let me Google it.'

I Googled 'eat puffin in Iceland' and got quite a few hits from Tripadvisor.

'I think we could be having puffin and French fries tonight,' I updated Brandon. He looked at me with a worried look.

'Er. Okay. If you like,' he hesitated.

It seemed that Brandon had limits to his adventurousness. He was exceedingly well-travelled – having been to many interesting places such as China – but he was still an American. Their idea of being adventurous with food was putting an extra patty in their burger. I found a well-rated restaurant on TripAdvisor called Grillmarkt and agreed with Brandon that we would meet there at 6 p.m.

After the 45 minute drive back to the city, we were dropped at bus stop 10 and I bade goodbye to Brandon. Back at the hostel, I downed as much water as I could, checked in online for my flight to Oslo then set off in the dreary conditions again. This was utterly miserable weather – way worse than Manchester – which was the dreary rain capital of England. The rain had been off and on by the minute since I had arrived. The only time it hadn't rained was the initial flurry of hailstone when I had arrived in Keflavik Airport.

The walk was longer than I had expected; perhaps a 25-minute walk. I observed the grey and miserable-looking residences along the way. They were typically two storeys with a half-sunken basement. The walls were pebble-dashed and faded to various shades of colour ranging from linen to vomit. All the windows appeared to be single glazed, which surprised me.

One thing that puzzled me was that half of the windows were left wide open. It was a chilly 4 Celsius outside – why would you let all the heat out – unless you were a Scandinavian millionaire with money to burn? I then recalled that the homes in Iceland were heated by geothermal water from underground. Around 90 per cent of Iceland's homes were heated this way – all for a fraction of the energy cost of the rest of Scandinavia.

I guess there were no controls for the stifling heat, so residents resorted to opening their windows to control the temperature. I pondered all that energy literally going out of the window, but then I recalled on my visit to Geysir, that the underground thermal vents were blowing hot steam into the atmosphere. There was lots of steam to go around.

Soon enough, I was at the crossroads of Bank and Laekjargata streets where the Prime Minister's Office stood. I crossed Laekjargata and found The Grillmarkadurinn Restaurant located behind an Italian restaurant with a smoking chiminea outside.

Inside, a pleasant greeter took my ski jacket and didn't bat an eyelid despite me being dressed in dirty hiking boots and jeans, which were unbefitting of a classy restaurant. The interior had dim mood lighting with rows of young birch logs for artificial walls, an open kitchen grill to my right and a sweeping spiral staircase leading to basement seating. I asked her to wait a while until my companion arrived, and soon enough, Brandon arrived in a sweat. He had ran most of the way from his hotel.

'You're puffin' for your puffin,' I told him.

'I think we're gonna have a whale of a time,' he replied.

We followed the waitress downstairs to our reserved table and were presented menus by a bearded and balding young fellow, who cheerfully greeted us.

'I'm fine with what you are having,' quipped Brandon.

'Are you sure? Let me read the menu to you. How about the grilled puffin with wild preserved blueberries for appetiser?' I suggested.

Brandon looked like he was about to jump out of a window – I could almost see a bead of sweat running down his forehead.

'I think that's okay,' he agreed.

Then I continued, 'we could have the grilled minke whale steak with Icelandic wasabi and soy sauce for another appetiser. Shall we share?'

Brandon made a slight whining noise, 'if that's what you want,' he agreed hesitantly.

I didn't think that Brandon was cracked up to be an exotic dish eater.

'Fantastic,' I confirmed,

Brandon let me choose the main course. There were no exotic mains, but the locally caught cod, salmon and flounder fish board sounded wonderful, so I ordered it from Beardy-Baldy-Waiter, along with two 40cl glasses of draft Viking White Beer.

'Cheers!'

After some sourdough bread slices with salted butter, the appetisers arrived. The smoked puffin was cut into small breast flanks the size of a lower lip and presented in a bowl of blueberry sauce and tiny vivid-purple blueberries. The whale meat was about the size of a butcher's sausage and laid on a stainless steel hot grill with spruce box sides. A clump of wasabi accompanied it with an eggcup-sized pouring dish of soy sauce sprinkled with chilli seeds.

Brandon didn't want to dig in and asked me to serve him – his hesitation was as evident as my absence of trepidation. I served us two chunks of puffin and berries each.

'Here goes,' I remarked as I popped one chunk into my mouth. I tried to savour and analyse the taste without laughing at Brandon, who grimaced with every chew.

'That's awful – it's like rubber,' grumbled Brandon.

'It's not that awful – it's like duck,' I tried to encourage him.

Indeed, it was like rubbery duck – very lightly cooked and with purple-brown flesh. I couldn't fully chew it into shreds and I swallowed the chunks. Then I caught an after-taste of fish, and we looked each other in the eye. Beardy-Baldy-Waiter returned.

'The puffins eat lots of small fish for their diet, so you may taste the meat is a little fishy,' he informed us.

'It tastes like sardines,' groaned Brandon.

'Yes, I think that's the name of the fish,' added the waiter, 'did you try the minke yet?'

'Not yet,' I replied. Beardy-Baldy-Waiter gave a slight bow and whisked away again.

'Time for some whale next,' I challenged Brandon, who looked as if he was thinking about asking for a sick bucket.

I cut two strips of the red-brown meat off the grill and placed them on his plate. Then the same on mine. We dabbed a dash of soy sauce each then Brandon looked at me hesitantly again.

'Come on – one, two, three,' I encouraged him. His mouth screwed up as he took his second chew.

'Oh no! That's *too* smokey,' he remarked.

The meat was tender but tasted very earthy and smokey with a wisp of fish flavour. It wasn't completely unpleasant – but it was definitely an acquired taste.

'I think this is roadkill,' I laughed.

I kept force-feeding Brandon, but he struggled and ate only a third of what I did. A few sips of the cloudy-white beer helped to wash down the whale meat, then we were ready for the main course. Brandon looked as if he was at a cannibal feast. The main course was delicious, and we skipped desserts and finished our beers. Brandon was still sweating as we stepped out into the chilly but light evening.

'Man. That was unreal,' he sighed, 'I couldn't eat that again.'

We ambled back to Snorrabraut Street via the concrete cathedral and shopping backstreets chatting about geopolitics, crime and Donald Trump. We bought some souvenirs along the way, then I shook his hand and bade him farewell.

Back at the hostel basement dorm, it was unwelcomingly hot despite the window being open in a futile effort to offset the ancient iron radiator, which was spewing enough geothermal heat to melt the Ross Ice Shelf. A slightly built Dutch youth had arrived and was appointed the single bed next to the enormous radiator. He stood there perplexed with one hand on it.

'It's not super hot, but man, it's just too warm. What can I do?' he warbled.

'Wear as little as possible and don't use the quilt,' I suggested.

I prepared my backpack for the morning, changed into my sleeping T-shirt and shorts then crawled on to my top bunk. The bedsprings crunched and the metal bed frame squeaked in protest as I got myself into position. I barely slept any better on my second night as the springs dug into my thighs and lower back.

The time was 6 a.m., and I couldn't suffer the murderous mattress any longer. I took a sulphuric-water shower, checked out and took the Gray Lines bus to the airport.

It was a rather uneventful end to my trip. I had seen quite a portion of Iceland on my short visit, from the lunar-like west to the glaciers, national parks, waterfalls and geysers. On reflection, the capital city was uninspiring and lacked charm, but this was compensated by the stunning natural scenery and the plucky Icelandic folk, who persevered the rotten weather to give a smile and make me feel welcome to their island in the middle of the North Atlantic.

That was European country number 49; two more to go, I thought to myself in glee.

And Iceland was country number 97. I was nervously close to my target.

14: A Stone's Throw to North Pole

Svalbard (No. 98)

For those unfamiliar, Svalbard is a bunch of islands located inside the Arctic Circle. *Way* inside the Arctic Circle. Imagine you were to travel to the northernmost country in mainland Europe, Norway. Then travel to its northernmost inhabited settlement on the European continent, Skarsvåg. At latitude 71 degrees 08 minutes north, Skarsvåg is 492 kilometres inside the Arctic Circle. Then keep heading north, and halfway between Skarsvåg and the North Pole is Svalbard – a frozen landscape that means 'Cold Coast' in Old Norse language.

Is it really another country, you may ask? The islands were tussled over by whalers of various European nations in the early seventeenth century – including England, Holland, France, Denmark and Norway. Following the whaling boom, mining arrived in the early twentieth century, and USA, Russia and Sweden also piled into the affray. Everybody wanted a piece of the action.

This was all sorted out in 1920 with a treaty which ceded sovereignty to Norway, but the mining rights were still doled out to every man and his husky. So there you go – Svalbard belonged to Norway. However, it was still listed as a territory by the United Nations: distinct from Norway. So it would have to be included in my list of countries and territories.

I flew from Reykjavik to Oslo, Norway, in preparation for my flight to the far north. Oslo was simply stunning in early May, and I stayed at the Gardermoen Airport Hotel and sat in the outdoor terrace with a gloriously blue sky and temperatures of 20 Celsius. I nursed a pint of Ringnes Norwegian lager for two hours because it cost me the price of a laptop computer.

I went to bed early – my first night in a comfortable bed on this trip. After two nights of tossing and turning on a bed of coils in a basement dormitory in Reykjavik, the spongy mattress and starched linen of the airport hotel was blissful joy. But I still could not sleep soundly – my mind was excited by the next leg of my journey – and I was also worried about missing the flight.

I gave up trying to sleep at 4:40 a.m., got washed and dressed then went down to the hotel restaurant for my breakfast. No munching on Sainsbury's brioche today, I thought. Bacon. Fried eggs. Baked beans. Sausages. That'll do nicely, I daydreamed as I descended in the lift.

Downstairs in the restaurant, I realised my worst fears – it was a European breakfast. A basket of lukewarm boiled eggs, dark rye bread, sliced peppers, liver pate, sliced ham, salami and cheese. What was wrong with them? No wonder the Viking Empire collapsed – they couldn't even rustle up a decent breakfast.

I disdainfully ate some mini-croissants, two boiled eggs and a slice of white toast. I grumbled at the waitress and she laughed at me heartily. I supposed I was not the first whinging Englishman who complained about the lack of a decent breakfast. Ah well.

The airport shuttle ran every 20 minutes from 4 a.m., so I was not too worried about the mile-long trip back to Goedermen Airport. I checked in at an efficient kiosk in the terminal, attached my printer luggage tag on my backpack and scanned it myself at the bag drop conveyor belt. Watched afar from Norwegian Airline staff – who filed their nails while I did all the work – I went through to the departures.

Inside, the electronic departure board advised that flight DY396 would depart from the international departure zone for non-European Union flights. Why wasn't it a European Union flight? It didn't even depart from the domestic zone.

I made my way to gate zone F and entered passport control. An enormous queue of about a hundred travellers waited in the queue marked 'European Union'. I looked at the 'All Passports' queue; there were only two passengers who waited. The UK was in the process of leaving the European Union, so I decided to demand my rights to not be a European Union Citizen. I sauntered past the long queue of folk proudly holding their identical red passports and walked straight to the front of the 'All Passports' queue. I then handed my passport to the immigration lady.

'We are Brexiting, so I want to use this queue,' I smiled to her.

'No problem,' she smiled back.

'Why do I need to go through passport control to fly to Svalbard,' I asked in confusion, 'I thought the territory belonged to Norway.'

'It is international,' she replied, 'there are Norwegians, Russians. Everybody.'

'Ah. Okay,' I replied.

There was my answer. It seemingly belonged to Norway but was treated as a separate country due to the

Russians. I think.

Just a few seconds later she waved me through.

At 8:25 a.m. the gate was open for boarding. I stood in the queue and recalled my flight from Punta Arenas to Puerto Williams at the southernmost tip of South America en route to Antarctica. I remembered observing my fellow passengers on that flight – wondering why they were flying to the end of the earth. Were they intrepid tourists? Or government officials sent to shuffle papers down there to reinforce sovereignty? Mercenaries?

This flight to Svalbard was just as remote. It would fly closer to the North Pole than my flight to Puerto Williams was to the South Pole. I took my seat 13D and observed my fellow passengers. Many were Norwegians dressed in tourist attire who cheerily greeted each other and the cabin attendants with a '*Hei hei*'. Some spoke in Russian, and a few looked like President Putin – so were probably Russian. A handful of blonde-haired Scandinavian kids of junior school age and a few roughneck types completed the manifest.

The Boeing 737-800 swiftly filled, and only a few seats remained empty. The seating capacity was 186, and I counted around 20 empty seats so there had to be as many as 166 on the flight. The official population of Svalbard was 2,214, so it was going to increase by 7.5% with this one flight. Svalbard was triple the landmass of Wales but with a smaller population than the village of Llanfairpwllgwyngyllgogerychwyrndrobwllllantysiliogogogoch.

This was my second flight on Norwegian Air Shuttle, and I was impressed by their level of service. There was no standing in boarding queues like infant school children. You weren't charged £40 for the flight and another £50 for your check-in baggage – it was all-inclusive. Nor was there intense scrutiny of your hand luggage in case it is was an ounce or an inch over the airline policy. Passengers on Norwegian were treated like grown-ups – and nobody took advantage in return. My only grumble was that the coffee wasn't free, unlike SAS, and the seats were as thin as an ironing board despite their posh appearance and leather covers. I had had a stiff back after my flight to Oslo, so in preparation, I had put on several layers of clothes and wore my double-layer winter coat to cushion my poor old spine.

The flight departed a little late at 9:25 a.m. and ascended into the brilliant sunshine. I bristled with excitement; country number 98 was in my grasp, and I hadn't given Andy a clue. Although, if he was sharp enough, he could spot my Facebook posting of the ghastly breakfast at the Gardermoen Airport Hotel. Would he spot that one, I thought?

I soon dozed off and was awoken with a jolt. One of the cabin crew was laughing and joking heartily with the passengers. I popped to the toilet, and on my way back to my seat, took the opportunity to chat with him.

'When did Norwegian start running flights to Svalbard,' I asked him.

'Oh, two years ago. They are really popular,' he informed me, 'there are lots of tourists going there. And this is the right time to go – the weather is beautiful with the sun. It's a bit scary to land in the winter when the weather is bad.'

'Did you stay there as a tourist?' I continued.

'Sure. I love the place. Are you going to see polar bears?' he asked.

'I hope I don't encounter any when I'm walking about,' I replied.

'Watch out the windows,' he suggested, 'sometimes

you can see them on the final descent. Keep an eye out, huh?'

I thanked him and returned to my row 13, which was all mine for the taking, and shifted from the aisle seat to the windows seat so I could look for polar bears.

By 10:30 a.m., the aircraft had left the mainland behind and I watched the fjords and snow-capped brown mountains fade into the distance. I was over the Barents Sea, and except for Svalbard, there was nothing else until the North Pole. The Norwegian flight advertised that it had free Wi-Fi access, but I couldn't get it to work.

'Excuse me,' I asked the laughing cabin attendant, 'the Wi-Fi doesn't seem to work.'

'Sorry about that,' he apologised, 'we are getting closer to Russian military installations so it has to be turned off.'

Shucks.

My first impression of Svalbard as the 737-800 approached the runway was its striking similarity to South Georgia: steep black mountains shrouded in glaciers. The plane landed soundly then did a U-turn off the runway towards the terminal. After the usual kerfuffle of passengers getting their act together, I walked out to the airstairs and was hit by a chilling breeze. It wasn't that cold, reportedly minus 1 Celsius, but it was certainly a surprise to me given the sunny spring weather I had been basking in back in England and Oslo.

After crossing the apron and entering the terminal, I collected my backpack from the single baggage carousel swiftly in a few minutes. The terminal was diminutive with the main arrival hall a little larger than the size of a tennis court. There was a governor's office and a car rental booth, but there were no shops. No tourist information desk. There wasn't even any passport control, which surprised me – I was free to enter the territory with no checks whatsoever. I supposed they knew who was arriving based upon the flight manifest, anyhow.

Despite no transport desk or tourist desk, I walked out of the terminal and was fortunate to discover that two airport shuttle buses were waiting outside.

'Guesthouse 102?' I asked the driver of the front bus.

'No. No. Behind,' he pointed at the other bus, 'route number four.'

The second driver confirmed this was indeed the bus heading in the right direction. I stowed my backpack, paid the 120 kroner (£11) fare and boarded. Within a moment, the SAS shuttle bus roared off, and I was left to absorb the scenery as it flew past. The roads were part tarmac part stone chippings, and the sides of the roads were mostly mud and compacted snow.

The bus passed the dockyard, turned right at the Longyearbyen town centre then drove up the valley along the wide road towards the coal miners' cabins. The road was marked with red canes like a ski run so that under snowcover the drivers didn't go off-piste. To the right was a secondary road, which I assumed was for snowmobiles.

The buildings were standard Scandinavian stock: painted in dull colours and with large Lego-style windows. They were mounted five feet off the ground with grey wooden slats covering the lower area, and wooden or metal-grilled steps leading up to the front doors. I assumed the clearance was to cater for deep snowfalls so the windows and doors would not be buried under snowdrifts.

The bus made one stop before performing a U-turn

at the top of the hill among the coal miner's huts. They were a cluster of two-storey cabins where the miners formerly lodged, and they had been sold to various businesses.

'Coal Miners Bar. Guesthouse 102,' shouted the driver as he applied the air-brakes.

He dashed off the bus and rapidly plucked all the baggage from the luggage hold. I found my backpack and paid him 120 Norwegian kroner (£11) for a return ticket.

'Which way is the Guesthouse 102?' I asked.

The driver pointed back up the hill to an amber-coloured miners cabin.

'*Takk*,' I thanked him then crunched 20 metres up the gravelly path to the guesthouse. There was a policy of no boots inside in the guesthouse, so I took mine off and presented my passport to the Thai *receptionista*. I was presented a key for dormitory room 7110, and I dropped my backpack there and realised that the only free bed was, again, the upper bunk. That should frighten my bunkmates, I thought.

I thanked the *receptionista*.

'How far is it to town?' I asked her.

'Over two kilometres. It will take you about 25 minutes walk,' she replied, 'it's okay. But the walk back...' she shook her head and tutted.

'Is it safe to walk?' I asked, 'I mean, are there any polar bears?'

'No polar bears [were] in town [for] two years. No worry,' she reassured me.

Nevertheless, I was still nervous. Svalbard was polar bear land; there were more of them than human residents. They were second only to grizzly bears in ferocity – up to eight times the weight of a man – and not frightened of humans. Svalbard law mandated that you couldn't leave the settlement without at least a 0.308 calibre rifle to protect against polar bears. I didn't own a rifle and the creatures could sprint at up to 25 miles per hour. I would be polar bear snacks before you could shout 'Ursus maritimus behind you!'

I thanked her and headed off down the valley. I passed miner's cabins painted in colours such as tangerine, teal and clay-red. A ditch ran parallel to the main road and was occupied with an old wooden conveyor belt that formerly hauled coal from the mines. I noticed former mine-workings halfway up the ice-strewn mountainside: wooden huts, conveyor belts and pylons all precariously clinging to the steep slope.

I passed a lady in yeti boots walking up the hill, and as she levelled with me, I noticed that she had a rifle slung over her shoulder. She was obviously not a tourist, so I supposed the threat of polar bears was higher than the *receptonista* had alluded to. I decided to hasten my walk and looked over my shoulder time to time in case a hungry polar bear had identified me as a large feast.

At the lower end of the valley were many residential houses – each with snowmobiles parked outside. They seemed to be laid up for the impending summer: some were mounted on wooden pallets but others had seen better days and looked knackered.

I passed the secondary school, which looked like a blue warehouse, then the primary school where the pupils were on their lunch-break and ran amok in the snow-covered playground. I supposed that they had grown bored of snowball fights a long, long time ago. I eventually reached the main town and joined the old main road, which was twisted and in a bit of disrepair.

The CO-OP supermarket was open, so I entered and had a look about. I bought a half-bottle of Svalbard

Vodka as a gift for my son, which it claimed was made from pure glacial water on the island. The sale of liquor was restricted, and the store had to keep a record of who was buying how much. I had to present my passport and flight ticket to be allowed to buy the bottle. Some souvenir fridge magnets made me smile – they had a polar bear picture with the legend 'Keep Calm and Play Dead'. Good advice in case they return to the town, I thought.

Back outside, a storm was brewing. The wind whistled like a winter gale and the thick snowfall blew almost horizontally down the main road. I zipped up every flap and plodded past the CO-OP to a tiny shopping centre. I bought a Svalbard T-shirt from a souvenir store inside then found an inviting coffee shop, the Fruene Café. I took a simple lunch of a cheese sandwich and a brewed coffee. The coffee was only 25 kroner (£2.30), which I thought was pretty darned reasonable for the Arctic Circle. Then I was back on the road.

Most of the residential houses were clustered in small estates around the town area. Some had Dutch-barn-style roofs in bright colours, whereas most others were larger and painted dull grey. I proceeded on, but with the storm worsening considerably, I decided to take a look inside the post office and the local bank, Sparebank 1, which were co-located in the same building. The glass front doors had a sign prohibiting rifles and handguns, which reminded me again to look over my shoulder for polar bears.

I was astonished to find a cash machine inside the lobby, and on its display screen it said 'Welcome to the world's northernmost cash machine'. Well, I just had to try it, naturally. After a lady bumped in front of me, I entered my UK cash card and successfully withdrew

200 Norwegian kroner (£18.40). I was mightily impressed – this was the closest cash machine to the North Pole – and it worked perfectly.

I passed a further clutch of shops, then after a few hundred metres bleak walk in the snowstorm, I reached The University Centre in Svalbard (UNIS), which was billed as the world's northernmost higher-education institution. These northernmost things were getting a bit repetitive. And sometimes tiresome. What next? The northernmost toilet in the world? Which contains the northernmost toilet roll? And the closest toilet brush to the North Pole? Officially though, Longyearbyen laid claim to the northernmost school as well as church, commercial airport and museum.

I thought I might have a look at the museum, which was co-located with the university, but couldn't find the entrance. By now, the blizzard was seriously worsening, and I decided to take cover. Where else but the bar?

I walked to the Radisson Blue Hotel and entered the comfort of the Barentz Pub and Spiseri, which was a cosy respite. I ordered a pint of Mack lager, which was brewed in Tromsø, and took the opportunity to warm up and dry my stuff. Time went by and the blizzard persisted, so I ordered a fish and chips for 145 kroner (£13.30), which I thought was wonderful value for a bar meal just 650 miles from the North Pole. Tucking into my delicious battered cod and sipping another pint of Mack lager, I figured out that I was closer to the North Pole than the road from London to John O'Groats. This was as north as it got.

After several hours, the storm seemed to weaken somewhat, so I decided to take the opportunity to return to my miner's barracks. I was not relishing the thought of the long trek back up the valley. I buckled myself up, press-studded each flap then braved the elements. The first kilometre wasn't too bad, with occasional gusts which blew down my coat hood. But once I was out of Longyearbyen town proper and was heading up the narrow valley, the wind whipped up and the snowfall became heavy enough to affect visibility.

The road was thick with snow and slippery underfoot, and I started to worry that an oncoming car may skid into me. Or maybe I would fall into the ditch? Or a marauding polar bear might take advantage of the snow cover and ambush me? I kept my head down to avoid the snow blowing into my face allowed my mind to wander on a vast array of remote possibilities that might stop me getting back to the safety of my hostel bunk.

I noticed footprints from some other intrepid – or foolhardy – pedestrian along the edge of the road, so I decided to follow them. The wind picked up so strongly that I had to hold my hood with one hand to prevent it from blowing off. After about 40 minutes of following the footprints in the blizzard, I made it up the valley and could see the orange cabin of 102 Gjestehuset.

Inside the hostel, the temperature was very cosy indeed. A Filipino lady manned the reception and told me that she had been employed there for five months. I felt sorry for her being so far from the tropical climate of the Philippines – she was almost 90% of the way to the North Pole.

I went to my room, 7110, where a young European fellow was stretched out on the lower bunk reading a book. He greeted me with some hesitation, then I noticed that he had moved my coat to the foot of the bed and grabbed every nook and cranny in the room to hang his stuff. I grumbled under my breath – I think he understood the word 'idiot' – and it embarrassed him to move his junk off my upper bunk.

The space-grabber was from Brussels and had been hiking the mountains and taken a walrus wildlife tour. He seemed a nice chap after all. In true Scandinavian style, my bedsheets were placed in a pile, and I had to struggle to make my bed. Then I laid down and listened to Queen on my smartphone. It was now the polar summer, and sunlight was shining 24 hours a day and leaking through our curtains, which made it impossible for me to sleep properly. I dozed off, and at some point in the night, two young girls sneaked in and took the opposite bunk beds. So I tried my best not to snore and emit gases in their company.

Morning came, and the highlight of my journey beckoned – the husky sledging. It was an expensive treat, at 1,350 kroner (£124) for a half-day, but I was expecting it to be an incredible experience. I arose at 6 a.m., showered in the large and clean bathroom, and noisily gathered my stuff together. I was warned by the husky company to wrap up with extra layers, so I put on my thermal long johns, thermal top over my T-shirt and two pairs of socks. Next, I wore a windproof shell jacket, acrylic cardigan and my double-layer Columbia coat. Six layers seemed rather excessive, but I could remove layers if necessary.

I waited outside, and just after 8 a.m., a crew bus arrived with a Green Dog Svalbard logo on it. I clambered inside the middle row.

'Hi. Name please,' asked the lady driver with mousey hair.

'Rice,' I replied.

She studied the papers on her clipboard, 'Ah yes. Rice Colin. I see. My name is Greta,' she said in a German accent, 'you are the only one for the journey today. So, we will go straight to Bolterdale.'

It transpired that Greta was Swiss and had only worked for the company a month. We drove downhill to the Longyearbyen town centre then right on to a raised highway, which passed marshy tundra with the odd white reindeer dotted here and there. After ten minutes drive, Greta turned right off the road and we parked in front of a compound surrounded by chain metal fencing. Inside were eight rows of dog kennels raised on stilts and each a little home to a husky dog. The dogs yelped and jumped as I alighted from the minibus; they knew they were going out for a ride.

'Follow,' Greta beckoned me, and we entered a Portakabin.

'Okay. Welcome to Green Dog. Please get your clothes from here,' she pointed to a rail of high-visibility yellow jumpsuits, baskets of leather mitts joined by string and fur hats with ear-flaps.

'You put on the mitts like this,' she demonstrated the cord loop over her head, 'then thread them through your sleeves like a kindergarten child so they don't get lost.'

Greta helped me to select a neck gaiter and Arctic muck boots then left me to kit up. I took off my winter coat because I had more layers than a wedding cake, then I met Greta in the compound where she was placing a red harness on one of the dogs.

'This dog is Power. This is how you put on the harness,' she demonstrated.

She made it seem simple, and I was given a handful of harnesses for the other huskies. I attempted to harness my first dog, a sand-coloured one called Jersey, but got her into a complete tangle. It got easier with practice. Greta then showed me how to unchain a dog from the kennel chain and walk them to the wooden sledge parked outside the compound. The other dogs went ballistic as I led Jersey outside, and some of them snapped at her in jealousy because they were not getting a chance to go for a run.

'Yah!' I shouted at the top of my voice, which seemed to calm them momentarily.

Greta then showed me how to tether Jersey to the end of the long wire harness, which was attached to the sledge. I waited with the two front dogs while Greta hooked up eight other animals. The back two were Power and Firefly; two enormous male dogs who were clearly the strongest. In the middle were two bitches: a sand-coloured one called Sandy and a black-and-white one called Barbie, who evidently didn't get along with each other. Barbie howled with excitement, which caused Sandy to growl and head-butt her.

'I have to keep these apart,' noted Greta as she hooked up Sandy further along the chain.

I sat down on the wooden sledge, and she led the front pair in a U-turn to face up the valley.

'*Deeba, deeba*,' Greta shouted in a high shrill voice, and the long harness of ten huskies looped around and yanked the sledge into action. The harness took the strain and straightened itself out, then Greta hopped on the back of the sledge and whooped more secret husky words to them.

The sledge glided and scraped across the six-inch deep snow and baldy patches of grassy tundra to pick up a steady pace of about a fast jog. I had somehow expected it to be faster, but the sledge twisted and bounced in and out of the potholes and patches of slush, which would have flipped the sledge if we were running any faster.

Away from the din of the remaining 54 dogs in the compound, there was silence except for the scraping of the sledge runners and occasional yelps of the dogs. The black and snow-covered cliffs towered a thousand feet over the valley – scarred by the glaciers that had created them a millennium ago.

After five minutes, Greta shouted '*stoppa*' in a low tone of voice and halted the sledge.

'Okay. It is your turn to mush,' she told me.

She showed me how to press the sledge brake with my foot, throw the anchor then retrieve and how to firmly hold on to the sled.

'You *never* let go,' Greta warned me, 'they will run away with the sled.'

Greta tramped through the deep snow to Power and Firefly at the front and beckoned them along, then she shouted at me.

'Push!' she shrieked.

I took my right leg off the sledge footplate, gave a push then the sledge creaked into action and we were off. It was an indescribable feeling to control the sledge and watch the long line of huskies yelping and pulling us along.

'Keep the line tight,' hollered Greta, 'brake if it is loose.'

She sat on the sledge and called out to the front dogs to change direction. Left. Right, in some Swiss gibberish language that must have made sense to her – or the mushing community. She commanded them to run slowly, fast and get a move on. The sledge started running up a slope parallel to the run, which caused Greta considerable alarm.

'Lean to the left side! Lean to the left!' shouted Greta.

After that, I got the hang of it. It could be steered by leaning heavily on the left footplate and vice versa: the opposite to skiing. It was vital to maintain a steady pace and keep the harness line taut, and if it started to droop then brake so the dogs would pull it taut again.

It was hilarious to watch the huskies urinate or defecate. Power got into the crouch position and started to do his business, and he hopped along as he was dragged by the others.

'Brake a little if they need to take a shit,' shouted Greta.

Urinating was much easier for them. Some dogs managed to pee and hop along while they squatted, but the middle two bitches seemed to be troublemakers who wanted stop and take their time. I had to slow the sledge to allow them to pee but keep the sledge in motion.

After a while, we reached a slushy river of glacier run-off, and Greta shouted at the dogs to take a crossing where it was shallow. Power and Firefly decided to jump straight into the broadest and deepest bit to Greta's exasperation.

'Stoooop!' hollered Greta.

I had trouble stopping because the lead dogs were now in the middle of the shallow river. They were up to their chests in freezing water and wanted to get out, but the harnesses had become tangled in the fracas.

'Stand with both your legs on the brake!' Greta shrieked while she waded in the freezing stream to unhook four of the tangled hounds. She unhooked them one at a time and tethered them to the harness again. When they were in a straight line again, Greta shouted.

'Sloow...ly...' she shouted to me then in husky-doggy-language to the pack. Slowly, each pair pulled out of the frigid stream until they were all free. I thought the sledge would sink in the stream, but it somehow floated across the slushy ice-water and we were on the way again.

'You are good at this,' Greta shouted as she hopped

back on the sledge.

'Its a bit like skiing,' I shouted back, 'just bend your knees and keep your balance.

I mushed the sledge for about five kilometres with no interruptions until Greta hopped off, then she walked Power and Firefly in a U-turn as I pressed the brake gently.

'Okay. Now we go downhill. You need to keep the speed down and the harness line straight,' she lectured me.

The downhill run was immense fun since I had got the hang of controlling the sledge and dogs. I ran the seven kilometres back down the valley, which was exhilarating. At one point, about halfway down, we were faced with three approaching sledges from another party. The riders were dressed in bright yellow waterproofs and each sledge had six dogs. Without question, there was going to be massive trouble if the dog sledges met each other.

'We must steer up the slope to let them pass,' shouted Greta.

She hopped off and led Power and Firefly by their collars to the left up a slope and gripped them tightly as we waved through the other sledges. When they had passed, she talked to the dogs in husky-doggy-language and we were off on a straight run again.

As the compound came into view, the dogs gained a renewed vigour and powered onwards to reach home.

'We go in slow – push the brake firmly,' shouted Greta, 'walking pace only – then stop just short of the entrance. Don't let the sledge go inside the compound.'

I laughed to myself as I imagined a runaway sledge hurtling into the compound and the dogs breaking out into a huge fight. I had to push with all my might on the brake to restrict the excitable animals to a walking pace, and my legs were now tired from two hours of knee-bending, pressing the brake and balancing the sled.

I stopped the sledge exactly as instructed and was rather proud of myself. I stood on the brake with all my weight while Greta hooked some loops of tugboat rope over the sledge rails to stop it moving. She then calmed down the dogs while I parked the sledge with the dangerous-looking, pointed red anchor.

Greta taught me how to unharness the dogs by unhooking the dog from the rear snap-hook, pulling the harness to their shoulders then lifting each leg in turn out. Then the final step was to pull the harness over their head, which was not easy because it was a tight fit over their ears.

I unharnessed Power and Firefly and chuckled to myself as they nuzzled my ear while I leant over them.

'Good boys,' I calmed them.

After they were all unharnessed, we took them back one-by-one to be chained up at their kennels, and I gave each of them a praise and ear rub. They were lovely animals and massively excited to have had a run.

'Here,' Greta shouted, 'they have a snack each.'

I walked across to two large plastic tubs at her feet and peered in to find them full of fish, each one about a pound in weight.

'Give one each,' Greta told me.

I grabbed ten fish and walked along the line of dogs, which had been out for the run, and the whole compound exploded into furious barking and jumped at the opportunity for a snack.

After that, I got changed in the Portakabin and felt quite knackered. Greta drove me up the hill along a precarious cinder track to another compound and parked among a line of other dirty vans.

'This is where we breed the dogs. These puppies

are about six months old now. When they are nine months old we train them. Then at the age of one year, we can start to let them go for a run with the experienced dogs.'

Several black puppies bounded across to me, a little cautious of my hand movements, and enjoyed a stroke and ear rub.

'Come, take a drink,' Greta led me to a log cabin where there were two log tables and bench seats.

I made myself a hot cocoa and ate two cookies for energy, while Greta chatted about husky sledging competitions in Norway and Canada including the 1,200-kilometre Finnmarksløpet race, which sounded like a gruelling journey taking five days. She seemed to love the sport and was living her dream.

It was time to go, and I said goodbye to the playful pups and Greta drove me back to the Gjesthuset 102 in Longyearbyen. I was shattered from all the exercise. I washed all the smells of husky dogs and dead fish off my hands and took a coffee in the kitchen of the guest house before going out to eat.

There was only one choice at this end of town. The Coalminer's Cabins was across the road from the guest house, which was another miner's barracks converted into a hotel. I found the bar-restaurant on the ground floor opposite the reception, where I chose a comfortable table and ordered a cheeseburger and a diet cola. The Coalminer's was far too comfortable, for I dozed off while doing some typing on my laptop and awoke with a start.

It was a pleasant lounge with rock music playing, so I decided to rest there rather than walk into town or return to the guesthouse, which was a bit niffy with teenagers and smelly socks.

I drank a celebratory Mack lager, then soon

enough, it was 5 p.m. and I ordered a pulled-pork tortilla. I was sat at a large window facing the southwest, and the sun shone brilliantly. It was steadily moving closer into direct view, but at the same time, it was gradually setting on the horizon as a couple of hours passed. Then I started to wonder – would the sun still 'rise in the east and set in the west' near the North Pole?

When I had planned my trip, I hadn't realised that Svalbard would have 24-hours-a-day sun in May. I had assumed it would occur closer to midsummer. I had been woken frequently in the night due to Belgian-Space-Grabber prodding my mattress every time I snored, and each time I awoke, I noted it was still light outside. I asked a waitress who confirmed that yes, it had been light round the clock since April.

The sun's trajectory seemed to be behind the mountain to the south-southwest. Would the sun set in the west as I would expect to see in England? Would it float on the horizon? Or hover below it? Another theory I had – if the sun was normally south at midday – then did it mean the sun would keep moving to the opposite side of the compass by midnight? That is, it would be at north? Would the sun still be shining? Or would it be a little dimmer? I tried to figure this all out in my mind, but to be honest, I had no idea.

I just had to find out. So I set my alarm for 11:53 p.m., finished my Mack beer then headed back to the guest house to do a bit of packing ready for the next morning. I fell asleep, despite the irritating Belgian-Space-Grabber waking me on one occasion. When my alarm went off, I noticed through the curtains that it was extremely bright outside. I was only wearing my sleeping shorts and T-shirt but thought it oughtn't be too cold outside. I took my room key and went out to the roadside.

It was as bright as day, and I looked around to find the sun. The mountains to the south were in partial shadow, and the sun was behind the mountains to the north. I couldn't see the sun itself, but for sure, due to the rays of light creating a halo effect on the mountain, it was at least 20 degrees above the horizon. It didn't feel too cold, but I think it was the psychological effect of the sun.

So, I concluded that in the Arctic Circle, 'the sun rises in the east, partially sets in the west and hovers in the north'.

I went back to bed on my thin mattress and thought to myself that I ought to visit the Arctic circle in winter so that I could experience 24-hours darkness and hopefully the Northern Lights.

I woke at 6:30 a.m., took a shower then headed to take my breakfast in the kitchen area. I had missed it the day before due to my husky sledge trip. One of the Thai women had prepared a buffet of the usual continental breakfast rubbish: cracker breads, cheese, salami, ham, tomatoes and the like – of which only Germans, Scandinavians and rabbits would be satisfied. I toasted two slices of bread and placed dollops of butter and strawberry jam on my plate.

'Have you tried the brown cheese?' suggested a lady who had joined me at the pine breakfast table.

'No. I've been thinking about it. It looks quite different. What is it?' I wondered.

'It is made from caramelised goat's cheese. It's delicious – try it,' she encouraged me.

The cheese looked like a brick-sized lump of fudge, and a handled cheese slicer was placed on top so that you could slice off a slither.

'Sure, I will give it a try. Thanks for the recommendation,' I answered.

I took a cracker bread, scraped off three slices of the fudge cheese and placed them on the cracker. I made a coffee and tried the cheese. It was sweet and not very cheesy – a bit like caramel fudge. The rest of the party joined the lady one-by-one, a party of Dutch tourists it transpired, and we chatted about husky sledges and Antarctica.

I did a final pack of my things and caught the 10:30 a.m. Flybuss to the airport chatting with Belgian-Space-Grabber along the way. I contemplated telling him frankly that he was a snorer as well but decided I didn't want to spoil his day or waste my breath to convince him.

I was impressed again by the speed and service of Norwegian Air Shuttle, and after the security check, I bought a coffee in the terminal café and contemplated my journey so far. Svalbard was in many ways a raw frontier: very similar in geography to South Georgia and increasingly accessible. You would have to be a tough cookie to live there due to its remoteness and limited infrastructure, but as a visitor, I had enjoyed its uniqueness and proximity to wildlife and raw beauty.

I compared it with Iceland in my head and decided that I would, given the opportunity, return to this fascinating territory to see some more wildlife – perhaps see some of the abandoned Soviet mining towns. But I had to continue my mission, to visit my last territory in Europe – the Faroe Islands. Country number 99 lay within grasp – just two flights and three airport transfers ahead of me.

I was buzzing with excitement. I was dying to let Andy know my next destination. But I had to hold my tongue. I would tease him in Copenhagen airport.

15: Final Dose of Vikings

Faroe Islands (No. 99)

What an oddity the Faroes are. The islands were originally settled by hermit Irish monks in the eighth century – presumably a peaceful bunch looking for somewhere quiet to pray – until they were ousted by Viking raiders, who we can presume weren't on a peaceful religious pilgrimage.

The Faroese language is based upon Old Norse – the language of the Vikings. The islands have no reptiles or indigenous land mammals – nor do they have native trees due to the windswept landscape. The Faroes have zero prisons, two international fast food restaurants, three traffic lights and more sheep than people.

Getting to the Faroe Islands was frustrating – the Faroes are a Danish autonomous territory, and almost every flight originated in Copenhagen. I had spent many many hours scouring Skyscanner for alternatives with no luck, which was hardly surprising since their airline, Atlantic Airways, only had three aircraft.

There was an infrequent flight from Aberdeen, however, it didn't fit in with my schedule and was too expensive. My trawling paid off – I eventually found a flight from Copenhagen for £60. So, I took my Norwegian Air Shuttle flight from Longyearbyen to Oslo then a short 70-minute flight from Oslo to

Copenhagen. I took the airport shuttle train to the city and stayed at a hostel just a stones throw away.

The Copenhagen Backpacker's Hostel was better than I had anticipated. I was booked in a room of 18 beds, so I thought I would have 17 bunkmates throwing shoes at me when I went into super-snoring mode. Thankfully, it was a quiet hostel and there were others gently snoring when I got my head down. I figured there would be a queue for the shower room in the morning, so I set my alarm for 6:20 a.m. so I could be done before the *kiddypackers* woke up.

The shower room had three stalls, each with old hardwood lockable doors and an internal shower curtain to stop water spraying over your stuff hanging from the door hooks. The centre one was empty, so I tiptoed in and hung my things.

To my right was someone – or something – taking a rather angry shower. They made growling and shuddering noises as they rubbed down their body and breathed with a deep, coarse rasp like a werewolf in a black and white Boris Karloff movie. Who or what was it? A human dog? Werewolf?

I desperately wanted to peer over the partition to see what it was. I was not to find out, for when I finished my shower and stepped out, Wolfie had already fled the shower room. I brushed my teeth then returned to dormitory one – on the way listening out for raspy breathing and watching for an overly bushy neck.

I handed in my key and walked the 50 metres to Koberhaven Hautbahnhov Station, enjoying a quickie McDonald's breakfast before finding the train to the airport. On the train, I was still hesitant to alert Andy where I was going. Anything could go wrong and ruin my devilish plan. I might be travelling on the wrong day, so I checked my itinerary documents anxiously. I could be late for the flight, so I checked my departure time on my smartphone. That was fine. The flight could be cancelled? I could fall asleep at the gate and miss the flight? I could be kidnapped by aliens?

Despite my anxiety, everything was going swimmingly well. At the airport, I printed my luggage label and boarding pass at an automated kiosk and correctly stuck the long ends of the label together – a first for me. There weren't even any ground staff loitering at the check-in kiosks and bag drop areas in Copenhagen – not even one – which beat even the efficient Oslo airport staff. The UK was way, way behind in automation.

I then went through to gate area without any passport checks and found a Starbucks where I decided to have a follow-on breakfast *pain au chocolate* and Americano so that I could skip the airline meal. Then it was time to head to the gate. I took a selfie in front of a Copenhagen Airport sign and posted it on Facebook to tease Andy that I was, in all probability, en route to my last territory in Europe.

Atlantic Airways flight RC 453 was scheduled to depart from gate B10 at 12:25 p.m., so I walked to the gate, read *The Telegraph* and checked my Facebook while apprehensively waiting. Andy had rapidly replied to my posting.

'Where are you going? Faroes? Greenland?' he posted.

'I don't know,' I replied.

'How much did you spend on flights this trip?' he persisted. He probably hoped by a long shot that I was en route to Greenland. His next post swiftly followed.

'Are you flying Manchester to Reykjavik to Oslo to Svalbard to Oslo to Copenhagen to Faroes to Copenhagen to Manchester?' he precisely stated. He had either hacked into my flight-booking account or had been thoroughly researching my trip.

'Boom !' I replied.

I kept one eye on the boarding gate. In Oslo and Copenhagen airports, the gates had turnstiles that were lit with red crosses. When the aircraft was ready for boarding, they turned green and you had to scan your boarding pass to release the turnstile. There wasn't even any ground staff at the gate; there was only one ground-crew fellow who flitted between the aircraft and the gate.

The cunning Scandinavians were hyper-efficient. I was a little irritated about having to do everything myself, but this was massively outweighed by not having jobsworth ground crew poking their noses in. I had positioned myself facing the gate and decided I was going to dash for the turnstile as soon as it turned green. At exactly midday, the turnstile flipped to green and I leapt up and self boarded.

The folk on the plane were amazingly friendly. A young woman with an infant and toddler, both ginger-haired and blue-eyed, sat in front of me next to a senior lady. They merrily chatted away, which made me conclude they were relatives, however they did not communicate later in the flight – so I suspected they were just uber-friendly islanders.

The flight was scheduled for a shade over two hours duration, so I settled in to enjoy the trip. The cabin service was impeccable. I was brought a glass of water and two cups of tea by the cabin attendants; I noted that they were piping hot – a first for an airline – and a jug of fresh milk was offered to top it up, rather than sachets of awful condensed milk or creamer. *Fantastisk!*.

The plane passed Oslo after about 30 mins into the

flight then Sumburgh in the East Shetland Islands after 90mins. I found it both amusing and confusing that I was crisscrossing Norway – the country of my second and fourth stop on my plane hopping, then the UK – which was my originating country and eighth stop, to reach an island owned by Denmark – which was the country of my fifth and seventh stop. The historical and linguistic borders were at complete odds with the political borders.

The lady next to me furiously crocheted a white square *thingy*. I had noticed ladies in Svalbard doing the same in the cafés. It must be a Viking pastime, I thought, unlike Brits for whom drinking is more prevalent. Maybe if Prosecco was cheaper in Scandinavia then the women would abandon their knitting needles?

The captain announced the descent to the Faroe Islands, after which I readied myself and carefully observed the landscape. It was much like Scotland with beautiful grassy mountains and cliffs, which were scarred with fresh mountain streams and plunging waterfalls. A gentle landing just after 1:30 p.m., and I was in country 99. This was my last and final European territory, and I was an airport-terminal exit from beating Andy to complete an entire continent.

I quickly fetched my backpack as soon as the luggage carousel sparked into life then passed into the compact arrivals area. Unlike Svalbard, the Faroes operated a tourist information office in the airport, albeit the size of a bathroom. An officer lady was manning the desk.

'Excuse me, is there a regular bus to Sandavágur?' I asked her.

'Yes,' she answered, 'it is the same bus as Tórshavn It's outside in a few minutes.'

I thanked her and darted outside into the crisp air. I took in a great lungful and congratulated myself on visiting every country in Europe. An entire continent. Despite me living in Asia for most of the previous two decades, and Andy living in Europe, I had beaten him on his own doorstep. A smug celebration was in order.

Soon, the blue bus arrived, and I paid the 20 kroner (£2.40) fare to the driver with my leftover coins from Copenhagen and took the front seat. A half-dozen other passengers boarded then he pulled away.

My first impressions of the island were highly positive: it was far greener than Iceland and the landscape was scenic – not barren. And the roads were new and well maintained. As we drove down route 11, the bus passed low hills then looped to the right around the long, thin Lake Letisvatn. Strange-looking, lonesome sheep dotted the landscape here and there, and the road headed towards Sandavágur, passing through the small village of Midvagur. A couple of passengers alighted and boarded at stops in the village.

'Can you tell me where to get off for Giljanes, please?' I asked the river.

'*Ja*.'

Past Midvagur, he stopped on a bend that overlooked the sea and a timber yard.

'Giljanes is here. I don't know where exactly,' the driver told me.

'*Tak*,' I thanked him and got off.

The sun was shining wonderfully with scarcely any clouds in the sky, and I could smell the fresh air and scent of grass the moment I stepped off the bus. This was a delightful place, I thought to myself. I studied Google maps on my smartphone, which indicated that the Giljanes was below the timber yard towards the seafront. That's a bit funny, I thought to myself, was the hostel in a light industrial estate?

I took the slip road 200 meters further along the road. Then I doubled back, and the splendid view of the entire bay came into view – a colourful village to the left hugging a green mountain, a tall rock island ahead in the distance and the mountains on other side of the bay, to my right.

Inside the hostel was a sign to remove boots, which was similar to the custom in Svalbard. The blonde-haired hostel owner greeted me with a mop in his hand.

'*Hej*. What is your name please,' he smiled. The Faroese folk were so friendly – I was smitten by their cheerful demeanour.

'Rice. I have a booking.'

'Ah yes,' he replied, 'I will show your room – I am just cleaning it actually.'

He showed me dormitory number two, and I agreed to keep out of his way in the common room while he finished his cleaning. The common room was as large as a squash court, bright and airy in Scandinavian style, with IKEA-type tables and a kitchenette at the far end. It looked fairly newly decorated. I whiled away some time on social media with free Wi-Fi until the owner returned.

'You can go to your room when the floor is dried,' he said, handing me the room key.

A while later, I visited my dormitory and found it typical of Swedish hostels: pine-and-white furniture with just enough room for bunk beds to each side of the window. I took the lower bunk to avoid collapsing on someone and hoped that my bunkmates weren't going to give me a hard time for snoring.

It was time to explore the island while the weather was in my favour. I removed the inner layer of my winter coat and set off back down route 11 towards

Midvagur.

The grass was similar to Cumbria: part green, part straw-coloured. The whole island was covered with babbling clear streams gushing down from the mountains, and every 100 metres or so, a stream emptied through the grass and down a rocky embankment into a gulley at the side of the road. A couple of the odd-looking sheep were munching grass five metres above me on the slope near a house. They watched me out the corner of their eyes, and as I approached, they sauntered away. They were in mixed flocks of traditional white, black and even tawny-brown coats with long, shaggy fleece and strange dreadlocks that draped over their faces.

There were quite a few houses along the way – neat and brightly painted with grassy gardens. Within a kilometre, I reached Midvagur village. I crossed the road to the path, which faced the bay, and noticed quite a few houses with turf roofs. I imagined my wife chastising me to mow the roof lawn because the grass was tatty.

Around the next bend, I passed two bank branches with amazing views of the sea and a pizza parlour, then I turned left toward a football ground and reached the end of the bay. There was a two-metre-high grassy embankment, presumably a sea break, between the soccer ground and the sea. I climbed up, took off my coat and sat there for a good hour soaking up the sun and admiring the view of the villages, which hugged the mountain. The houses were capped in either Dutch-barn or turf roofs in a wide variety of colours like you can see in Scandinavian picture postcards: clay-red, black, sage-green, mustard-yellow, steel-blue and white.

The panorama was magical, and it was a wonderful way to spend the afternoon after freezing and fighting blizzards in Svalbard. The sun shone warmly on my shoulders and face, and I felt grateful that this was the final destination of my trip – my last territory in Europe. This was a befitting grand finale.

After my period of contemplation, I walked back towards the hostel passing an old woman who was pushing a pram carrying a toddler in a pink outfit with a knitted hood like a motorbike helmet. The little girl looked just like the one on the plane journey. The grandmother gave a friendly smile and got the baby to wave at me.

I returned to the pizza parlour and ordered a 12-inch Havana pizza and a diet cola. It was the best pizza I had ever tasted, and the owner, who looked Turkish, chatted about football. I told him I was a Liverpool FC fan, and he was a Madrid fan, so we were both waiting for the UEFA Champions League Final, which was scheduled to play in Kiev.

I continued my walk past Faroese walking their dogs, a few more cheerful toddlers and babies being ferried about in stout 1960s-style prams and more odd-looking, dread-locked sheep, which gave me suspicious stares.

It was still warm and sunny at 7 p.m., so I occupied a picnic table at the grassy camping area of the hostel and celebrated my completion of Europe with a Montecristo torpedo cigar, which I had bought in the Oslo duty-free shop. I spent a good 45 minutes admiring the bay and savouring my fat Cuban. When it was expired, I walked to the roadside above the low cliffs and lobbed the stub as hard as I could into the sea.

'Bloody hell,' I cursed aloud. The cigar stub was too light and had fallen short of the sea - landing in the clumpy grass just above the rocks. What if the grass caught fire, I thought in a panic. I would be prosecuted for arson. I stared intently down the embankment to see if there was any smoke. I became apprehensive after five minutes and decided I *had* to find it. I placed my rucksack against the crash barrier and climbed over.

The embankment was rather steep, and I was sure I was so clumsy that I would tumble down to the rocks below. I climbed down sideways and began my search. 'Damn it.' I spent ten minutes searching for the stub with no luck. I decided to give up and return to the hostel common room.

I checked in online for my return flight – looking out the window every few minutes in case the embankment was ablaze. I spent an unnecessarily long time in the common room so I could be certain the fire risk was gone, met and chatted with a young fellow from Hong Kong then retired for the night.

My bunkmates in the dormitory were already in bed. One bloke was in the lower left bunk and reading a book with a torch, and the other on the right bunk above me was already asleep. I felt slightly apprehensive, not wanting to suffer another pesky bunkmate prodding my mattress due to my snoring.

Morning came, and I woke at 6:20 a.m. and lay there for a few moments straining to recall if anyone had prodded or protested at me in the night. I think I was safe – phew. Today I planned to take the bus to the capital of the islands, Tórshavn. It was Sunday and there were very limited services, so I had decided to take the 8:40 a.m. bus. I showered while performing a bit of a balancing act since the cubicles had nowhere to place my clothes or any toiletries. I found a plastic laundry basket near the washing machine, upturned it outside the shower curtain then intricately balanced my clothes and washbag on the top.

Clean and changed, I went to the common room with my dwindling stock of Sainsbury's brioches. They were pretty flat after enduring six flights and nine airport transfers inside my backpack. Still, they were soft and edible despite being misshapen, so I ate two chocolate and one regular one with a cup of coffee I conjured up in the kitchenette.

I turned right out of the hostel and marched down the hill to the nearby village of Sorgavur, where I could see a blue bus shelter in the far distance. The rain was persistent but not too heavy, so I just kept my hood up and head down to keep a bit dry.

By 8:06 a.m., one minute late, the blue number 300 bus for Tórshavn arrived.

'How much to Tórshavn,' I asked.

'90 kroner,' the driver replied. That was £10.80.

What! You must be joking?' I countered. The driver gave a wry smile.

It was going to cost me almost £22 for a return bus ticket. I could get a National Express bus ticket from Manchester to London for that.

I reluctantly coughed up the 90 kroner and took the second row behind an Asian woman and the bus set off. It continued on route 11 through the village and along a pass over the hill to the eastern half of the island of Vagur. The scenery was as equally stunning as the previous day, with high cliffs, tumbling waterfalls and the shaggy-dreadlocked sheep with a few timid black lambs. The bus then entered the tunnel under the sea to the next island, Streymoy.

I overheard the two women chatting in Filipino, so I took the chance to ask them about life in the Faroes.

'Oh, I love it here,' claimed the older lady, 'I have lived here for 25 years and already used to it. It's so safe and peaceful here,' she beamed.

'Don't you get homesick here – especially with the winter?' I asked.

'Yeah, it's very cold in the winter. The last winter was mild, but in the winter before that, the road out of Sørvágur was blocked with snowdrifts up to here,' she held her palm level with her neck.

'Did you manage alright?' I displayed concern for someone who had grown up on an island in the Philippines with temperatures rarely below 30 Celsius and was now up to her neck in snowdrifts.

'Yah, and we ate all the food in the fridge and cupboards,' she laughed.

'Does it get very dark in the winter?' I continued.

'Yes,' she replied, 'it gets light at 10 a.m. and dark at 3 p.m., but I just do my work and don't think about it,' she cheerfully replied.

'Do you find it a bit isolated from the rest of Europe?' I persisted with my sombre line of questioning.

'We had some holidays to Denmark, boat trips to Europe and once to Scotland. I enjoyed it.'

Well, there you are, I thought. If someone from such a sunny and busy place as the Philippines can enjoy life here.

The bus had now crossed another tunnel to Eysturoy Island, and soon enough, we arrived at the blue terminal building at the port. I bid the lady and her friend goodbye and that they would enjoy the church service they were heading to. It was still drizzling in Tórshavn, so I pulled up my hood and traipsed off towards the town centre.

I passed the narrow harbour where various boats and modest yachts were moored. Spying some clay-red buildings on the other side on a low hill, I recalled that the buildings in the Tignanes historical area were that colour, so I made a beeline for them. I entered a narrow lane, which ran up the hill, and reached a sign announcing that this indeed was Tignanes.

The area had developed in the seventeenth century to manage the trade in the port area and several of the houses had turf roofs. I supposed the turf must be a great insulator since some new houses were also built that way. I took a few turns until I reached the main road, or rather alleyway, where some government buildings were located. A long, clay-red building was name-plated as the Ministry of Finance – it looked quite unusual to see a key government building with grass poking out of its parapets and main roof.

I returned through some even narrower alleys, which were barely wide enough for a motorbike to pass through. Some tiny houses were not much bigger than a two-berth caravan with wooden clap-boards and turf roofs. I walked past a navy-blue one and could clearly hear the couple talking behind the wooden wall.

Leaving the port area behind and heading to the town centre, everywhere was closed. I read some opening hours posted in the windows and noted that a few were opening in the evening. After some more exploration, I was getting absolutely soaking wet and the rain became more persistent, so I decided that I would try my luck in a hotel and dry off a bit.

I found the Hotel Hafnia was open for breakfast from 7 a.m. to 10 a.m. so ventured inside to get a cup of coffee and perhaps some fried eggs. Upstairs, the small restaurant was busy with about 20 guests taking buffet breakfast, and the waitress confirmed there was no à la carte menu. I was flabbergasted to find the buffet had bacon, sausages, beans and scrambled eggs – no paltry European cold meat and cheese – so I decided I would treat myself and skip lunch.

I took a table and dined on two small plates of crispy bacon and the latter delights, drank a few glasses of orange juice, a cup of coffee and ate two slices of apple strudel for a finale. I thought I had done rather well for the 150 kroner cost (£18). I settled my bill and continued on.

Back on the streets, I decided to head in the direction of Vidarlundin Park, which was highly recommended on the travel web-sites. I thought it would be rather interesting because the Faroes had no native forest species, and the government had brought in trees from South America to forest it.

I walked along Torsgota Street past various shops with beauty salons and clothes shops, which seemed quite befitting of a cosmopolitan town rather than a frontier town halfway to the North Pole. I continued until I reached the park area, where a stream with a series of weirs provided a calming backdrop to the town. Mallard ducks paddled about in the crystal-clear water and the scent of pine trees and moss was welcoming.

Some of the paths were very narrow, and I took a turn towards the small hill in the centre to look for statues. I climbed up, and at the top found a statue to the Faroese folk who had perished in the Second World War. Eventually, I reached the art centre at the far end of the park. An unusual statue of a heavily pregnant woman standing on a plinth caught my attention. An exact duplicate statue was suspended upside-down with their feet flat together. It was time to give up and head for the fort.

A good soggy 20-minutes walk later, I recognised the port area and identified the short red-and-white lighthouse on a small hill. I passed the bus terminal on my right and climbed the hill, or rather, it was a big mound. This was Fort Skansin, which was built in the seventeenth century to protect the trading port. The fortifications had been grassed over – I wasn't sure whether deliberately to make it into a park, or whether it had grown over with time. The fort had been occupied by Britain in the Second World War to protect the shipping lanes in the North Atlantic, and two huge artillery guns from that era were mounted on the lower ramparts facing towards the sea.

At the peak were four old cannons dating back to much earlier times. I savoured the views of Tinganes, the docks and the city from the top, but it was still raining, and I was becoming soggy and irritable again. So I walked back to the terminal to dry off and wait for the bus back to Vagur Island.

Fortunately, there was free Wi-Fi from the Symbil Shipping Lines office, which ran ferries to Iceland and Denmark. I caught up with some social media for a while in the waiting area, then I heard a 'hello'. It was the two Filipino ladies back from their church service. They were making a near-100-kilometre round trip costing 180 kroner (£22) to visit the Catholic Church – which I felt was admirable.

The scenery on the way back was as splendid as ever. The older Filipino lady told me that she was working in the salmon farming industry, and that the large circular pens in the bay near to Midvagur were for fattening the salmon. Each fish was already 6 to 10 kilograms when they were moved there from the breeding facility on land.

Back at Gjesthuset, I decided to have a cup of coffee in the common room and do some writing. I found a comfy sofa and was soon joined by the Hong Kong guy. We had an interesting discussion about the freedom of Hong Kongese.

It had been an interesting, but soggy, day. I realised I had been most fortunate the previous day to enjoy brilliant sunshine and blue skies, but that day I had to endure the typical weather of the Faroes. I became hungry but was too lazy to walk the two-kilometre round trip to have another pizza, so I reluctantly ate the remainder of my brioche and retired to my bunk.

The next morning, I caught the number 300 bus back to the airport and took the Atlantic Airways flight back to Copenhagen. Then after four hours loitering in the terminal, I flew the final leg back to Manchester.

Despite the damp ending, I was enamoured by the natural beauty and friendliness of its inhabitants. My final destination on this cavale to the lands of the Vikings was my favourite, and the islands had an irresistible charm.

Mission now complete, my thoughts on my long trip back home to Manchester were about where, how and when I would visit my country number 100? How on earth could I persuade my wife to go? And how quickly could I go in order to beat Andy to the magic century?

There was also another bonus. I read in the newspaper in Copenhagen airport that Michael Palin had just visited North Korea for a new television series. He had now been to 98 countries and territories. I had beaten him as well.

Eat my dust, Michael. Watch out, Andy.

THE GRAND FINALE

16: Howdy There, Hezbollah

So there I was – gloating at 99 countries. But I hadn't reached my target of 100 – I desperately needed to visit one more country before Andy did something dramatic.

On the positive front, I had completed every country and territory in the continent of Europe. But that was a double-edged sword: taking a trip now meant I needed to fly to another continent. I was aiming for trips of less than a five-hour flight away – which effectively meant North Africa or West Asia.

Then in September arrived the news I was dreading: Andy had been granted a four-month sabbatical leave. He swiftly locked in a trip to the Middle East, and I anxiously watched Facebook as he ticked off some exciting destinations. Jordan was his country number 84. Israel and Palestine 85 and 86. Lebanon 87. I was tied up at work with a major project and couldn't take any leave until December. Could Andy reach 100 before me?

I sat down with a pencil and a sheet of paper. He would start his next journey in November. His Middle-Eastern trips were an average duration of five days each, so at that pace, it could take him over two months to complete 13 countries and reach 100. That was too close for comfort.

I analysed the worst-case scenario. Could he complete his remaining 13 countries in November? That would be an average of 2.3 days per country. Hmm. That was theoretically possible – but not highly probable.

I had noted with interest Andy's posts from Lebanon. Bombed out buildings in Beirut. The Temple of Baalbeck. Hmm...I wonder? I searched Skyscanner for hours until I found a flight to Beirut on the 1 December and locked it in. My son Eddie had decided he wanted to visit Lebanon as well, so he booked his own flight. I just had to hope that Andy would not accelerate his pace.

November arrived, and Andy began his sabbatical tickfest. I pensively made note of his travels: Greenland 88. Faroes Islands 89. Gulp.

Lebanon (No. 100)

The 1st December 2018 arrived, and I was joyous that Andy had not progressed his tally past 89. I was travelling to my 100th country, and Andy had no inkling of my trip whatsoever. He had booked a Caribbean cruise for December, which he hinted would be a tickfest of up to ten countries, and he probably thought I was wrapped up with my job.

Pegasus cheapo airlines flight 862 hit a wodge of turbulence and startled me awake from a snooze. I looked out to see dense white clouds – I thought there would be no rain in the Middle East? Fortunately, the plane burst through the cumulus cloud layer, and I was greeted within minutes by a pitch-black, crystal-clear sky and a view of Beirut to my left,

'It looks like Hong Kong,' exclaimed Eddie. I

leaned across him to inspect the view more clearly. The glowing twinkle of amber streetlights illuminated the shape of the city, and skyscrapers and tall buildings indicated the centre.

'Is that a Christmas tree?' I wondered.

'Yeah,' replied Eddie, 'I think it is.'

Beirut must be a pretty tolerant Muslim city, I thought, to allow an enormous Christmas tree to stand in the very centre of the capital. The surrounding hills were also dotted with street-lights, and I surveyed them for more Christmas decorations.

The captain announced the final descent, and within moments the plane walloped the runway with a great thud. The runway was densely lined with residencies just 200 metres away. What if the plane was blown off course? It would probably wipe out a shopping-centre-worth of people.

Beirut airport was rather small – which was unsurprising given it was buried into the city limits. After a short taxi off the runway, the plane neared the passenger boarding bridge and immediately about half of the passengers sprung up and began fighting for their overhead baggage. The plane jerked half-a-dozen times as the air-marshal guided it into the bay, and each time, the standing passengers sprawled onto each other and walloped their fellow idiots with their baggage. I chuckled to myself.

I was not going to be able to disembark quickly due to the mad scuffle, so I took a few moments to read the Foreign and Commonwealth Office travel advice website on my smartphone. The airport was to the south of Beirut city, and the entire southern area between the airport and the central district was shaded in red. In FCO parlance that was rated as 'no travel in any circumstances'. Yikes. There was a single green line through the no-go area – designated safe – which was the airport road that ran from the terminal through South Beirut. I imagined there must be something terrible lurking in the city.

By now, the passengers were disembarking and contorting themselves past each other. Most of the passengers sprinted to the immigration counters, so that by the time we filled in our embarkation cards and joined the queue, there was only a little old man and a family with young girls in the queue. Sods' law, we were guided to a counter behind a troublesome couple who quarrelled over their passports, and we were even overtaken by the little old man.

'It's 11:40 pm – our taxi driver might clear off. We are over an hour late,' I sighed to Eddie.

'Chill out,' he replied, 'he's not going to leave without his money.'

Sure enough, when we exited immigration to the arrivals hall, the driver was leaning on the stainless-steel barrier holding a sign 'COLIN E RICE' in wonky handwriting. I greeted him, and we nipped around the barrier to meet him.

'I need to get some cash,' I told Eddie, 'how about I pay for the taxi to the city? You can pay for the return?'

He made a melodic response in confirmation.

I approached a cash machine of Banque Libano-Française and inserted my bank card. After selecting English and punching in my PIN, I was greeted by choices of 10,000 to 200,000 pounds withdrawals. The local currency, the Lebanese pound, was worth about 2,000 times less than a British pound. In my fatigue, I struggled to calculate how much local cash I needed and made two withdrawals by mistake, paying 7,500 pounds bank surcharge per withdrawal. Fortunately, the Lebanese type of pound.

We followed the taxi driver out of the terminal to a battered 1980s Mercedes C240. The blue car was well bumped and scraped – it looked like it had been rolled down the side of a mountain. The driver opened the boot for us to throw our backpacks in, then we trundled off.

The driver left the airport perimeter, and we passed our first military checkpoint. The concrete sentry box was painted in red-and-white stripes with a cedar tree painted over it, like the Lebanese flag, and three soldiers in camouflage fatigues suspiciously peered into our taxi. After a cursory check, we passed through the checkpoint and hit the airport highway into the city.

It had four-lane carriageways and ten-foot-high concrete walls segregating it from the low-rise houses of South Beirut. The car barrelled along at a fair old pace down the straight highway, through underpasses and overtaking a few buses. I avidly watched the darkened suburbs on the other side of the concrete wall for any signs of car bombs or rocket attacks. After five miles, the taxi reached Beirut city centre and took a right turn then a left.

'Hey, Eddie. There's the Christmas tree we saw from the plane,' I called out as we passed the great tree, which was about ten metres high.

Peculiarly, the tree stood right outside a mosque – which seemed a wee bit too tolerant for the Middle East to me. A moment later, the taxi stopped at a hot-dog wagon, turned right down a narrow lane between two buildings and stopped outside a narrow staircase to an apartment block. There were no signs that this was the Talal Hotel. Or any kind of hotel or hostel.

'Talal Hotel?' I asked the driver.

'Yes,' he confidently replied as he opened the door.

I looked Eddie in the eye. It was a dodgy-looking

building, and I didn't fancy spending five years in captivity like John McCarthy who was held hostage in a tiny cell by Islamic Jihad. However, the area was brightly lit and there were diners at the hot dog wagon. We would probably not be kidnapped today.

I paid the driver 30,000 Lebanese pounds, and we climbed the stairs, which were cracked and broken marble. I imagined this must be precisely like the building where the British journalist John McCarthy and envoy Terry Waite had been detained from 1986 to 1991 during the civil war. A very French-looking pair of narrow brown doors were labelled with a small hotel sign. We ventured inside the old-fashioned lobby, where a young man with a short beard and a horsey grin of huge teeth appeared. He spoke softly – almost effeminately.

'Good evening. You are Rice?' he asked.

'Yes, we are Rice. We have two bookings,' Eddie replied.

After some confusion as to why we had not booked together, Horsey-Receptionist led us up two more floors, past an ancient water-cooled air conditioning unit the size of a mini car and into a small dormitory where one of the three single beds was occupied by someone sleeping. We dropped down our backpacks, and Horsey-receptionist showed us to the shared bathroom. It had evidentially been stripped of previous fittings and had a simple sink and a toilet bowl. The shower faced down over the rusty floor drain, and the ceiling was barely six feet high with peeling white paint. Horsey-Receptionist picked up a long-handled squeegee and swept it towards the drain.

'Like this. See,' he motioned calmly.

Ah. So the bathroom would become flooded.

We thanked him and he scuttled away.

'I'm hungry,' lamented Eddie, 'we only ate bread in Istanbul Airport.'

'Sure,' I replied, 'let's go.'

Eddie got directions to an all-night café from Horsey-receptionist, then we walked out into the mild Beirut night. At the main road, a Porsche Panamera roared past at probably over 100 miles an hour, closely followed by a bumblebee black-stripe-over-yellow Chevrolet Camaro. We turned down Charles Helou Road, right at the Port Bar and steeply downhill towards the port road – which was also confusingly called Charles Helou.

On the left, we located the Makhlouf Café, which had a white-and-pale-blue awning and advertised that it had been open since 1948. Inside the open café was a line of laminated wooden tables and chairs down the left, and to the right, a high glass counter like a New York delicatessen. A portly middle-aged man behind the counter looked overjoyed.

'Hey my friends,' he shouted, 'where are you from?'

'London,' I replied.

'Welcome to Beirut. Sit, sit,' he beckoned us to take a seat at a table, 'my name is George.'

'Do you have any beer?' asked Eddie.

'Yes, of course. Almaza is from Lebanon. The best,' George replied as he stepped to a cabinet fridge and plucked two 50cl bottles of amber lager out. He opened the bottles and placed them on our table.

'What food do you have?' Eddie asked.

'Shawarma. It's Lebanese – good food. I have beef, chicken, ham?' George suggested.

We settled for one beef shawarma each, and George scuttled off to the kitchen to the rear.

'Cheers, Eddie,' I announced raising my beer bottle to his, 'to surviving the red zone from the airport. To not getting kidnapped – yet. To Beirut. To me reaching 100 countries.'

The Almaza beer was cold and delicious, as was the shawarma, and we polished off two more bottles of beer before making the climb back up the hill to our hostel. Or hotel. Or deserted building – to the sounds of sports cars racing along the road.

I didn't sleep soundly that night – despite the beers. I awoke feeling chilly in the early hours and had to pull the blanket over me, and the sound of the supercars racing past all night didn't help either. I awoke later that morning to the sound of our bunkmate; he held a quiet conversation with me while Eddie still slept. It transpired his name was Haru – he was Japanese – and had arrived the same day as us. He hadn't planned what he was going to do for the day, so we agreed he would return to the hostel after breakfast to talk about going somewhere together.

I pulled the blanket further over me and dozed off again. Later at 10 a.m., I properly awoke to the racket of Eddie still snoring so decided to take a shower. I grabbed my washbag and hostel towel, put on my flip flops then quietly shuffled out of the dormitory into the chilly common area. I turned on the 1950's Bakelite light switch outside the bathroom, stepped inside and locked the rusty door bolt. It was as bare as a prison cell with assorted tiles in various shades, a chipped mirror affixed above the basin, a toilet bowl and a few measly hooks on the door and wall.

The ceiling was so low there was barely room between my scalp and the peeling paint to insert a Lebanese shawarma sandwich. This was probably a three out of ten on the crappiness scale. I gingerly removed my clothes and hung them on the hooks. The shower was a simple handset that hung off the wall by a flimsy plastic drill plug. There was no shower curtain or screen – nor shower tray to stand on. The shower just sprayed on to the grotty tiled floor next to the toilet bowl. I took a shower in the cool water and took care not to touch the toilet or stand in the rusty drain.

Back at the dormitory, Eddie was awake. After performing his ablutions, we tramped down the chipped stairs and walked back to the Makhlouf Café for breakfast. A different but eerily similar middle-aged chap was manning the counter.

'Hello. Come inside. Where are you from?' he cheerfully enquired, 'I have lots of food here to eat.'

We took the same seats at the same melamine table, and he sauntered over clutching two menus.

'My name is Maheer. Where are you from?' he cheerfully asked. This was déjà vu Beirut-style.

'We are from England. We came here last night – we were served by George,' I replied.

Maheer gave a warm smile and waved the menus in the air, 'We are brothers. George is manager in the night, and I am [the] manager in the day,' he explained, 'you know – we can't work together at the same time. It is better we are apart: he has his way, I have my way. You understand?'

I sympathised with him – I had worked alongside my brother when I was younger. We had worked in a store together and had even thrown tin cans at each other.

'What do you have for breakfast?' enquired Eddie, 'can you do an omelette?'

Maheer sighed, 'I am sorry my friend. I can only serve omelettes after 11 a.m. How about ham and cheese on bread? Or Lebanese breakfast?'

'What is a Lebanese breakfast?' asked Eddie

excitedly.

'It has olives, tomatoes, mustard...' Maheer replied.

'That sounds tasty. A Lebanese breakfast and a Lebanese coffee for me, please,' I ordered.

Yeah, me too,' furthered Eddie.

Maheer scuttled off and busied himself behind the counter.

'It sounds better than a ham and cheese toasted sandwich,' I optimistically told Eddie.

A few minutes later, Maheer returned with two plates, each with a toasted bread sandwich on greaseproof paper.

'OK. Lebanese breakfast,' he said and walked to the coffee machine to get our drinks.

Eddie and I looked at each other. I had expected something like a Turkish breakfast of olives, tomatoes, cheese and so forth on the plate like a salad. I took the knife and lifted the edge of the bread up. It was exactly the same ham and cheese toasted sandwich we had eaten the previous night, except for a sprinkling of sliced green olives and smears of green mustard. Eddie and I looked at each other in disbelief.

'Maybe we should try the Beirut breakfast tomorrow,' I smiled at Eddie, 'it probably has black olives instead of green.'

Despite the limited variety, our breakfast was delicious, and after sipping the Turkish-style coffee with ground beans at the bottom, I paid Maheer and stepped out to the mild, sunny Beirut day.

'You are navigating,' I reminded Eddie, 'lead the way.'

'We'll head east to the port then double-back to the city centre,' he confidently told me.

Beirut was an architectural mixed bag. Older French-era low-rise buildings that were predominantly dilapidated, awful 1970s office blocks, crumbled foundations where buildings had presumably fallen during the civil war, partly-built high-rise buildings adorned with cranes and flashy-new mirrored glass office blocks. They were all cheek-by-jowl with few homogeneous blocks.

We headed down the main Charles Helou Street and along a newly-built overpass. I was delighted to watch the American Chevrolet Camaros, Cadillac Escalades and Dodge Cherokees roaring past with their V8 engines growling, while Eddie studied his city map and raised his gaze at cars that interested him.

'An Audi S6,' he excitedly announced.

'Whatever. Lame. There's a bumblebee Camaro,' I replied.

Lebanon was rapidly becoming an adorable oddity of a country. I hadn't known what to expect given the bad press it had had. As a teenager, I had watched the nightmare of the Lebanon Civil War unfold on British late-night news. This tiny state, half the land area of Wales and with twice the population, had exploded into gunfire and bombing as the factions of the Maronite Christian and Muslim communities fought for control.

The tinderbox was lit in 1975 when the Christians, known as Phalangists, attacked a busload of Palestinians heading for a refugee camp. This escalated into a full-scale civil war between the Phalangists and the Lebanese National Movement, or LNM, who fought ferociously in Beirut city centre – which morphed into Muslim West Beirut and Christian East Beirut.

The whole conflict was inflamed by neighbouring states, including Israel – which provided arms and finances to the Christians – and Syria, who intervened with assistance to the Palestinians. The war resulted in over 100,000 deaths, over a million refugees and billions of pounds of damage to the country's infrastructure. The physical scars of that conflict were still clearly visible, although I couldn't discern if there was any tension between the two ethnic groups.

We walked to the end of the overpass and doubled back across a bridge, which passed under the expressway. At this angle, I could see that the brand spanking new overpass was laid upon a decrepit three-storey bus terminal, which was disused. As we walked past, I peered inside and could see rubbish strewn here and there. The Charles Helou Bus Station was an enormous and largely derelict facility, which was testament to the troubled city. From the side view, I couldn't even see the far end of the station; it must have been half a kilometre long.

The French-built bus fleets had been destroyed at least twice: once in the Lebanese Civil War and the second time bombed by the Israelis. The bus station was re-commissioned in 1996, but in the following decade, the myriad of private bus companies crept away to their informal transport hubs, which had arisen during the Civil War. The place was giving me the creeps and there was no-one about, so I increased my walking pace.

We continued under the overpass then along Pasteur Street, which headed back west towards the city. Block by block, the narrow street became more lively with cafés, coffee shops and bars becoming more frequent. The buildings were mostly French-style low-rise in pale colours. The European influence was oddly undermined by the wealth of American cars; Camaros, Cadillacs and even a couple of Dodge Charger police pursuit cars, which delighted me.

Just before we reached George Haddad Street, I encountered the first evidence of the Lebanese Civil

War. An old French-style building, four storeys high, had artillery holes across the tiled facade. Two storeys had been blown away and the enormous gap crudely patched with hollow blocks.

We proceeded along in the direction of the city centre following the minarets of the main mosque as a beacon.

'We are almost at civilisation after that mystery tour,' I teased Eddie, and he grumbled back under his breath. I decided to send a text message to Haru.

'We are near the city centre. Where are you now?' I asked him.'

'American Beirut University. Meet There?' he replied quickly.

'How far are we from the university?' I asked Eddie.

'Maybe 20 minutes I think.'

I updated Haru, then we reached the Mohammad Al-Amin Mosque, which was a golden-sand-coloured building topped with a 48-metre-high light-blue dome and 65-metre-high minarets. It was also known as the Blue Mosque. We passed the mosque towards the Martyr's Statue where the enormous 20-metre-high Christmas tree stood in the shadow of the mosque. A Christmas festival event was being constructed with a Christ in the manger nativity scene.

'They must be pretty tolerant of religion to allow this,' I exclaimed to Eddie as I stared at the minarets of the mosque in the rays of the afternoon sun streaming over the nativity set right in front of me.

We then headed 200 metres downhill to the Martyr's Monument. Unveiled in 1960, this statue became Ground Zero during the Civil War. The area became part of the Green Line that divided the city between Muslim West Beirut and largely Christian East

Beirut. The monument was of a woman holding aloft a torch, Statue of Liberty style, with her arm around a man. They stood on a plinth above a wavy-haired man who resembled a drunk boy-band member trying to get to his feet. The statue had taken the full brunt of sniper fire, and it was riddled with bullet holes and the man's left arm was blown away.

In the interest of time, we hurried on past the Roman ruins, Nijmeh Square, with its sandstone clock tower then through the restaurant district. The whole area was obviously where tourists and businessmen dined, and the entire pedestrianised zone was cordoned off. We passed an army checkpoint at the northern edge guarded by a concrete bunker painted in red-and-white stripes and several soldiers swaggering M16 assault rifles. The road barrier was the heftiest I had ever seen, with three beams the size of railway girders. It must have weighed several tons and could have kept out a T-34 tank.

We walked for 15 minutes up Omar Daouk Street, past a McLaren car dealer, until we stumbled upon the abandoned Holiday Inn building. This hotel was probably the most visible sign of the Civil War and had lain damaged for 40 years. The eastern end of the 26-storey building was riddled with heavy-artillery fire.

Fierce fighting took place in the hotel district from October 1975 to March 1976 as the various Muslim and Christian factions fought for control of the high vantage points in the area. On 27 October, Christian Phalangists moved into the Holiday Inn and around 200 staff and tourists were trapped in the artillery crossfire. After two days, a ceasefire was called by the Prime Minister Rachid Karami to allow the evacuation of the hotels. In November 1975, a ceasefire was agreed and Prime Minister Karami started to demilitarise the Hotel district, but Phalangists dug in at the Holiday Inn. In March 1976, Palestinian PLO commando units successfully drove out the Phalangists from the hotel.

We continued along Omar Daouk Street to the rear of the building, and I decided to take some photos of the damaged building.

'That's interesting. There are armoured vehicles in the ground floor car park,' noted Eddie as I surveyed the building with my camera lens.

'Cool,' I replied.

'Stop. Stop!' cautioned Eddie after a moment. I grunted in response as I stared through my lens. He then started to tug my T-shirt.

Suddenly, I was confronted by a soldier brandishing an M16 assault rifle.

'No photo! Show me!' the soldier challenged us.

Eddie was closest and showed him the photos on his smartphone. He swiped through them.

'Delete. Delete,' commanded the soldier sternly.

The soldier then approached me, and I showed him the first photo on my SD-RAM card, which happened to be a family photo in England.

'No problem,' he told me. Whatever he wanted, I would do for a man with an assault rifle.

After a good ticking off, we thanked the soldier and continued.

'Phew. Let's not do that again,' I told Eddie.

After another ten minutes walk, we arrived at the entrance to the university campus where we were greeted by Haru who sprang from the shades of the checkpoint.

'Hey, Haru,' greeted Eddie.

'Sorry we are late,' I apologised.

It was already dark, and we decided it was not worth to visit the university grounds at this hour. So we agreed to go and find something to eat and have a couple of beers. We walked all around the Hamra district until finding a bar-restaurant where we ordered a plate of cheese tacos, but the mains were way too expensive at 30,000 pounds (£15) each.

'Do you have draft beer?' I asked the waiter.

'Yes, Almaza,' he replied. This seemed to be the one and only local beer. Eddie ordered a pint of Almaza as well.

'How about you, Haru?' I asked.

'I can't drink beer,' he answered, thumbing through the drinks menu, 'a Moscow Mule,' he ordered from the waiter.

We chatted about our travels over drinks and tacos. Haru had been working in Dubai and was on a three-month tour of the Middle East then he planned to return to Tokyo. I told him that I was on my 100th country and was going to officially celebrate. I had bought a Montecristo robusto from the duty-free shop in Stansted airport, and I joyfully puffed on my Cuban and sipped chilled Almaza as we exchanged stories and chatted away. I told Haru about my competition with Andy, and how Andy had no idea I was in my 100th country already.

Haru became as red as a beetroot due to his alcohol intolerance and put his head in his hands with pain.

'So, where should we visit tomorrow?' I asked the others, 'We can visit Tyre – which is in the bible, Sidol – with it's Crusader Castle or the Temple of Baalbek.'

Eddie and Haru looked at each other.

'Baalbek looks really cool,' I continued, 'it has some of the best-preserved Roman temples in the world. However, it's in the no-go area of Lebanon'

'What does that mean?' asked Haru.

'The UK Foreign and Commonwealth Office

website advises against all but essential travel to the area around the Syrian border and the area surrounding Baalbek town.' I advised, 'Still, my friend Andy visited Baalbek a few weeks ago and came back alive.'

I took my Lonely Planet guidebook from my rucksack and read the chapter on Baalbek.

'Cool,' I noted, 'the town of Baalbek is a stronghold of Hezbollah'.

Haru wasn't concerned about the security situation, which seemed to be a common trait of Japanese I had met on my travels, and Eddie said he would go along with the decision. So, it was decided.

'We're going to Baalbek. Cheers!' I raised my bottle of Almaza.

'Kanpai!' cheered Haru in Japanese with his Moscow Mule.

'Kanpai,' copied Eddie.

We continued to talk and drink, and Haru became redder and redder until he started to hold his head in his hands again,

'Shall we go to a club?' Haru suggested.

'I don't think you will survive another drink,' I told him. Haru made a loud teeth-suck noise.

We decided to look for something for dinner, but everywhere sold beef shawarma, chicken wraps or club sandwiches. This was sandwich city. We ate at a sandwich-cum-burger cafe then talked and walked miles back towards the hostel, along Waygand where we reached the bridge over George Haddad Street. We were just a stone's throw from the giant Christmas tree. Groups of young men loitered around the bridge engaged in talking, smoking and laughing. They seemed a bit shifty, but we didn't need to be concerned – there were soldiers dotted everywhere.

We crossed the road bridge, and the neat street

turned into a more crumbled road with potholes and damaged verges. This bridge was the demarcation of the well-guarded, well-heeled city centre and the more dodgy periphery. We walked past a dark-green M998 Humvee that was manned by several soldiers wielding M16 assault rifles. One soldier was peering into the windows of passing vehicles entering the centre.

After another 200 metres, we were at Charles Helou Street near the hostel.

'Shall we have another beer?' asked Eddie.

'Sure,' I replied.

'Me too,' chipped in Haru.

We tried the Mexicana Bar, which was decked out in *Day of the Dead*-style ornaments. We sat at the bar, which was strewn with potted cacti plants and hand-painted skulls. We whiled away a couple of happy-hour Almaza beers while Haru stuck to an iced cola, then we padded back to the hostel at 11 p.m. so we could rise early for our trip to Baalbek.

Today was our big day. We were going to be either triumphantly successful at seeing one of the best-preserved Roman temples in the world or chained in a basement by Hezbollah and held for ransom. Everyone we had met in Beirut had said that Baalbek was safe, and I knew Andy had safely arrived back in England from his visit. Still, I had nagging doubts about the warnings on the FCO website.

After cold showers, we left the hostel. The morning air was hazy, but the sun was warming up nicely. We predictably ate breakfast at Makhlouf then walked downhill towards the port, where we caught the number 15 minibus to the Cola transport interchange. After 20 minutes, the minibus screeched to a halt under an overpass.

'Cola!' the driver shouted at me with a toothy grin.

A lady in a black hijab headdress pivoted in her seat and talked to me in excellent English.

'This is Cola. You get the bus from here,' she advised.

During the fighting in the Civil War, Beirut's transport hub in Martyr's Square had become a virtual war zone. Consequently, informal transport hubs had evolved in faction-controlled areas. Cola became the hub of Muslim West Beirut.

We alighted, and to the chagrin of Eddie, I asked several-hundred random pedestrians for the bus to Baalbek, and they consistently pointed us down Salim Salam Road to a lay-by with buses in various stages of filling up with passengers.

'Baalbek?' I asked one minibus driver.

'Yes, yes,' he excitedly replied and herded me towards the steps.

'How much?' I asked.

'8,000 pounds. No problem. Let's go,' he replied.

Haru led the way inside and sat on the rear seat, Eddie took the middle, and I sat on an end seat so that I could stretch my legs along the aisle. The minibus began filling up, and by 8:40 a.m., the final passengers climbed aboard and we were ready. Our fellow passengers looked like a motley crew of freedom fighters and vagabonds.

We took a couple of turns down side streets then hit the dual carriageway, which ran to the east. We passed one of the military checkpoints with red-and-white concrete pillar boxes adorned with cedar tree emblems, then the road hit a steep incline and twisted and turned up the mountains, which were desiccated and covered with yellow boulders and dark-green bushes. After the initial ascent, the road became a pass snaking along the steep mountain slopes until it levelled out into the Bekaa Valley. This was a fertile plain between the mountain ranges of Mount Lebanon to the west and the Anti-Lebanon Mountain Range to the east that marked the Syrian border.

After 90 minutes journey, which included a change of minibus, we reached the town of Baalbek.

The Temple of Jupiter was enormous, with a giant staircase, 20 metres wide and 6 metres high, leading up to the plinth upon which the temple was built. Huge columns, the largest in the ancient world at 2.2 metres diameter and 30 metres high, supported the remains of the facade.

We spent a few hours exploring the huge temple, which was 90 metres wide and 135 metres long, then the Temple of Bacchus, which was a smaller but perfectly formed temple – in itself huge at 35 metres across and 66 metres long. This tiny part of the Temple of Jupiter was larger than the Parthenon of ancient Greece.

By early afternoon, we found a direct bus back to Beirut and were dropped a ten-minute walk from the Corniche, the three-mile-long promenade that ran along the northwest coast of Beirut. We walked along the modern, neat promenade with granite block paving and steel-tubed handrails, past a restaurant, until we reached The Rocks. They were just offshore and lit-up for decoration.

'You can go down there to the rocks,' said Haru, 'see the people down there?'

'Hmmm. I think so,' I answered.

'It's not very impressive...' said Eddie.

'Well,' said Haru, 'this is probably impressive for Beirut. What else is there to see?'

Our thoughts turned to food, and we settled for a

Kentucky Fried Chicken dinner – which was hardly local food – but I couldn't stomach another Lebanese sandwich. After finishing our non-Lebanese, non-sandwich meal, we took a number 15 minibus back to Charles Helou Street and were dropped in a quiet spot near the port area.

'One for the road?' asked Eddie?

'I need to go and change for a party,' declined Haru, 'you guys enjoy.'

'Sure, let's find a cheap place to drink,' I agreed.

We walked 50 metres down the port road and found a convenience store with some melamine tables outside, a fridge full of cold beer and a clear plastic canopy to keep out the rain. We were greeted by one of the men who worked there.

'Take a seat. Here,' he offered a metre-square table.

They were serving 50cl bottles of chilled Almaza, which we duly ordered.

'Cheers,' we clinked our bottles together.

We decided to buy some menthol cigarettes with flavour balls, which Eddie recommended, for fun. I tried to buy some in the store.

'These have flavours of both menthol and blueberry. You can choose which you like,' the sales guy told me.

'Cool. Give me a packet.'

We enjoyed popping the little flavour balls between sips of chilled Almaza, while a party of men next door were getting rowdier. Two of them entered the canopy and talked loudly in Portuguese tones.

'Where are you from?' one asked me. They were dressed in green military fatigues.

'Guess?' I quizzed him. He wasn't holding an assault rifle so I could be cheeky.

'USA?' he answered.

'No. England,' I answered after wondering if he was packing a handgun somewhere, 'how about you?'

'We are from Brazil. We are United Nations peacekeepers,' he pointed to the docks, 'See – that's our ship.'

We exchanged more banter before we shook hands and they returned to their noisy little party.

After our third bottle of Almaza and much popping of blueberry fusion balls, we clomped up the hill at 1 a.m. to our hostel.

I slept reasonably well through the nightly F1 races and awoke at 10 a.m. to the sound of Haru rummaging through crinkly plastic bags in the bowels of his pink suitcase. We woke up later at 11 a.m.

'What's our plan for today?' I asked Eddie.

'Order the taxi to the airport tonight. See inside the mosque. See the souk. Take it easy,' he prescribed.

'Right you are,' I agreed, 'Lebanese breakfast at Makhlouf?'

After we ate fish and sardine sandwiches and two Turkish coffees, we set off down Gouraud and arrived at the Mohammed Al-Amin mosque.

'You should have worn trousers,' I cautioned Eddie, 'they might not let you inside wearing shorts.'

He replied with a head wiggle. Sure enough, as we climbed the dozen steps to the melodic call to prayer by the muezzin, the sign at the entrance stated that bare legs or shoulders were not allowed.'

'Don't worry,' I reassured him, 'there's usually some loan clothes for tourists.'

I headed for a garment rail adjacent to the entrance and flipped through the assorted black garments.

'Here – a sexy gown for you,' I said handing Eddie a long cloak.

He groaned and put it on while I untied my boot laces.

'Right, let's go,' I said.

Inside, the 11,000-square-metre mosque was beautifully carpeted with a neat grid pattern of spaces for worshippers to pray. Around two dozen worshippers were in various states of prose around the mosque, and there was a trickle of new arrivals behind us. I placed my walking boots in the shoe rack and skirted around the edge to view the interior of the dome. An enormous chandelier hung from the 48-metre dome, which was inlaid with Koranic scripts.

After admiring the mosque, we passed the ancient Roman main street, Cardo Maximus, and headed into the Maronite cathedral, Saint Georges. We walked around the perimeter to view the chapels, paintings and figures, but sadly, many of them only had Arabic legends. I returned from the altar along the right-hand side of the church and noticed that the frescoes were sprayed with bullet holes.

'I guess they retained these holes for the tourists,' quipped Eddie.

'Or maybe they ran out of wall filler in Beirut?' I answered.

We departed the cathedral and turned right into El Maarad, which was a narrow street at the entrance to the restaurant district. The road was guarded by an armed military checkpoint and a road barrier. I stopped at a cash machine to withdraw some Lebanese currency since I had ran out of cash and had borrowed from Eddie. I withdrew 200,000 pounds of currency (£100) and handed him one of the two banknotes.

'Here, 100,000 pounds for you,' I joked.

'I could buy an Audi R8 sports car for that,' chuckled Eddie.

We continued up the clean street to the centre, Nijmeh Square, and visited the St. George Orthodox Cathedral.

'Should we find the souk?' asked Eddie.

'Sure,' I replied, 'lead the way.'

We travelled up Waygand and arrived at Beirut Souks. It was totally rebuilt after the Civil War, converted from a traditional souk selling spices, produce and fish, to a posh shopping centre.

'This isn't a real souk,' I moaned, 'there are no donkeys carrying baskets or stalls selling sheep heads.'

Eddie was politely ignoring my grumbling.

'This is a decent mall,' he continued, walking further inside the upmarket building that was adorned with marble floors, expensive fashion stores and international restaurants with well-heeled patrons.

It was already dinner time by now, and we ate in the food hall near the cinema. Since we were now worn out from marching about Lebanon for several days, we decided to watch a movie in the brand spanking new multi-screen cinema.

We walked back to Charles Helou Street at 11 p.m. and enjoyed a final bottle of Almaza at Makhlouf Café, before ordering a taxi to the airport and retiring to our crumbling hotel.

We needed to take an early flight to Istanbul. At 1:30 a.m., we dragged our backpacks down the damaged stairs for the final time and placed them on an enormous four-foot-cubed concrete block near the hot dog van. The hot dog guy waved and smiled at us. We only had to spend 15 minutes watching the stray cats and boy racers until a white Toyota hatchback drove the wrong way down the city-bound lane and reversed up to us. Given that the Porsche Panameras must have

Printed in Great Britain
by Amazon

been zooming past at 100 miles per hour, I didn't rate his choice of manoeuvre.

A moment later, we were driving along the streets of Beirut, past the fake souk then entered the airport expressway. The taxi's warning light was flashing furiously, and I realised that although he was now reaching 110 kilometres per hour, he was not wearing a seatbelt.

That was the quickest airport transfer I had ever taken. Except for an Iraqi woman on crutches asking me to fill in her departure card, and the immigration officer intensely scrutinising my passport pages for Israeli stamps, the boarding to Pegasus Airlines flight 963 was uneventful.

Beirut and Lebanon had been as fascinating as I had wished for. It had more supercars than a thousand Top Gear shows, more concrete barriers than the Berlin Wall and more sandwiches than every Subway on earth added together. The people were friendly and tolerant – except towards the state of Israel – and it had been great fun.

Oh yes. And I had reached my 100th country. Before Andy had. And I had still maintained my radio silence on social media. And Andy had no inkling that he was beaten to the century.

I smirked to myself smugly and waited to savour the moment I shared my photo at The Temple of Baalbek with him.

Game over. I had won. I had quietly celebrated my personal achievement in Beirut, and upon return to England, I was going to reveal all to Andy.

EPILOGUE

Epilogue: Continuing the Cavales

I had now pretty much visited every country and territory within five hours flight of the UK and would need to start planning long-haul destinations for my future trips. That was going to take a lot more time – and a lot more funds.

And how about my next target – which famous personality should I challenge myself to overtake? Her Majesty Queen Elizabeth? According to royal historian Kate Williams, The Queen has travelled the equivalent of 42 circumnavigations of the Earth – visiting 120 countries. Perhaps in a few more years, I might be able to meet Her Majesty's grand tally?

What about Andy?

Well, he did take my burgeoning tally as his Pearl Harbour – he took out his threat to book an island-hop in the Caribbean. We agreed to meet for a meal before his cruise, and he had prepared to gloat over his forthcoming tick-fest, which would vault him to 98 or possibly even 100 countries. He was girding to overtake me and had absolutely no idea that I had been on my trip to Lebanon. My family had kept absolute radio silence on social media, and Andy thought I was preoccupied with my work.

I was smirking to myself about the moment I would pop his balloon and tell him he was too late – I had made 100 countries first. I bought a large 100 birthday badge, which simply said '100 Today' on it, and a framed photo of myself standing in front of the Temple of Bacchus in Baalbek – the very same pose he had posted on Facebook months earlier.

We met in an Italian restaurant, and he proceeded to gloat about how he would soon add nine Caribbean countries and territories to his tally.

'Hmmm. I'm going to be only two countries away from 100 by Christmas,' he teased, 'and I have booked a flight after Christmas before I return to work.'

'Ah well,' I sighed, 'you are going to beat me. I'm such a loser.'

We sat at our booked table and ordered a bottle of Italian wine and our main courses. After the waiter poured the wine, I pulled out a gift wrapped in Christmas paper.

'What's this for?' Andy asked in surprise.

'It's a gift for your cruise. A going away present, you could say,' I replied.

Andy looked at me puzzled but not with suspicion. He proceeded to tear off the wrapping paper, which I had deliberately double wrapped with a whole roll of sticky tape to make it difficult to remove. He got the wrapping paper off and then unfolded the tissue paper around the picture frame. An enormous grin sprung from one ear to his other ear.

'What's this?' he asked, 'is this a Photoshopped picture?'

It did indeed look like it was composed in Adobe Photoshop, since I had taken a professional-looking shot with fill-in flash.

'No. It's real,' I replied as I opened my jacket to reveal the pocket lining where the giant '100 Today' badge was pinned.

Andy's grin widened from earlobe to earlobe and

he turned slightly red.

'Smile,' I said, 'hold the photo frame up,' which he duly did in mild shock.

حلو النصر

LIST OF COUNTRIES

What constitutes a country? According to the United Nations, 'The recognition of a new State or Government is an act that only other States and Governments may grant or withhold.' As a result, the membership of some countries to the United Nations is blocked by one or more other members, for example, Taiwan. Does that mean if you visited Taiwan, you never even visited a country?

The United Nations also defines "Observer States" – do you tell the people of Palestine that they are not a country?

On the other hand, some territories have their own government, immigration and print their own currency. For example, the Isle of Man has all of the above – even a parliament which is older than that of the United Kingdom.

Then there are disputed states, which have declared independence but are not widely recognised by United Nations member states. These include South Ossetia and Abkhazia.

Finally, there are also endless frivolous claims of statehood, such as Westarctica – don't even get me started on those.

To avoid endless debate, Andy and I agreed to reference ISO 3166, which is derived from United Nations sources, to count how many countries and territories we have visited.

It's not perfect, but it's free of frivolity.

Here are my first 100 countries and territories based on ISO 3166. This book covers most of the countries from number 74 to 100.

1967	United Kingdom	1
1974-75	Spain, Tunisia, Greece	3
1983-86	Netherlands, France, Italy	3
1989-1990	First Cavale Morocco, Algeria, Niger, Mali, Nigeria, Congo / Zaire, Uganda, Kenya, USSR / Russia	9
1990-1991	Second Cavale Belgium, Germany, Denmark, Luxembourg, Gibraltar, Monaco, San Marino, Holy See (Vatican City State), Liechtenstein, Switzerland, Austria, Hungary, Czechoslovakia / Czech Republic, Poland, Mongolia, China, Macau, Hong Kong	18
1991	Thailand	1
1992	Third Cavale Philippines, Malaysia, Singapore	3
2000-02	Brunei Darussalam, Guam	2
2004-06	South Korea, Taiwan, USA, Australia	4
2008	New Zealand, Indonesia	2
2012-14	Saipan, Vietnam Japan	3
2015	Fourth Cavale Chile, Antarctica, South Georgia, Falkland Islands, Argentina	5

	Fifth Cavale	
2015	Mexico, Belize, Guatemala, Honduras, El Salvador, Nicaragua, Costa Rica, Panama, United Arab Emirates, Oman	10
2015	Cambodia	1
	Sixth Cavale	
2015	Kuwait, Qatar, Sweden, Finland, Aland Islands, Norway, Slovenia, Croatia, Bosnia & Herzegovina, Montenegro, Serbia, Bulgaria	12
2015	Bangladesh, Ukraine	2
2016	Ireland, Isle of Man, Andorra, Malta, Turkey, Moldova, Romania, Jersey, Guernsey, Portugal	10
	Seventh Cavale	
2017	Slovakia, Belarus, Lithuania, Latvia, Estonia	5
2017	Albania	1
2018	Macedonia, Iceland, Svalbard, Faroe Islands, Lebanon	5
	TOTAL	100

THE END

конец

ALSO BY COLIN RICE

7 Continents

A travelogue about Colin's mission to visit every continent on earth. This is a collection of some of his favourite travels across all seven of the continents. From a boat ride up the Congo River in the Central African jungle to swimming in the source of the Nile in Uganda. Bicycle riding among thousands of Chinese people in Shanghai and exploring the Great Jaguar Temple in the lost Mayan city of Tikal in Guatemala. And on his greatest journey yet, on an expedition ship to Antarctica, which sailed through pack ice in the Weddell Sea and visited an Antarctic research base.